Let's Party! San Francisco

PUBLISHER
Mark J. Maxam

AUTHORS
**Sam Khedr   Mark Maxam
Jessica Fernandes   Mike Wm. McColl
Kevin Afuso   Randy Bancroft**

EDITOR
Don Maxam

COVER
Mark Maxam

The City By the Bay
Some call it OZ

WHERE IT ALL BEGINS!!!

"Welcome to the Land of Oz," the signs should read as you cross the bridge and alight in the city of San Francisco.

"Toto, I don't think we're in Kansas any more!" – says Dorothy.

Munchkins and witches, scarecrows and wizards, tin men, cowardly lions and, of course, flying monkeys! They're all here – all marching to the beat of a different drummer ... if not riding the horse of a different color!

That's right, whether born here or arriving by tornado, San Francisco hosts an eclectic trove of vagabonds found nowhere in this world. So, what better place to begin our *Let's Party!* U.S. Tour than in The City by the Bay; the land of Sourdough, Cable Cars, and Apple Pie (whoops ... that's Kansas), and, of course, the home Montana built (whoops, that's also Kansas).

Just thank the Wizard that Toto got loose, or you may have ended up in one of those other California towns (which would be enough to make you click your ruby slippers,

and make your way back). Instead, the golden-brick road has landed you in this beautiful city of 'natives' and transplants, vagabonds and house plants. All we can say is, "There's no place like home."

Welcome to San Francisco – the city of the Golden Gate, the Pyramid; the *most visited* city in the United States. This is The City tourists swarm to in January expecting heat, beaches, and ... well ... California! But don't be disappointed – we may not have the warm-water beaches, but we do have some of the best clothing-optional beaches you'll find anywhere (there ya go!).

Yes, this is the city of Broad Appetites. It's the city where you'll not only find the nation's oldest 'organized block party' (North Beach), but also 'Dykes on Bikes' riding down Market Street leading the Gay/Lesbian Freedom Day Parade every June (don't miss it!).

San Francisco – the city that some say is "the most beautiful city not of this Earth." Sure, we have a few witches and monkeys to deal with but, as in *The Movie*, the witches aren't all bad, and the monkeys are just basically stupid! (Remember, we're surrounded by water!)

So, latch down those doors, the storm's a-brewin', and – although it's been a while since The City was shook by a tornado – *the ground moves here, folks!* And, be careful, because on those "San Franciscan Nights," "when the lights ... go down ... in The City," you may find yourself "sittin' on the dock of the bay," "with flowers in your hair."

When you reach that place, do yourself a favor and look around. In this city built "on R-o-c-k and Roll," you'll soon discover why it was here, in San Francisco, where Tony Bennett left his heart.

And, oh, that thing you're looking for ...? Don't worry, you're sure to find it here. Welcome! – *And don't forget to "follow the Yellow Brick Road ..."*

3

Helping Let's Party!™

1st– Buy this book.

2nd– Convince all your friends to buy this book.

3rd– Send us your questions, comments, corrections, suggestions, recommendations, marriage proposals, or junk mail (we really like mail) to:

Let's Party! **San Francisco**
Vagabond Publishing, Inc.
2131 Third Street
San Francisco, CA 94107-3123

Phone: 415-241-9085
Fax: 415-241-9188
eMail: party2max@aol.com
http://EntertainNET.com

4th– Look for Let's Party! Europe (in bookstores now), Let's Party! Chicago coming fall of 1996, Let's Party! New York coming in Spring of 1997, and other Let's Party! titles in the near future. ••• ALWAYS – Beware of slackers and cheap imitators •••

Vagabond Publishing, Inc.

2131 Third Street
San Francisco, CA 94107
eMail: party2max@aol.com

ISBN: 0-9644467-1-5

Let's Party! San Francisco
Copyright © 1996 by Vagabond Publishing, Inc.
10 9 8 7 6 5 4 3 2 1 ∞

All rights reserved.

ISBN: 0-9644467-1-5

Publisher: Mark J. Maxam

Editor: Don Maxam

Authors: SamKhedr
Mark Maxam
Jessica Fernandes
Mike Wm. McColl
Kevin Afuso
Randy Bancroft

Cover Art: Mark Maxam

Photos: Jon Zimmerman, the San Francisco Visitor and Convention Bureau, and Mark Maxam. Photo Manipulation: Mark Maxam

Maps by: Liz Romo, © 1996 Vagabond Publishing, Inc.

Distributed by: ICS BOOKS, Inc.
1370 E. 86th Place
Merrillville, IN 46410
1-800-541-7323

Bulk Purchases of *Let's Party!* San Francisco are available at special discounts.

Let's Party!™ & **Party Passport**™ are trademarks of Vagabond Publishing, Inc.

CONTENTS

First, I'd like to thank everyone who purchased our first book, Let's Party! Europe. Without you, there's a good chance we wouldn't be able to share our home – The City – with you.

Yes, San Francisco – *The City* – is *Let's Party! headquarters*, U.S.A. – and we're glad you're here ... or about to be here ... or, are at least here in spirit.

Let the truth be known – no matter our reputation for being world-party animals, *The City* has something we've found nowhere else. San Francisco is the *true* embodiment of a *WORLD* city, and has extended its arms wide to welcome ... *you!*

It doesn't matter who you are, or where you come from. It doesn't matter what color your skin, your religion ... or your political persuasion, for that matter. And, as far as your sexual preference is concerned, well – *you already know the answer ... that really* doesn't matter!!!

And why not? Who am *I* to tell you who – or what – you should be?

Yes, this is The City at the end of the rainbow, the proverbial pot of gold. After all, we're *all* looking for some place ... *aren't we!?!*

Before we begin to enjoy the *fun* San Francisco has to offer, however, I want to personally pay tribute to the Ohlone Indians – The Bay Area's original residents.

The beauty you've seen here, before this pristine beautiful land was 'discovered.'

I want to thank you for sharing – even if by force of will – this land, your home ... and I wish to extend to you my gratitude, that of my ancestors, and that of my children.

And, I'd like to thank all native peoples for preparing for us this land we call "America," as I believe your spirit lives with us still.

As we seek peace and happiness for humanity, I hope – and believe – our paths will find their fork.

Until next time,

Mark J. Maxam

P.S. If I've discovered one thing when making this book – no matter your personal vision, no matter how *He/She* appears to you – what you need comes from God. *Just ask!*

B elow you will witness the cast of characters who put this book together for you. We are all Bay Area residents, and we all call San Francisco home. Look carefully at the photos on the following pages, some of the people 'depicted' are written about below. The others are our friends.

If you see any of us, please say hello – and tell us what you think of this book. We've done it for you, and we really wish to know. Other than that, we hope you will join us at our *Let's Party! Parties* that we will be having from time to time (you can hear about them by dialing our *PartyLine* (415-979-4FUN).

You can also find out what is happening with us by wiring to our World Wide Web address (http://EntertainNET.com), and we would appreciate your eMail any time of the day or night (party2max@aol.com).

Here's looking forward to the 21st century. We don't know about you, but we're going to party *"like it's 1999!"*

Sam Khedr

H aving encountered this book's publisher in the summer of 1993 at Oktoberfest in Munich, Germany, Sam signed on to become the major contributor of *Let's Party! Europe* (now in bookstores). Overcoming the egregious hardship of traveling around Europe drinking complimentary beer, Sam agreed to take on the daunting task of drinking free beer throughout San Francisco.

Thankfully, through the haze, Sam again managed to contribute his insightful wit and skewed perspectives to the accomplishment you hold in your hand. Be assured that if you read something in this book that causes your brain to do something akin to a belly-flop in a swimming pool – *it's Sam's.*

Jessica Fernandes

H aving had the publisher literally *stumble across her* on the island of Corfu, Greece, in the summer of 1992, Jessica continued on her personal party-trek until being called on to contribute to the France, Spain, and Portugal chapters of *Let's Party! Europe* (now in bookstores). A self-affirmed *'party girl,'* Jessi Mamba'd her way East and West of the Pyrenees in-search-of *"marcha marcha"* and … *"je ne c'est qua."*

When the opportunity to continue her search presented itself, Jessica responded by finding a guy and settling down.

… *Okay,* she didn't *quite* settle down, so between dispensations of *"coffee, tea, or me …?"* on transcontinental flights, she 'hustled-buns' through many a San Francisco club. And we thank her for her *sacrifice.*

Jessica's reviews are the ones that sound like they're from the woman's point of view *(even though we **tried** to edit them to the m-a-l-e perspective).*

Mike McColl

"So who is this Mike McColl dude, anyway. The guy just keeps calling and calling, and he won't leave me alone ..."

Well, it didn't go *exactly* like that, but when the need arose to knock off some quality reviews before we could put this baby to bed, Mike was the man we knew we could count on.

Ya see, Mike wrote this book called *The Worldwide Guide to Cheap Airfares,* and – although that sounds like a *really* dry subject – he throws some *great* parties! So we *knew* he could handle the task – especially after hearing that he *was going* to call his book *The Hitchhikers Guide To Cheap Airfares* until he became worried that Douglas Adams would sue him or something.

Mikes reviews are the most descriptive and *flourishy* in the book, having taken advantage of his acute sense of observation, attention to detail, and tendency to *wax poetic.* Thanks, Mike, for being 'The Man.' You'll find ordering information for Mike's book in the back of *Let's Party! San Francisco.*

Kevin Afuso and Randy Bancroft

It may seem odd that we talk about Kevin and Randy under one heading. And those of you who know they're gay may just choose to think we're acting within some stereotypical reference of gay business partners as ... well ... *partners* (if you get our drift – "wink, wink, nudge, nudge").

Well, we don't care. All we know is that they're the creators writers and publishers of San Francisco's *Oblivion Magazine* – and yes, it's a gay rag ... !

We also know that *we* certainly knew of no better persons to author the gay section of our book – and we're very glad they did (not that we would find it hard to go to *those* clubs, only that – in good faith – we knew we can't give you the true flavor of *gay San Francisco* the way gay men can). By the way, we want to apologize to San Francisco's lesbian population that this book doesn't entertain their perspective. We promise to add it to a future edition.

Besides, Kevin and Randy wrote their stuff together, and *please* don't ask us which reviews they wrote. You'll find information about *Oblivion* in the back of this book.

Brad 'Santosh' Olson

Brought from ... * ... to San Francisco to assist in completing the *Let's Party!* mandate, Santosh came, with *World Stompers* book in hand, primed to show our small band of galactic party travelers the best way to get this *Let's Party!* ship off the ground.

Spouting inspiration and advice (which you can personally derive from his newly published guide to *World travel on an Ultra-Budget)* he showed us *European travel on a Beer-Budget* folks a thing or two, assisting in our worldwide party assault.

His fascinations also became an inspiration for our fantasy cover.

You can read his austere jottings in *World Stompers* – a book we predict will change the way *good* travel guides will be prepared forever. You'll find ordering information for Santosh's book in the back of *Let's Party! San Francisco.*

Juri Koll

"*So ... ya want something about the arts in The City ... do ya? It's gonna cost ya, moneybags ...*"

Oops, there we go into fantasy land again. Juri, a *jack-of-many-talents* appeared out of the dusk when we were merely *hoping* to include editorial about the excessively-hip underground art scene in San Francisco. We call it *underground* because ... well, it's not like that other stuff you find near Union or Ghiradelli Squares.

So,. we're at this party at Blausthaus (that is the only mention you'll get from us ... we're keeping *it* a secret!), and hanging-out with the other cool people dancing and enjoying the scene was Juri. The scenario:

We meet Juri; he asks us what we're up to; we say we're almost finished, but we have to research some stuff on the San Francisco art scene ... and can you believe it? – Juri had the angle (doesn't that beat all!).

Coincidence? All we can tell you is that after so many 'coincidences' with this book, we're really opening ourselves up for *anything.*

If you're reading, and you get the itch to check out some art, good chance that's Juri (and sorry, he has nothing for sale).

Liz Romo

"*I'm rubber ... and you're glue ... whatever you say bounces off me and sticks to you ...*" (I have to tell you, it's awful sometimes being a child stuck in an adult's body. Well, not always – only that responsibility stuff is awful.)

So what can we say about Liz, Elizabeth, *Beth* --- %@!&$%#%!-*NO!!!*---Liz! Well, what we should say is that she's a good worker, conscientious, well groomed ... ...

But that just wouldn't cut it. You see, Liz is *not only* the glue that has kept this little product of ours from flying off somewhere in the universe – she is easily one of the best people we (cumulatively) have ever met.

You know, sometimes you meet someone who you just want to tell to quit being so nice, because they make you look bad by comparison? Liz is one of those people and, while we are sadly looked upon by others when we are in her light, it's worth it.

Okay, so we're laying it on a bit thick, but what do you expect – after all, she's the *Liz-ard of Oz!*

Mark Maxam

Can you believe it, I almost forgot to mention myself. *Hey, if I don't do it ...?* Besides, I really like seeing my name in print (it must have something to do with that *palindrome* thing.

You see ... there I was ... a young man in search of an adventure. Lo and behold, before I knew it, I'd caught this bug. Oh, no! It's not like I hadn't had an infection before, and, well, sure ... they warned me that it could happen. But sometimes you have to take chances in this life, and although there's no vaccination for this sort of thing, I just had to go for it. Besides, I was "a man ... a strong man, at that. I could handle it!"

So off I went. Sure – ignorant, like many, but determined to make it through ... to endure ... and to do it – **to do it all!**

And, let me tell ya, fella, "When you get this one ... it stays with ya – it stays with ya for life." At least so far, because there's no cure. But the best advice I can give you is to be careful ... use precautions ... and *don't goof around!* This is serious!

Because when the travel bug gets ya, you just gotta honor that 'jones!'

So I – ignorant as are so many – set out to conquer a beast of another kind. One called The Publishing Industry. No, *I couldn't be happy just taking my little royalty, and spend my time traveling the world* – as I had originally hoped. *No ... I* had to publish *Let's Party! Europe* myself!

After all, it was my idea, and our efforts, and we did a good job, and people wanted it ... and like it! Wouldn't ya think the industry would appreciate that?

Well, you *would* hope so, but remember, folks, what you were taught in Marketing class in University. This is a *mature* industry. To those of you who skipped that academic accolade, what it means is that the powers that be have set up a multitude of *Barriers to Entry*, as my marketing professor used to say (at those times when my head was on the desk from the big beer bash the night before).

So what's the big deal? David took out Goliath, didn't he? And he only had a string of leather and a little stone. *I had* **an idea!**

So, somewhere between *"Party!? Our youth shouldn't be going to Europe to* **party!**" and some (unscrupulous) publishers trying to buy your efforts with a nickel, you find that you missed with that first rock.

It's a damn good thing there are more where that came from.

So, hurling at you from a small office South of South of Market (SoMa) in San Francisco, CA – The City By The Bay – we fling *Let's Party! San Francisco.*

Sure, *Let's Party! Europe* has had success, finding reviews in Playboy, USA Today, Details, Detour, High Times, The Washington Post, and dozens of other publications, but this time, we're goin' for the eye.

Everyone listed above wishes to thank you personally for reading this far. It gives us hope.

Yours,

MAX

P.S. Look for *Let's Party! Chicago* in the fall of '96, and *Let's Party! New York* in 1997 *(beware of cheap imitators!)*

Editorial Mishmash

T he English language is full of stringent rules and principles that both restrict and facilitate our ability to communicate ... **R-r-r-r-r-r – Clunk!**

Geez, that was painful. Kinda felt like we passed a gallstone (Ouch!).

When it came to the name of our book, we got all sorts of (unsolicited) suggestions. But even with all that input, the problem of naming a book clearly and concisely – so that it communicates its contents – is not easy. We went through a number of themes, including:

- 'Through the Looking Glass' *(... but the queen scared us!).*
- 'A Guide to Middle Earth' *(... Mordor scared us, not to mention that evil, mean, slimy little Gollum).*
- 'Xanadu' *(... but Kane scared us ... hell – Orson scared us. Megalomaniacs ... and alien domination of the earth ...! What was this guy thinking? We don't call that fantasy. We'll stick with the Samuel Taylor Coleridge classic of the same name), and ... Let's Party!*

And what are we really trying to say with a name like *Let's Party!?!* The truth of the matter is – no matter what Mr. Webster tells you – as far as we're concerned, the definition of the word 'party' is *fun!*

With that in mind, in naming this book we bowed to the demagogic principles of marketing. *(There, we said it!)*

Thanks

A s you can imagine, there are tons of people we need to thank, starting with our mothers – *"hi, Mom"* – *and ending with the guys who delivered pizzas during those all night 'jam-sessions.'*

Just as with the Academy Awards, there's limited time and space to do this, so we'll make it short and sweet. We'd like to thank:

- Our Parents – because no matter the work and effort involved, when you have parents who support you in your efforts, the mere knowledge alone is enough to steel you in times of hardship. Don Maxam – for working hard to *accurately* keep us from splitting too many infinitives (we just had to slip that in!). Liz Romo – for being all, and doing all, and acting as a stabilizer around the office when Mark had his temper tantrums. Eric Stampfli – for his 'unique' brand of humor and input. Erik Sayle – for *being* unique. Mike Wm. McColl and Brad 'Santosh' Olson – for their respective books *The Worldwide Guide to Cheap Airfares,* and *World Stompers,* and for our alliance in the *Travel Publishers Network.*

- Kato Space – You are the soul, you are the sky, the sun and moon in Our Father's eye. You are the wind that sweeps across our face, a beautiful spirit, an embodiment of grace. Your energy soars, into our land, from the Heavens upon high. And knowing you, gives us hope, we need not know ... nor question why.

- and, Ahmed Azzam, Alex, Ben, Devin Black, everyone at Blasthaus, Jodi Brast, Breeze, Elisha Bucko, Carla, Chill, Keith Christy, Dave Dean, Harry & Margo

DeWildt, Stephanie Devins, Karen Evans, Samantha Ferro, Daphney Georghiou, Aki Georgiou, Gulgun (gigi), Claire Hall, Wayne Hoy, Kurt Kawasaki, Margaret Kenny, Dino Koullapis, Juri Koll, Kyra, Leah Ladd, Alf Marcusson, Marion, BriAnna Marie Maxam ☺, Julia Millan, Dale Miller, Moe, Mike Munoz, Kelly O'Connor, Cindi Oppheim-Colon & the House of Sirens, Petrina, Chris Powell, Nabiel, Raphael, Ubaldo Rodriguez, Allie Russell, Eric Sayle, Craig Scheftel, Robin Schuster, Scott, Scotty, Sebastian, Karl Sevdas, Carolyn Shipes, Steven, Jair Stokes, Pam Strawgate, Amber Tellez, Tiny, Martel Toler, Baha Turker, Josie Valderrama, Dave Vasquez, May Wu, Paul & Bonnie Young, Michael & Mimi (will they stay together?), Kelly & Martha, Tony & Maria, the boys in the band, the Wicked boys, all the people we've met over the years, and all the people we failed to mention.

- *Ourselves,* of course – for not giving up.

The Disclaimer!?!

Adhering also to purloined precepts of publishing principles, we'd like to say: The information in this book was collected on the straddle of '95/96, and the information we collected ...

... was accurate at the time of collection *(and things change, blah, blah, blah)* ...

... contains individual author opinions *(so you may disagree, blah, blah, blah)* ...

... is based on our experiences *(and you may not have as much fun as we did, blah, blah, blah)* ...

... actually took a lot of work to compile and write *(so we hope you like it).*

And, before you get into it, we'd like to leave you with ...

A sobering thought

Here's a sobering thought – *God knows we need one.* While scouting for the social haunts that made our cut, two things became clear.

- Any establishment worth the 'note' of its notoriety has seen its share of walking wounded.
- You don't want to be one!

Let's Party! (the book) has many goals. Among them is our aim to rage and let rage. It is *not* to trash and get trashed.

So, in a rare appearance for this book, on your trek through San Fran, keep in mind the concept of *"moderation"* There, we said it. Moderation, moderation, moderation, moderation, moderation! *(whew, it feels good to get that out of our system.)*

Moderate? Inebriate? Moderate? Inebriate? Moderate? Inebriate? – the choice is yours. Just remember, it would be a neat trick – *at best* – to mingle and flirt while passed out under the table.

After all, we here at Vagabond Publishing use the word 'party' as a verb. You know, *it's an action word!*

It's Time ...

T he time has come! Ba–bum-m-m (the sound of rolling drums in the background) ... it's time to go out. *WooHoo!*

Jubilation! Freedom!! Mayhem!!! *ANARCHY!!!!*

Yes-sirree-Bob, this is it! You're so excited you're actually looking forward to the long lines waiting to get into the *cool new club*.

This evening is going to be one to remember. Who knows ... maybe you'll meet your next boss, or fall 'forever in love' with some visiting Spanish señor or señorita

and fly off to Madrid. Perhaps you'll embrace your 'other side' and move to the Castro, or wake up on the beach in the arms of a beautiful friend.

All we can say is, before you fly off to Paris, do yourself a favor and pick-up a copy of *Let's Party! Europe.*

Other than that, these times provide the perfect opportunity to *just let go.* Life is hard enough, much less carrying all that other pragmatic bullshit around with you all the time. So relax – your day-time will take care of itself ... take *our words* for it.

And when you have let your mind escape from all of those things (like survival ... and your boss) that drag you down, close your eyes, take three deep breaths, and *BLAST OUT!*

So, whether or not you find Nirvana, the fact that you're using this book as your entertainment companion speaks volumes for your character. So now, let us tell you ...

How to Use Let's Party!

A s you wind your way through this glorious achievement we call *Let's Party! San Francisco* (please take a moment to pay homage to ... us ...), *ahem* – Anyway, as you read through this book, you'll notice we use such words as: best; greatest; rowdiest; funniest; coolest, etc. That's right, *Let's Party!* is your oracle of superlatives.

Unlike most guides, we find no wisdom in wasting your time (not to mention the paper on which this book is printed) covering anything that's not among the best in its class. We know you don't want the name and address of a club, and then to be told that it's as much fun as being in a coma. So, rest assure that, if it's in *Let's Party!*, it's happening. All you have to do is read each description, and decide what's your speed.

Let's Party! is written conversationally. Like a friendly 'local' you meet in a bar, we fill you in on the in's and out's of The City's amusements and diversions. We've dug deep to give you the inside scoop.

Sure, *Let's Party!* researchers have exposed some daytime amusements, however *Let's Party!* is really about diving into The City's nocturnal jungle of social haunts. In other words, while entertainment sections of other guides may require a magnifying glass to decipher, our whole book is just that – *one big entertainment section.*

Editorial Mishmash

What may surprise you, is that you hold in your hand *more* than your guide to San Francisco's best clubs and bars. If for no other reason than to sound like enlightened individuals, *Let's Party!* has gone one step further by including snippits of The City's history and culture (at least *our* rendition of it's history and culture).

Rest assured that it's only enough to give you a feel for the scene. With this info, you'll be able to plug into the Who's, What's, Where's, and How's of what makes San Fran's diverse and wacky natives tick.

That's right, *Let's Party!* is your guide to the scene behind the scene! (Hmmm, that's a pretty lofty title. Perhaps we should stick with ...

Let's Party!
Your Guide to Fun in **San Francisco**

... it works for us!

Orientation and Getting Around

The delight of exploring a city is all about that element of uncertainty you can expect to find behind every corner. With that in mind, who really wants orientation in this disoriented world?

Nevertheless, we have provided you with a map of each neighborhood, and most are marked with items of interest: BOOM! – *'X' marks the spot!* These maps are not comprehensive, nor are they your have-all and end-all. You can use them to mark the map you get from local retailers or the Visitor Office. As for our advice – *Go with the flow!*

Practical Information

i ••• The best – *no bullshit* – information we can give is the location and hours of San Francisco's Visitor Information Center. You'll find that they really are there to help, and seasoned travelers prefer their information and maps over those provided in travel guides. If they covered entertainment and night life, you wouldn't need us, either *(whew!)*. Look for the *'i'* on our maps.

Their "multilingual staff will be happy to answer your questions. Just drop by and see us in Benjamin Swig Pavilion on the lower level of Hallidie Plaza at Market and Powell Streets. We're easy to find." the brochure reads "And we're there to help weekdays 9:00 a.m. – 5:30 p.m., Saturday until 3:00 p.m., Sunday 10:00 a.m. – 2:00 p.m.. Or you may call 415-391-2000. You can also phone us 24-hours a day at 415-391-2001 for a recorded message listing daily events and activities. For information in Français, 415-391-2003; in Deutsch, 415-391-2004; in Español, 415-391-2122; and in Japanese 415-391-2101."

Attractions

Ever wonder why most travel guides bear the weight and dimensions of the stone slabs Charlton Heston lugged around in 'The Ten Commandments'? Do they sometimes feel heavier than a pile of paper should ever weigh? At *Let's Party!*, we have pin-pointed the answer to this weighty issue. A case in point:

"The museum contains volumes of historical artifacts, paintings, sculptures of monarchs, frescos, portraits, and religious icons of all sorts and sizes. They are housed in an impressive Neo-classical structure designed by Brian Hither III between 1934 and 1938 and modeled on the gothic fortress of OZ ... Look for Dürer's wood etchings of 'Witches in Flight' ... or Brueghel's 'Tin Man with Ax'."

God, that's heavy!!! If this sort of (real) information tickles your fancy, read this, and more, in any number of other travel guides. Meanwhile, you'll find us at the bar down the street doing the *jive-thing* with some locals.

Accommodations

Accommodations? What, are you kidding– *we're a party guide, find your own accommodations!* (Sorry, but we can get a little uppity at times.) For accommodations, talk to your travel agent, or call the San Francisco Visitor Information Center (see 'Practical information, above).

If you're really strapped, give us a call, and we'll put you up for a while – *NOT!*

Dining

As an entertainment guidebook, it only stands to reason that a bunch of the places we wrote about have food – great food in many cases! If you find a food spot listed in this book, odds are the place also has a party scene. Our writers have also snooped, scooped, and (where possible) revealed late-to-close munchy pit stops. We know it's at those times it matters most.

Entertainment

What, are you kidding? This whole book covers entertainment! The clubs, bars, pubs, cafes, and other haunts and events featured in this edition of *Let's Party!* have, in fact, undergone the strictest scrutiny en route to having our bus stop at their door. Our selection process was based on a formula developed by several professors emeritus from the Brookings Institute of Controlled Mayhem. An establishments 'fun factor' was derived in the following manner:

$$C^2 + \frac{((S*3)/(E+L))-(A-T) = P*\pi}{2D+10G*\sqrt{B}} = X$$

Where: C represents Capacity in numbers of people; S is the raw Size of the establishment; E is the appearance of the Exterior; L equals the Length of the bar in meters (if there was no bar we entered 0); A is the quantity of Alcohol available on premises; T calculates the quality of Tune-age, live or electronic; P is the average Price of beer; D is the Decibel level (measured at full capacity); G is the layers of Graffiti found in the men's room; B is how often the establishment gets Busted by the cops, and the upshot; X is any damn thing we please.

LET'S PARTY!
Editorial Mishmash

Okay, we're just having fun – but this hair-brained formula exemplifies the kind of the wacky suggestions we've received as criteria for listing a social haunt. Let's face it, there's no such thing as the perfect formula for guaranteeing a 'happening' scene.

Without opening a Pandora's box of philosophical mumbo-jumbo, everyone has their own subjective reality – including, we suppose, Pandora. Therefore, *Let's Party!* researchers went forth seeking a wide variety of establishments. So be it cool blues and jazz, frat party revelry, dance fever, or a park where to kick back, we have something for you

If there's one thing you can be sure of, it's the level of pulse found on Friday and Saturday nights. So, while we can't guarantee every place we've listed will be 'happening' every day of the week, show up anywhere with the right attitude, and you won't need to find the party – the party will be looking for you!

Just Remember ...

The man who follows the crowd, will usually get no further than the crowd.

The man who walks alone is likely to find himself in places no one has ever been before.

Creativity in living is not without its attendant difficulties, for peculiarity breeds contempt. And the unfortunate thing about being ahead of your time is that when people finally realize you were right, they'll say it was obvious all along.

You have two choices in life: you can dissolve into the mainstream, or you can be distinct. To be distinct is to be different. To be different, you must strive to be what no one else but you can be ...

– Alan Ashley-Pitt

SAN FRANCISCO

Straddling the western edge of the Western Hemisphere, a city exists of such rare quality, she is referred to by most as simply *The City*. Her profound presence stands alone, yet belongs to all. With little argument, she is the 'favorite darling' of this United States – her prominence deeply echoed around the globe as a shining example of 'progressive diversity.'

Embracing, *not just tolerating,* the traditional *and* wacky sides of human culture, she is admired by all and cherished by the lucky few who come to call her home. Some may claim she is the rediscovered lost city of Atlantis, while others see her as the new Shangri-La. But for us, she's simply ... *OZ.*

Yet, as with every city, she's made up of metal, marble, and glass ... and as such, vulnerable to the ills of any big city. Nevertheless, she is ... *San Francisco.*

High atop any of her undulating hills, you're treated to a barrage of endless post-card views and dangerously stunning sweeps. At the tip of a thumb-shaped peninsula, covering an area of 47 square miles, San Francisco is framed on three sides by water. Her northernmost rim is curbed by the deep waters of the bay – home to Marin, Angel Island, and the Rock of Alcatraz. To the east, the Bay Bridge reaches out through Treasure Island to Oakland and into Berkeley. To the west lies the fading blue hues of the Pacific Ocean, where the Japanese current begins its wrap-around journey destined for Asia.

Separating Ocean from Bay is the famed portal, the Golden Gate Bridge, which shares its name with the largest city park in the United States. Thickly sprinkled throughout The City, is an endless collection of Grand Victorian homes – a city trademark. To the immediate south, Twin Peaks towers above the city below the ominous shadow of the Sutra Tower (The City's only downright eyesore). To the east, Mount Diablo (Devil Mountain) towers imposingly. In Marin to the north, Mount Tamalpais provides a perspective shared by only a few urban centers – none of which can match this beauty.

The Fault

E ven with all of natures ingredients at his disposal, no wizard could have created a finer masterpiece. But beauty of this caliber doesn't come cheap, and the signature on this painting reads: *San Andreas* – the fault, that is! Deep within the earth's crust, deep cracks separate the Pacific Plate from the North American Plate. Though violently rocking San Francisco only twice this decade, the area's faults are constantly at work touching-up the landscape. Every now and then they release faint, yet stirring, reminders of their presence ... and ominous, brooding, force.

The Habitat

N o less amazing than the magnificence of San Francisco's panoramic views, has been The City's growth. As with many great discoveries, she was first stumbled upon by accident. In 1769, leading an expeditionary force on an overland trek heading north to Monterey Bay, a Spanish captain named Gaspar de Portolá overshot his destination, and discovered the bay peninsula.

White man had arrived, and what started as a fledgling community of tents, sprinkled atop a small patch of hill, soon replaced the tribal villages of the Ohlone Indians, and became the precursor of what would eventually be San Francisco.

Things didn't heat up, however, until January 28, 1849. A day seen by many as 'Day One' ... a day when James Marshall first screamed "GOLD!" ... and the rush was on. Word of his finding spread like wildfire to the furthest reaches of the globe, and a single yellow nugget had seduced untold thousands of fortune hunters to endure long, dangerous journeys over mountains and across oceans.

A rmed with the lust for that proverbial 'flash-in-the-pan,' willed to the 49th parallel by blind determination, migrants quickly streamed into the Bay Area. For the first time, streets teamed with a motley mix of people with varied languages and cultures – all looking to 'strike it rich.'

Gambling, prostitution, and crime reached epidemic levels as more and more prospectors – and those that preyed on them – became feverishly wealthy. In a short time, the modest, quiet community that had become San Francisco was greed-shocked into 'big-city hood.' By 1890, The City's population had mushroomed to well over 300,000 Americans, Mexicans, Australians, South Americans, and Chinese. And, San Francisco's lawless character resembled a pirate's cove, earning it the dubious nickname 'the Barbary Coast.'

We can only imagine the scene on the streets – perhaps sounding like the lunatic rantings of Daffy Duck … *"I'm rich! I'm rich! It's Mine! Mine! All Mine!"* … after finding a magic lantern.

Well, that's the picture – and enough talk about the habitat. Now, we'll cut to the chase, side-step the remaining historical bits, and shift to 'today' – *after all, we're a party guide!* But don't worry, at the beginning of each chapter you'll find a 'quick, don't-blink' summary of each neighborhood's history.

Just be sure to arm yourself with at least a half dozen roles of film when you visit.

Peerless San Francisco

S an Francisco's distinctive and volatile beginning has blended into the flavor and character of The City today. It's no coincidence that the United Nations Charter

was born here. Next to New York and London, San Francisco boasts one of the richest, most diverse selections of ethnicity in the world. With storybook perfection, The City perched on the edge of a continent is a global village where you'll find different cultures and lifestyles coexisting in relative harmony. It is a quality made clearly visible due to San Francisco's compact, user friendly size.

As you walk from one neighborhood to the next, your senses are ambushed by the sights, sounds, and smells that hallmark each cultural microcosm. As if it were part of one's character, residents – upon meeting for the first time – are eager to discover which neighborhood each calls home. The same is true in this 'potpourri of transplants' when San Franciscans seek to discover another resident's birthplace. Realizing that diversity brings cultural enlightenment, and hence understanding, residents revel in The City's impartiality. Most of them seem to know that only through understanding the differences and opinions of others can we, as the human species, find oneness – *and,* diversity makes for better parties!

And there's much fun to be had:

- If you're the type who prefers Italian-style lingering at some street-side cafe with cappuccino in hand, check-out North Beach.
- If it's Dim Sum and dragons you seek, enter the small enclave of China Town.
- If you crave Mariachi music and taquerias, find your way to the chaotic Mission neighborhood – San Francisco's largest, oldest, most-populated area.
- If there is hob-nobbing to be done, you'll find it in the affluent Pacific Heights, Marina, and Cow Hollow neighborhoods.

- To check out the birthing-grounds of flower power, venture down to the 'street called love' in the Haight. Although diminished, this area has doggedly held on to its Bohemian flavor.

- If you're armed with plastic and intent on a trailblazing shopping spree, let the ringing sound of cash registers guide you to the big-name consumer temples of Union Square.

- If the alternative-slant of gay life is more your speed, seek the trendy and progressive Castro district.

- To check out one of the country's most-visited tourist attractions, loaded with 'stuff' shops (and sea lions), make your way to the hype-powered Fisherman's Wharf.

- And last (but first priority in our party-on hearts) comes our favorite neighborhood – South of Market, popularly known as SoMa. This is most likely where you'll find us, late-night, playing with the rest of the *kids* 'til sunrise.

I n addition to those rippin', rockin', roarin' spots you're beginning to expect from *Let's Party!*, throughout The City you will find an ample selection of time-out parks, overviews, and chill-zones where you can take stock and rest up for your evening's adventures. You'll also find festivals, street fairs, and other events where you can go and meet the people – which is, after all, what it's all about!

One thing for sure, is that San Francisco offers both its residents and visitors a wide and diverse selection of entertainment offerings. Set in a center of open-mindedness, the scenes in the clubs and on the streets give testament to the belief "to each his/her own" – a basic tenet of human co-operation. After all, if it's not hurting anyone, what's the problem?

All we can say, as we send you into the fray, is, "Get out there … and do it *your* way."

If you wish to have fun, both inside and under the sun, you must make your own path, and look out for number one:

But one thing is for sure,

As we dangle *'party!'* as a lure

Is to keep an open mind

For it's *humanity* we must cure.

S o do your thing … with your brothers and sisters join and sing … lock arms and hold to hands … in the end we'll *all* find the golden ring!

Cheers!

THE CASTRO

The Castro has not always been the 'hustle and bustle' center of gay life it is today. In fact, as we know – and love – it, The Castro is only about 25 years old.

Polk Street (from the Civic Center north) was San Francisco's *original* gay neighborhood. Many of the old-timers remain, and a great gay life certainly thrives there. Many bars and businesses are gay owned, and cater exclusively to the gay community.

With the late 1960s and early 1970s came urbanization – and a great influx of new white-collar workers who liked the Polk Street neighborhood, and it's proximity to downtown and the financial district.

As "The City By the Bay" evolved from an industrial city to a city of service and industry, San Francisco attracted a young, upwardly mobile crowd who began moving into the Polk Street neighborhood. Simultaneously, the Gay Rights movement was making great advances, and the 'new city' feel of San Francisco was attractive to gay men and lesbian women, who also began moving here in ever greater numbers. However, this well-educated, enthusiastic, and politically active young crowd of gays and lesbians were reluctant to settle in the Polk Street neighborhood, and instead searched for a new place to call home.

Enter 'The Castro' district.

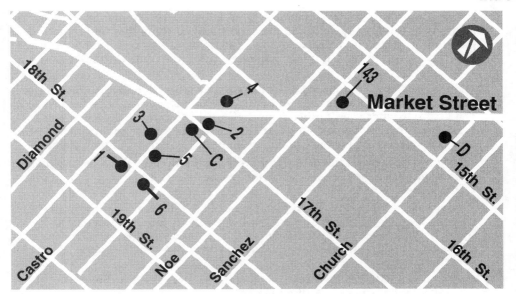

As the rapid urban sprawl of San Francisco in the 1960s began pushing the suburbs further from the city, the Irish-American families – who had first settled the outlying areas along upper Market Street in the 1880s, following completion of the Castro rail line – left their once-beautiful Victorian neighborhoods for greener, more-suburban pastures. Gays found these Victorians, nestled at the foot of Twin Peaks, to be aging but ideal homes – full of charm and character – and breathed new life into this dying neighborhood. And, The Castro became the home of choice for many gay people.

Men were walking Castro Street arm-in-arm, and San Francisco became known as 'the gay capital of the world' because ...

In 1972, San Francisco was the first U.S. city to pass an ordinance forbidding sexual-orientation discrimination in housing and employment.

In 1977, local Castro Street business owner Harvey Milk – the first openly gay man to hold office in The City – was elected to the San Francisco Board of Supervisors. One year later, he and liberal Mayor George Moscone were assassinated in Milk's City Hall office by anti-gay ex-supervisor Dan White. The community mourned, and began an evening candlelight vigil – a walk from Harvey Milk Plaza (at the corner of Castro and Market Streets) to City Hall to commemorate his bravery. This ceremony is repeated every November 27th.

In the early '80s, AIDS made it's devastating attack on The Castro and San Francisco. As the numbers of ill and dying climbed, so did the strength of the community. Education is 'the name of the game' today, and – among the many businesses in The Castro – AIDS and HIV organizations and services occupy Victorian store fronts and upstairs flats.

By the 1990s gays and lesbians had adopted the attitude that being gay was no longer just a lifestyle, but a life. In 1990, San Francisco passed the Gay Partners Ordinance allowing same sex couples to register their committed relationships at City Hall. A year later, voters elected several gays and lesbians back into city government.

Roberta Auchtenberg, a lesbian member of the Board of Supervisors, later moved to Washington, D.C., to work for the Clinton Administration's Department of

Housing and Urban Development. As a lesbian, she deeply understood the meaning of community, and had the opportunity to share that understanding at the highest level. She returned to San Francisco in 1995 to run for mayor, and received a substantial number of votes from the entire San Francisco community.

Today, The Castro and it's residents have a new label: Not gay. Not lesbian. But 'queer.' This 'queer' social and economic influence is growing wider and wider as The Castro extends even farther from the corner of Castro and 18th Streets than ever. Traveling up Market Street on the newly restored (1995) vintage F-line streetcar, you feel the presence of the 'community' as early as Church Street.

As you pass through the gateway marked on the right by the red Safeway sign and on the left by the blue S&C Ford sign, *you've arrived*. Everything in front of you ... that's The Castro!

Several places are worth checking out here, but the most noteworthy for the party crowd is Sparky's Restaurant, located just a few doors south of Market on Church Street. It's your basic all-American bill of fare, and they're there to serve you 'with a smile' at all hours of the day or night. After you've been out 'clubbing,' it's a great place to fill up.

Continuing up Market Street on the F-line, the first few blocks include a mix of gay and straight businesses. By the time you get to Noe Street, however, businesses become almost exclusively gay owned and operated. Get off the F-line as early as Sanchez Street (look to the left for Image Leather) and walk the rest of the way. You won't want to miss a thing.

As you walk, you'll pass some of the best shops, eateries, and bars The Castro has to offer. At the corner of Market and Noe, for instance, there's a lot to take in:

• There's the Baghdad Cafe' – open 24 hours for your late-night/ early morning munchies; behind it (on 16th Street) is Josie's Cabaret and Juice Joint – the best place to catch a cabaret or stage show in The Castro.

• Across Market from Baghdad is another famous landmark and stop over. If you feel the need for a late-morning or early afternoon Italian soda (or just love people watching), stop in the Cafe' Flore – the totally 'queer' inside / outside cafe / eatery.

• Further along Market are more specialty shops catering to the 'queer' clientele. If you're staying in town for a while, you may even consider joining one of the gyms, which offer short term packages for travelers.

• At the end of the block, just before the intersection with Castro, is the famous body-piercing studio known as The Gauntlet; and above that, The Cafe'. This hot-stop is one of the few places in The Castro where dancing is in order. If it's warm, there's also a great little balcony for checking out the crowd below.

• The Detour bar, located across the street at 2348 Market, will definitely be a stop after dark. This is *'the'* Castro bar.

The intersection of Market and Castro is now just a few more steps along – you can't miss it. Turn to your left, and watch out for the F-line hurling itself around the corner in front of Orphan Andy's (another 24-hour eatery) and back onto Market Street.

The grand marquee of the stately Castro Theater, built in the 1920s (and currently home to the San Francisco Gay and Lesbian International Film Festival) makes it official: This is the heart of The Castro. This vital street seems to change by the season, and more and more of the aging Victorians are giving way to the 'mallification of The Castro,' as local political commentator and 'drag queen' Joan Jett Blakk wrote.

If you continue down Castro, the next intersection is Castro and 18th – referred to by many as the 'gayest intersection in the world.' All the 'queer' stuff you've seen so far radiates from this point.

And, there's another block up Castro to check out, and at least one block in each direction along 18th. Walk it all, and check out the people ... it's quite a show.

As important as The Castro is to the 'queer' community, it's only part of what San Francisco has to offer:

- SoMa is home to the very best 'queer' night clubs and most of the 'queer' leather bars. There's a great trio of nasty leather/Levi bars grouped within walking distance of one another near the corner of Folsom and 8th Streets. The Hole in the Wall Saloon is located on 8th Street just off Folsom, and only a half block away are My Place and Powerhouse – and that's just the beginning.

- SoMa is also home to the *major* 'queer' clubs in The City. Club Townsend, located at 177 Townsend Street at Third, is home to The City's largest Saturday-night party, Club Universe. It's sweaty, it's beautiful, and it's hot! Sunday night, Club Townsend also hosts the city's longest-running 'queer' club, Pleasuredome.

For the 'queer' tourist, there's *never* a bad time to visit San Francisco. There are, however, outstanding highlights and special events to remember:

- Gay Pride Celebration and Parade – the world's largest 'queer' celebration, is traditionally held on the last Sunday in June. It's a great time to be in San Francisco. Have you ever experienced the Dykes on Bikes? Reason enough.

- Two other dates to watch for are the Folsom Street Fair, held on the last Sunday in September, and the Castro Street Fair, held one week later. Drastically different events – but each worth its title –

  - The Folsom Street Fair is the wild one, with the best stretch of Folsom Street laced in leathermen and leatherwomen dressed to shock and impress while savoring the Indian Summer The City often enjoys during this event.

  - For the Castro Street Fair, it's back to jeans and a T-shirt, and one of our more traditional Street Fairs, loaded with food, booths, live music, and wall-to-wall people!

1: Badlands   Gay Bar

4121 18th St. (at Castro). 415-626-9320. Castro. **HOURS:** Daily, 11:30a.m.-2a.m. **SPECIALS:** Happy Hour. **RESTRICTIONS:** Cash only.

Badlands stands out as one of the most architecturally intriguing gay bars in The Castro. It's spacious, nouveau-western decor is highlighted by soft lights filtered through gorgeous stained glass built into the ceiling, giving it the appearance of natural light coming through a skylight. Check out the extensive collection of U.S.

license plates suspended from the wall behind the bar, but (most important) don't forget to check out the gorgeous late-20 to 30- and early 40-something guys packing the bar every night of the week.

This bar gets very cruisy and, to the delight of most patrons, no other bar is apparently designed specifically for such activities. There are two pool tables at either end of the space, with elevated, wooden-bench-like seating ideal for checking out and being seen. These elevated benches are also abundant throughout the back

of the bar, so don't be surprised if you see the same person walking and casually staring back and forth throughout the back bench area – he's just looking for the right guy to sit next to.

The toilets are situated between the back and front areas, and accessible from both spaces. They feature one of those long, porcelain-trough urinals that seem so popular (obviously!) in gay bars.

Aside from the heavy cruising possibilities, don't miss their great weekend DJs, who spin a high-energy selection of current House music that keeps the crowd *moving!* Too bad there's no dance floor.

2: The Café   Gay Bar/Dance Club

2367 Market St. (at Castro & 17th). 415-861-3846. Castro. **HOURS:** Daily, noon-2a.m. **SPECIALS:** Happy Hour. **RESTRICTIONS:** Cash only.

The Cafe' is like ... coming home. Coming home to friends, coming home to family ... coming home to a relaxed, unpretentious hangout where you talk, laugh, dance, flirt, and just be yourself. I propose they slap a sign onto the back of the Powell Street Cable Car line that reads, "Meet me at *The Cafe'*." It's where *everybody* goes to meet friends or make new ones. It's at least as popular a meeting space as any 'coffeehouse' cafe, only this one's open 'til 2 a.m.!

This is a melting pot for locals and tourists of all ages, genders, economic, social and ethnic backgrounds. It's more like going to a big party than a bar or night club.

One of the most outstanding features is the dance floor –one of only two in the entire Castro area. It's small compared to SoMa standards, but – due to it's distinct reputation as a place to dance in The Castro (and because there's never a cover) – the Cafe is usually packed every day of the week. On weekends, expect a 30- to 60-minute line of people waiting to ascend the nondescript stairway that opens into the best party in The Castro.

I'd also like to mention their weekend DJ, Phil B. As the late-night DJ for the legendary Sunday-night SoMa Queer Club, The Pleasuredome, and as one of the premier DJ names in Australia before he moved to The City, hearing Phillip spin at this relatively modest club is a rare delight not to be missed by club-music afficionados.

3: Castro Station   Gay Bar

456 Castro St. (between 17th & 18th). 415-626-7220. Castro. **HOURS:** Daily, 6a.m.-2a.m. **SPECIALS:** Happy Hour. **RESTRICTIONS:** Cash only.

You may hear *Castro Station* referred to as a leather bar, but it is, in fact, much more diverse, catering to anyone and everybody in search of a good drink, some upbeat House music, and the chance to cruise. *Castro Station's* prime Castro location and wide-open entrance entices locals and tourists alike into the sizable bar to mingle with a crowd that ranges from pretty Castro boys to rough-looking leathermen, to middle-aged, chain-smoking transvestites, to care-free tourists.

The place is consistently busy, and the diverse, often-cruisy 30- to 40-something clientele creates a fun, dynamic environment ideal for curious people watchers. *Castro Station* also periodically lends it's ample wall space to local 'queer' artists (usually photographers) and, at any given time, there's a selection of intriguing work to hazily gaze upon should the carnival-like weekend atmosphere become a bit too much for drunken senses to handle.

4: Detour   Gay Bar

2348 Market St. (between Castro & Noe). 415-861-6053. Castro. **HOURS:** Daily, 2p.m.-2a.m. **SPECIALS:** Happy Hour, 2p.m.-8p.m. **RESTRIC-TIONS:** Cash only.

The bar scene, as all fags are aware, is the center of the social scene for most of us involved in the gay lifestyle. And, *Detour* is the center of the bar scene in The Castro, as all bar flies inevitably end up there at one point during their weekend bar hopping escapades. And, for good reason. *Detour* is quite possibly the most popular bar in the entire Castro area. You'll not find a more packed, sexually charged bar anywhere.

This is also where the most-gorgeous 20-something locals hang out to cruise, cruise, cruise. *Detour* is a madhouse on the weekends, and the back-alley, chain-link-fence motif, jet-   black walls, and loud DJ-ed House music elevate this bar to the status of the ultimate fag bar in San Francisco for a Generation X crowd desperate to party until it positively *hurts!*

Detour is also the only bar I know of that features Go-Go dancers, so – if the friendly crowd fails you (an unlikely possibility) – you'll always have something gorgeous to look at.

5: A Different Light Bookstore   Bookstore

489 Castro St. (at 18th). 415-431-0891. Castro. **HOURS:** Daily, 10a.m.-Midnight.

For socially and politically aware 'queer' living in San Francisco – or anywhere for that matter – *Different Light Bookstores* (they also operate in Los Angeles and New York) are like shining stars, burning brightly in this dark era of conservative madness and right-wing fanaticism, guiding us to a higher consciousness where it's not only okay to be 'queer' – its something we can actually be proud of in all respects.

A Different Light Bookstore reminds me of a photo that was taken during the 'Million Man March' in Washington, D.C., in 1995. It depicts several African-American men, standing tall, basking in the midday sun, boldly grasping a sign that reads, "Black by birth, Gay by God, Proud by Choice." That's really what *A Different Light* is all about – pride, awareness, and equality.

A Different Light not only provides a space where enlightenment-thirsty fags can go to quench their thirst for knowledge, but also an important social space where small, community events can be held and important 'queer' role models go to sign books, meet people, and read excerpts from their latest work. Such public figures as Martina Navratilova and Greg Louganis have appeared at *A Different Light,* as well as important gay and lesbian literary figures, all of whom usually cause quite a stir within the confines of our humble gay ghetto.

A Different Light Bookstore is one of the essential elements that shapes and binds us together, and I highly recommend a visit to experience the magic that creates such an important force in our community.

6: Midnight Sun   Gay Video Bar

4067 18th St. (at Hartford). 415-861-4186. Castro. **HOURS:** Daily, noon-2a.m. **SPECIALS:** Happy Hour.

The idea of video bars has blossomed into such a huge business that no big city would be complete without several in every district. The Castro is no exception. *Midnight Sun,* however, stands out as *the* premier video bar in The Castro, which is why no guide book would be complete without a description of this nicely sized, beautifully designed (must have been decorated by a fag!) bar that, in addition, attracts quite a unique Castro clientele.

Midnight Sun is basically one, large, square room, sparsely yet tastefully designed in muted natural tones, accented with large floral arrangements and seasonal decorations. On either side of the space, framing the long bar, are two giant screen TVs (or two very small movie theater screens, if you prefer) hanging on the walls just below the ceiling. They screen dance-music videos, with regular breaks featuring HBO-style 'queer' stand-up comics as well as campy or 'queer'-oriented sitcoms and nighttime soaps. Either screen is visible from any point in the bar and, due to its omnipotent presence, is often the primary focal point for a large portion of the 20- to 30 -something, upwardly mobile, button-down, white-collared, financial-district-centered, cologne-scented, freshly manicured, three-shower-per-day-patrons.

Oh, did I mention the customers? These beautiful boys come to unwind (and drink) after a hard day's work at the office. However, despite their clean-cut, medium-starched-collared appearance, the place is extremely cruisy – and you should have no problem making new 'friends' on your night out at *Midnight Sun.*

Additional Gay Lifestyle Reviews:

SOMA:

- The Box
- The Endup
- Hole in the Wall Saloon
- The Stud
- Club Universe
- Girl Spot
- My Place

FISHERMAN'S WHARF

H ere we are, at Fisherman's Wharf – a neighborhood solely, completely, and (to be totally clear), *entirely* devoted to San Francisco's tourist trade.

Many moons ago, before there was such a *thing* as tourism, The Wharf was primarily *work* to Italian and Chinese fisherman. Once upon a time, they plied their trade, harvesting the bounty that Bay area waters provided, and earning a handsome living off the once-fertile waters. It was a time when these waters were frequented by trawlers, leaving at dawn, often returning before noon, with holds filled with fresh fish, prawns, squid, and crab.

Well, those busy fishing days are gone, the result of pollution and over-fishing. At Pier 45, as a token truce with the environment, you'll still find a few fishermen pulling up with their early morning catch – *that is, if you can drag yourself out of bed by 6:00 a.m.*

Mostly, however, the Chinese and Italian fisherman of yesterday are the shopkeepers and restaurant owners of today. Their catch these days is the flood of tourist dollars that flow in daily.

The power of hype has mutated what once was a small enclave of fisherman into one of the country's most-visited tourist attractions. Last we heard, it's number three after Disney World and the Mall of America in Minnesota (where, if you're not indoors, you're just plain *cold!*).

Okay, we have to admit it … San Francisco is *Let's Party!* central command – and our home. So visions of The Wharf do not necessarily conjure up images of raging entertainment and 'party 'til you drop' action. What's there is a landscape 'jungle thick' with moderate-priced motels, t-shirt shops, fast-food stalls, and amusements are smeared with the fingerprints of a theme park (yet without the cool rides).

THE WHARF
Intro

You may not be caught dead wearing one, but many tourists *do* leave here sporting their new "I Love Fisherman's Wharf" t-shirts ... feeling they've experienced San Francisco. It's a pity. Sure, it's a famous area, but to San Francisco natives, Fisherman's Wharf and cable cars alone do *not* represent this city of broad and diverse tastes. If you see any real locals at The Wharf, they'll be standing behind cash registers, taking your order, or providing entertainment for this city's out-of-town guests.

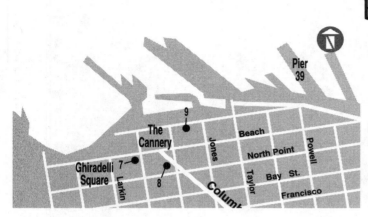

But you know you're going to visit The Wharf – if only to see Alcatraz – so we've prepared a *Let's Party!* QuickTour for you. To start you off right, we want to tell you that parking at The Wharf can be a big pain – especially at certain times of the year. So, during the winter months (when visitors falsely imagine that San Francisco is in *California* – with hot temperatures and all that), take a cable car from Union Square. If you must drive, plan to spend time looking for parking (or quite a bit of money at the tourist-priced lots in the area).

If you've found accommodations in the area, you're lucky. You can walk. Just be sure to bring your jacket in preparation for that cold snap that hits The City daily about 4:00 p.m.

Our QuickTour starts at the infamous *Pier 39*. A World-famous, wood-planked novelty shop, it's jammed full of game arcades, and specialty stores packed with novelty trinkets. If you must go, use the kids as an excuse – you know ... "Junior just had his heart set on riding that double-decker carousel ..." If you have no kids, just grab one from someone else. In all fairness, however, Pier 39 *does* offer some decent restaurants.

Be certain you have your camera loaded, because you're going bypass the restaurants, candy stores, and knick-knack shops, and head to the end of the pier – and The City's number one "take my picture" spot. That's right, ya just gotta have your picture taken with Alcatraz – the most notorious prison in American history – in the background. Now *there's* a tale to tell your grandkids!

After you've finished with that, head around to the west side of the pier, and get that 'other' Wharf shot – the one of sea lions lying around on floating docks. *Sea lions?!?* That's right, for some unexplainable reason, after the earthquake of 1989, these sleek, whimsical creatures no longer felt comfortable on their traditional Island home. So they appropriated several of the docks in the marina to the west of the Pier. As you approach, you're likely to *hear* them first – and they *are* worth seeing and hearing! It may not be *The Call of the Wild,* but it's probably the closest you'll ever get to these true loungers.

Breaking away from the griping buzz of Pier 39, hop on **Jefferson Street** (it runs along the marina and waterfront). In this area, expect to dodge other tourists while encountering a relentless barrage of kitsch boutiques, more t-shirt shops, and even more t-shirt shops. Scattered between are such attractions as the Wax Museum (do you think Michael posed for that?), the Guinness World of Records, and Ripley's "Believe It or Not."

On your way, before you get to the heart of The Wharf, you'll pass the Boudin Bakery store, where you can load up on some of that great sourdough bread you can only get in San Francisco. *Hey, we don't know if it's the active yeast thing or what* – and, sure, we may prefer a French loaf while walking along the Champs Elysées in Paris (for more, pick up a copy of *Let's Party! Europe* at your favorite book store) – but the bread in The City is *really* that good!

As you continue, cut across at Taylor Street – and enjoy the fishy smell of ice-laden display cases, stew pots loaded with such scrumptious offerings as shrimp or crab salad, whole crabs, and easily the best clam chowder you've ever eaten. Have it in a sourdough bread bowl, add a little tobasco and pepper to taste, and experience your taste buds reaching gastronomic highs.

Now, pause a moment to re-live the moment.

Okay, now that you've picked up some energy, continue on past *Lou's Pier 47* (at the turn-off to Scoma's Italian seafood restaurant ... even *we* recommend Scoma's, but go hungry, and plan to put your name in an hour or two before you plan to eat – pretty much every night of the week!). On your left you'll see *The Cannery*. Retaining its name from the days when it was a fruit packing factory, The Cannery has been renovated into a three-floor shopping mall offering a maze of walk ways and elevators. In the summertime, the courtyard of this complex hosts free concerts of ethnic music from around the world.

Further down, past Victorian Park, the cable car turnaround, and entrepreneurs selling jewelry, sits the hulking brick complex of buildings that make up *Ghirardelli Square.* This is a shopping Mecca that's not very shy about announcing itself. The one-story-high, well-lit Ghirardelli sign has become a landmark for this area. For generations, the name Ghirardelli has been associated with quality chocolates, and this is where the busy factory once pumped out the dark dairy delights by the ton. The factory has moved, replaced by a very-crowded Ghirardelli chocolate and ice cream boutique sitting among fashionable shops, galleries, and specialty stores – some with Native American crafts. Besides being a browser's heaven, this square also offers a couple of notable restaurants with notable chefs.

Cutting to the chase, we found some social points that make for a great escape from the street-side swarm. Lou's Pier 47 is one Wharf haunt that has real locals venturing in for a healthy daily serving of live R&B, Rock, and Jazz. Or, if you're looking to meet fellow tourists in a historic setting, check out *Jacks Cannery Bar,* where you can join in a beer splash that offers one of San Francisco's largest selection of brews.

If you're ready for some comic relief of the no-holds-barred variety, pay a visit to one of San Francisco's most famous houses of laughter, **Cobb's Comedy Club**. Or, check out Ireland's Wharf envoy, and stop in at **Fiddlers Green** – a pub that pulsates with revelry.

While we're on that Irish *thing*, last – and certainly not least – across the street from the cable car turnaround is the **Buena Vista Café** ... recognized as the originator of Irish Coffee, that steamy dark brew that is so appealing on cool San Francisco summer afternoons. As long as nobody comes up to prove a challenge to that noteworthy accomplishment, we'll continue to stop in from time to time to experience the best ... from the original.

So, there's your tour of The Wharf. Now, hop back onto your car now (the cable car that is), and head back over the hill. The *real* San Francisco awaits you.

7: Buena Vista Cafe   Restaurant/Bar

2765 Hyde St. (at Beach). 415-474-5044. Fisherman's Wharf. **HOURS:** Mon-Fri, 9a.m.-2a.m.; Sat-Sun, 8a.m.-2a.m. **RESTRICTIONS:** Cash only.

So here you are at The Wharf ... *tourist central*. And those kids – the ones pretending to be robots with that little buzzer thing in their mouths – are beginning to get on your nerves. What do you do?

If you are on the *Let's Party!* track, and visiting The Wharf because you 'just gotta' (plus for the clam chowder), and need a place that makes it all worthwhile, step into *Buena Vista*.

Beside having a very cool name, *Buena Vista* (Pretty View) has the best Irish coffee you're likely to find anywhere. Said to have invented the stuff some time back before any of us remember, it's no wonder their petite concoction of coffee, whiskey, and cream is enough to take the chill off a naked Hawaiian in Alaska.

Sure, we'll stop in whenever our tour-guide obligations necessitate that we visit this part of town. It's in the colder months (November through February, May through August), however, that we often stalk down for a glass ... or two ... *just to take the chill off!*

So don't fret your fate. The Wharf isn't *that* bad, and the T-shirt shops will still be there when you get back. So head on over to *Buena Vista*, ask them "is this *really* where Irish coffee was invented?" And play the tourist. You'll be glad you did.

8: Fiddler's Green   Irish Pub/Resturant

1333 Columbus Ave. (at Leavenworth). 415-441-9758. Fisherman's Wharf. **HOURS:** Mon-Fri, 10a.m.-2a.m.; Sat-Sun, 8a.m.-2a.m. **SPECIALS:** Daily, live Irish folk music, 9:30p.m.-1:30a.m.

Among San Francisco's global family of social haunts sits the proud Irish entry, *Fiddlers Green*. Although located in the tourist-drenched jungle of the Wharf, this pub offers home-away-from-home to a slew of local expat-Irish. From the floor to its low ceiling, this pub is heavily laden with classic pub-decor (of which the color green, what else, is very evident). It is to *Fiddler's Green* where throngs of revelers come to bend elbows with a hardy brew of Guinness in hand while enjoying the merry happenings and acoustics of live Irish folk.

We recommend that you take the short jaunt upstairs to a roomier space, offering not only a pool table but – most importantly – the restaurant. Heed our warning, and coat your stomach first with a traditional Irish dish before you depart to Planet Guinness (your body will love you for it!).

On weekends, while the lower floor resonates with the makings of live music, a DJ reigns upstairs. And, if you're into classic photography, the walls of *Fiddlers Green* are sprinkled 'head to toe' with turn-of-the-century photos of the Emerald Isle. It kinda makes you yearn for the potato fields back home – and wonder about the rumor that over 50 million Americans claim some Irish heritage. The rest of us will just have to wait until St. Pat's day, when we can don our "Kiss Me You're Irish" buttons, and get sloppy with strangers.

Pasport: 20% off the Lunch or Dinner menu per table.

9: Jacks Cannery Bar   Beer Hall

2801 Jefferson St. (In The Cannery, North Entrance, street level). 415-931-6400. Fisherman's Wharf. **HOURS:** Daily, 10a.m.-2p.m. **SPECIALS:** Live Music: American Folk, Mon-Thur, 3p.m.-10p.m.; Pop & Blues, Fri-Sat, 9:30p.m.-1:30a.m.

Whether you're a beer connoisseur or merely in search of a rambunctious good time, stop-in at *Jack's*. At this wharf-side haunt you can wet your whistle to a selection of 110 different brews comprising a who's-who of northern Californian micro breweries. *Jack's* reputedly offers the largest variety of draft beer in The City … and, in case you're thinking about it … it's been done! A former bartender holds the record, having sampled (in 5-oz glasses) the entire beer menu. His inebriated journey was achieved in under two hours – top that!

The interior is dominated by a 16th Century Elizabethan decor. From an interlaced fleur de lys plaster ceiling, to a Jacobean oak staircase, oak paneled walls, and an elegantly carved fireplace, you won't find a more courtly setting. History buffs will be interested to know that the interior of Jack's comes from the estate of the late-great William Randolph Hearst, as he pursued his feeding frenzy on European antiquities. They are pieces that were presumable destined for San Simeon – the Hearst Castle – o-o-o-o-o-h, a-a-a-a-a-h! By the way, we've been there and, short of actually going to Europe (with your copy of *Let's Party! Europe*, of course), "it's the next best thing to being there!"

At *Jack's*, you'll be treated to the schizophrenic offerings of Grateful Dead music mixed with German beer-hall revelry. Upstairs you'll find a stage, pool tables, and an inconspicuous looking 16th Century bed frame that has been altered to … to … *naah* – figure it out yourself On the beer menu, the El-Toro-Poppy-Jasper-Amber-Ale is not only their longest name for a beer, it's the most popular (and first to run dry). If you're looking to coat your stomach before beginning your drinking orgy, try the Grilled Salmon on Sourdough Roll ($6.95), or Grilled Crab Cakes ($8.75).

THE HAIGHT

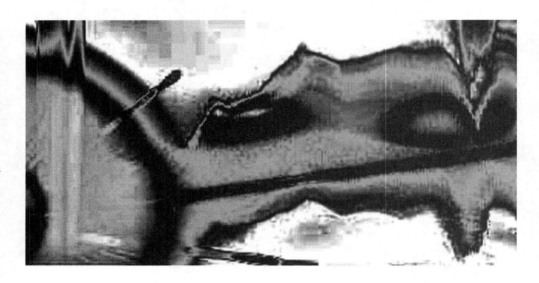

For many, the words **Haight & Ashbury** evoke memories of a time when a collective consciousness of youth, armed with "flower-power," yelled "Revolution" and bulldozed their way into the spotlight of media attention which, at the time, had its hands full with race riots, assassinations, and war. A window in time had opened and, as with North Beach of the 50's, it was Haight & Ashbury's turn to leap through.

But first let's shoot back to a time when the only things here were a few squatters and a rolling countryside that was content to innocently roll into the ocean. It was a time when the first guitar-wielding hippie to walk down Haight Street wouldn't arrive for another 115 years. But we'll get to *him* later.

During *The Haight's* infancy, nature conspired to satisfy the squatters' needs. Ah, but just over the hill, San Francisco was rapidly becoming a city. By the 1860's, The City had swelled to the point where city planners found it necessary to plan for a peculiar new idea – a public park ... and what would later become **Golden Gate Park** was born.

In the 1880's, the fashionable activity of the day was to explore nature. And, endowed with a park, The Haight became increasingly attractive to affluent San Francisco families. The idea caught on so well, in fact, that some families decided to build what have survived today as one of this neighborhood's hallmarks ... grand Victorian country homes. With the advent of an amusement park and a Haight Street cable-car line, the area reached its peak as San Francisco's most fashionable resort area.

But that all ended in the 40-second explosive rumble known as the 1906 quake. As two-thirds of San Francisco either crumbled or burned out of existence, The Haight was among the few areas left standing. What was once a nature retreat, away from an overpopulated San Francisco, became a desperate retreat away from The City's advancing fires. Like a sponge, The Haight and park area absorbed the homeless masses in tent villages. During the reconstruction, many stayed as tents

matured into homes. The tranquil charm of nature had given way to the construction sounds of machinery and hammering.

That catastrophe compounded with the Great Depression of the '30's to strike with the impact of two 6-foot, 350-pound wrestlers. It was a tag team that beat The Haight beyond recognition. Urbanized and overpopulated to ghetto proportions, any fond memories left of a once-fashionable resort ultimately fell with the obscurity of time. The Haight was sucked-up into Central San Francisco.

In the early '50's – while The Haight was down for the count – tour buses were filing in across town at **North Beach**, there to witness a three ring circus of beatnik antics. Media hype had caused the beat-born scene to turn on its own daddy-os. Life became too expensive to sit around cafe tables all day discussing the woes and ills of a disillusioned generation. With prices on the rise, many beret-topped hipsters packed up and moved their camps to The Haight, where rent was cheap and cafe tables were plentiful.

The beat movement had uprooted the entrenched norms of the day. As for the good old days, they were just that – old, and gone, and (for many), that was good. The trend was set for a tumble-wash of new ideas, and as one generation paved the road for the next, everyone was wondering ... *what next?*

With the anticipation of a million eye's fixed on a single egg, a bird finally appeared. Out of its crumbled shell, and in true muppet style, the hatchling flashed a wicked smile ... and the '60's were born.

In the early 60's, The Haight had been as calm as a country meadow – that is, just before it is assaulted by a tornado.

As beat turned to pop, the hipsters began to notice a following. One day, as the story goes, some beatnik noticed a guitar-wielding, long-haired kid walking down Haight Street. The beat thought to himself, "This kid is trying very hard to be a hipster, but he's just a wannabe, and that makes him a hippie." The label stuck, and was to become the label of a generation.

By the mid-60's, years of neglect had turned The Haight into a run-down district, yet it's princely (now subdivided) Victorian homes, marred by only a few scars and wrinkles, had survived. Rent was affordable, the ground was fertile, and more and more cafes and bars appeared. With its neighboring park, many saw The Haight as a poetic setting for a new bohemia. Many left the shelter of their suburban and small-town upbringings, and moved in increasing numbers to the student and art communities springing up around the corners of Haight & Ashbury.

Across the nation, stretch marks of a troubled time began to show. Racial strife, slain leaders, and warfare had done a number on America's collective psyche. As the nation fell into a state of disarray, The Haight bloomed with the concepts of peace, love, and freedom. It was a three-word manifesto that rang with an evoking echo.

Music spread the gospel of a new Shangri-La, and talented young bands were catapulted into the spotlight by Bill Graham's promotional genius and financial support. The first group to hit the scene was the Charlatans, followed closely by

Jefferson Airplane and the Warlocks, who later changed their name to the Grateful Dead. Janis Joplin joined the celebration of music, along with Santana, Joan Baez, Bob Dylan, and Jimmy Hendrix – and that's mentioning *just* a few. What DJ's across America casually labeled "the San Francisco sound" had matured into the voice of a generation.

Then one day –stage left– entered Timothy Leary, and the plot thickened. His prescription, "Turn on, tune in, drop out (with LSD)" took the place by storm. The popularity of this *yet to be criminalized* chemical lifted The Haight scene to *seemingly* religious heights. The world of Psychedelia had been born. Suddenly, reality became an option between acid trips:

- Many were claiming 'the answer' was slipped to them while having tea with God.
- Ken Kesey and his Merry Pranksters hosted acid parties – their promotional leaflets asking "Can You Pass the Acid Test?"
- The Grateful Dead and other bands provided musical sermons for concert halls full of trippers.
- The entire of the collective consciousness had collected under an umbrella of hallucinatory images and ideas.

Against and detached from the political madness of the 60's, The Haight scene had become one big hippie commune. Word spread quickly across the nation of a new way of life. The Haight began to experience a Renaissance. Boards were coming off storefronts, which reopened as book shops and cafes. The famed acid-induced sojourns into the soul seduced many to journey across the country. VW vans with New York plates pulled into the neighborhood for the first time and, as Haight & Ashbury became the symbol of freedom, the next wave of hippies initiated a tidal wave of uncontrollable force.

As schools let out in the spring of 1967, The Haight was swamped with a mass pilgrimage of over 100,000 youths. The streets and park pulsated with what the media christened the "Love Generation." Flowers and peace signs were handed out and paraded through the streets; incense burned from every shop; and acid was passed out like candy to bare-footed face-painted flower-topped hazy-eyed bell-bottomed hippies. Golden Gate Park turned into a campground where the hypnotic beat of drum circles filled the night time air. Tribal-like gatherings, free concerts, free food, free love, free expression, and just a bunch of free-falling wackiness presided over a time known mythically as "The Summer of Love."

The ongoing carnival of street and park happenings, accompanied by a blaze of new ideals, peaked in the summer of 1967. Yet, as autumn rolled in, the blaze diminished into a small brush fire. What had attracted middle-class kids in search of alternative life to The Haight also attracted the Hells Angels looking to cause hell, heroine dealers looking to deal, and crazies such as Charles Manson looking to recruit. Just as the Vietnam war began to take a heavy toll on human lives, the criminal element in The Haight took its toll on human souls. The Haight sang its swan-song. With no cosmic-sized aspirin in sight, the party was over. The neighborhood that popularized the concept of collective consciousness fell into a collective hangover – requiring 20 years to recover.

By the mid-70's, the once flowery Haight had wilted back to its pre-60 days of boarded-up storefronts and high crime rates. Gun wielding drug dealers replaced flower-bearing hippies. The few that stayed on from the 'Summer of Love' and the 'Be In' of '66 had either fallen prey to heroin, or had taken one too many acid trips, only to become burned out MIA's ... lost in their own world of flashbacks.

The subject of numerous books and documentaries, the script is still being written for this neighborhood, which has bounced back and forth between the realms of Greek Mythology and Tragedy. To this day, the cultural revolution that upended the 60's and defined The Haight remains fresh in the minds of yesterdays' hippies. For some, 'Flower Power' and 'Love Street' magically chime with a nostalgic tone. For others, the nostalgia has crumbled into a lingering legacy that stands in the way of advancement.

The commercial spin-offs of flower-power and hippie-hoopla have given Haight Street a schizophrenic quality, with one foot firmly set in a lyrical past, and the other foot pushing-on into a yuppified future. You'll run into head shops, anarchist book stores, used clothing stores, dive bars, and thrift stores sitting shoulder to shoulder with art galleries, glossy fashion boutiques, trendy cafes, and artsy shops with pricy knick-knacks.

Golden Gate Park

Stretching from the West, pulling the ebb and flow of the sea breeze into the heart of The City, Golden Gate Park resides as San Francisco's crown jewel. From the once hard-working windmills, to the eastern Panhandle, this park *anchors* San Francisco to the Earth.

As lofty as that may sound, it's important to remember that San Francisco is merely a concrete and asphalt 'crown' that has come to rest upon this once pristine setting of old-growth forests, streams, lush meadows, and sand dunes.

The park – finely tuned by the arboreal genius of the horticultural wizard John McLaren – holds as firmly to The City's essence as a newborn suckles firmly to a mothers breast. The park's agrarian wonders feed more than air to The City's populace, reminding them of the greatness of nature.

Declared a city park in 1852, 'negotiations' with squatters held up efforts to start work on an area that appeared more like a big sandbox. By the time his work began in 1890, and until his death in 1943, McLaren (better known as *Uncle* John) was a feisty devil. Throughout his tenure as superintendent of gardening, he doggedly cajoled the dunes into the abundant presentation of life found in the park to this day. He held viciously to his original intentions – that the park be reserved for the enjoyment of *nature,* and – unlike the parks you'll come across in Paris –

Uncle John would not permit a "Keep off the Grass" mentality.

Nestled within the 1017-acre park are roads, paths, and trails; glens, gardens, and forests; fields, ponds, and monuments. More than a million trees, shrubs, and plants freshen the air, and include over 6000 varieties of flowers – many of which are not indigenous to northern California. Yes, the park is one expansive greenhouse, preserved from modern-day pioneers and profiteers ... forever.

So, Golden Gate Park will remain, and continue to pay this city's homage to Mother Nature – an honor she so deserves. This is more than we can say for the Presidio – perhaps the most valuable real estate in the United States – which is now subject to an enormous land-grab. What disheartens us, is that the desire of *the many* to retain and enjoy our natural wonders can so easily be subjugated to the whims and greed of *the few.*

Oh ... sorry! ... we didn't mean to wax political. What was that we were speaking about? Oh, yea, *The Park!*

Whether you hike to the top of Strawberry Hill in the center of Stow Lake, or spend some time sipping tea in the Japanese Tea Garden, the air somehow seems different in The Park. Gone are the smells of exhaust and sounds of blaring engines; present is the chirping of birds – and the wail of a three-year-old child chasing ducks. Like a big sponge, the park seems to suck fresh air from the neighboring Pacific Ocean, presenting in abundance to fuel the jogger, tennis player, or bicyclist.

Sporting and recreational opportunities abound, as the park hosts such daily activities as baseball, soccer, tennis, bocce ball, miniature boating, and horseback riding – and many, many more. Sundays, The Park screams with the sound of blades – roller blades, that is – as its roads are closed to motorized transportation.

Undeniably, The Park is also the domain of a small percentage of The City's homeless, who hide themselves away in the more-remote sections. Yet it offers to all a lush alternative – *an escape-zone,* if you will – to the busy metropolis that surrounds.

The large Polo Field, in the western half of the park, has historically hosted music festivals featuring such acts as the Grateful Dead, Santana, and Pearl Jam. And, The Park at large, is often the site of spontaneous, impromptu gatherings of all breeds of people who come with drum, guitar, or flute in hand, and while away the day in the company of friends.

Golden Gate Park offers a myriad of choices to The City's natives, many of whom make ritual sojourns into this, San Francisco's lungs. There is so much to The Park, however that only but a few discover everything it has to offer. *But that's not the point!* The Park is here for you to *escape*, using its ample inventory of seclusion and serenity to break away from the torment of our pragmatic, everyday existence.

So, find your personal sanctuary, light some incense, assume the lotus position, and start to repeat your mantra – or practice your Tai Chi. We guarantee The Park will do *its* part to help you find the world of peace, love, freedom, and hope. It's all here ... and it's all good ... and we're glad you came by for a visit!

The Upper Haight

Eight blocks up, past the sloping edge of **Buena Vista Park** and **Masonic Avenue**, lies the gateway to historic **Upper Haight**. The remaining six blocks that lead to Golden Gate Park constitutes this neighborhood's commercial hub. Partially gentrified and slightly sanitized of its former infamous reputation, Upper Haight has matured along with the generation that first lit its spark, but today's revolution is fought more with tax petitions and cellular phones.

Re-restored Victorians and glossy storefronts – including that of the GAP clothing store – have become part of Upper Haight's present-day reality ... *but has the dust really settled?* As with anything legendary, The Haight's cultural revolution is hardly forgotten, and if you attempt to dislodge it from your memory, you'll surely be reminded. Fueling the legacy, radio stations with a classic-rock format entertain the latest crop of disillusioned youth with such staple tunes as the Fifth Dimension's 'Age of Aquarius' and Scott McKensy's 'Wear Flowers in Your Hair.'

Between camera toting tourists, grocery lugging locals, and hustling workers, you'll discover a micro-cosmic world of stray-cat run-aways, grungers, crusties, and grifters. Conjuring images of Oliver Twist, these teenage gypsies are clad in baggy gruff-wear, schlepping their rolled-up sleeping bags in one hand and hustling for hand-outs with the other. They're among the many who converge daily on and around the 'promised land' of Haight & Ashbury, joining in a feeding frenzy on the romantic ideals of Bohemian-freedom.

On the corner of Haight and Clayton sits the **Haight-Ashbury Free Clinic** – a profound remnant from the 60's; profound because its still free, and its in America ... Wow!

Get a jump-start on your Upper Haight maraud and down a *'Depth Charge'* at the *All You Need* (1466 Haight). Return to the retro 50's-of-swing at the very cool *Club Deluxe*. As you near the park, you'll find *Kan Zaman* – rated tops in the city for Middle Eastern dishes and delights. If that crescent moon cuisine just doesn't do it, cross to *Cha Cha Cha* where there's a large selection of tapas (and a long wait). A few hops down sits *Nightbreak* – a brash 'divish' live music bar with a most trippy painted interior. Across the street is *Boomerang* (across from Nightbreak), competing with Nightbreak for the areas 'dive' title.

Okay, now that you've reached the finish line, take a break in the park.

10: Cha Cha Cha   Tapas Bar/Restaurant

1801 Haight St. (at Schrader). 415-386-5758. Upper Haight. **HOURS:** Sun-Thur, Lunch, 11:30a.m.-4p.m.; Dinner, 5p.m.-11p.m.; Fri-Sat, open 'til 11:30p.m. **RESTRICTIONS:** Cash only.

This hip, not-to-be-missed upper-Haight restaurant serves Caribbean and South American Tapas, and an *awesome* Sangria. It got so busy, in fact, that they had to move down the block to a larger corner building for additional space – *oooh, the sweet taste of success.* Even with the extra room, it's still *always* packed – so expect long waits around dinner time (no reservations accepted, and cash only!).

People come from all over The City to hang out amid the folk-artsy decor and loud conversations. Bright-colored Mexican altars hang on the black-painted walls; miss-matched tables and chairs are place closely together under several palm trees. They have a few booths for larger parties, but you can expect an even longer wait for them.

So is it worth it? Well, it depends on your mood. You may opt to wait for your table while sitting at the bar in back – which also gets thoroughly packed as well by 6:00 or 7:00 p.m. – but that's a *good* thing!. We don't have to tell you ... but we will – get the Sangria! A pitcher, or two, of this delicious blood-red concoction, dipped out of a larger bowl with a few slices of fresh orange and lime, will ease your wait (as you spend that special *Let's Party!* time socializing). A few glasses and you'll be feeling it.

Food portions are fairly small, since what they serve are Tapas (Spanish appetizers), but they're great to share as everyone at your table gets a chance to sample a wide variety of flavors. We also don't have to tell you this, but *order the Caribbean prawns! Even if you don't like prawns!* They come served in a deliciously spicy coconut curry in a large skillet. Get plenty of the hard crusty bread to dip in the sauce, cuz this baby's got sauce!

Also try patatas bravas – always a classic – and the chicken quesadillas with fresh verdant salsa. You should try *Cha Cha Cha's* mainly for the experience – the blasting Latino beat, funky ambiance, and plenty of chatter. It makes for plenty of fun, and it's right on the Haight (where walking down the *street* can be an experience).

11: Deluxe Club   Retro Bar

1511 Haight St. (at Ashbury). 415-552-6949. Upper Haight. **HOURS:** Mon-Sat, 4p.m.-2a.m.; Sun, 2p.m.-2a.m. **ENTRANCE CHARGE:** For live Music $2.00-5.00. **SPECIALS:** Live music, Wed-Sun, 10p.m.-2a.m. **RESTRICTIONS:** Cash only.

Retro becomes trendy with the happy faithfuls who walk into this locale. Continually in business since the mid-40s, *Club Deluxe* has been a virtual shrine for that nearly extinct era of Swing. On most nights of the week, the tiny stage at *Club Deluxe* is home to the sweet musings of live music. Usually, you'll find a small band paying homage to the Big Band era – and such notables the likes of Cab Calloway.

On the other side of this split-room haunt, you'll find a bar that both barflies and fashion-junkies claim is the proverbial home of '*The*' Bloody Mary. We don't know if that's true – *nor do we care* – but for $4.00 you'll get a 'meal-full' of vegetables and fruits with your drink. The bartenders, dressed in shirt and tie, are also known for their famous cocktails and Martinis ($3.00-$4.50). On weekends after 10:00 p.m., the band plays to a standing-room-only crowd, so come early and grab yourself a booth.

12: Kan Zaman   Middle Eastern Cafe/Restaurant/Bar

1793 Haight St. (at Shrader). 415-751-9656. Upper Haight. **HOURS:** Mon, 5p.m.-Midnight; Tue-Thur, noon-Midnight; Fri-Sat, noon-2a.m.; Sun, noon-Midnight. **SPECIALS:** Belly Dancing, Fri, Sat & Sun, 8:30-10:30p.m.; occasional palm reading on Wednesdays. **RESTRICTIONS:** Cash only.

What do you get when you mix our laid-back California lifestyle with Middle Eastern pleasures? Poof!... *Kan Zaman* ('Yesterdays'). The exotic delights that can be found in the land of the crescent moon have flourished like a Lotus in this Haight-area restaurant and bar. On weekends, *Kan Zaman* undulates to all corners with a merrily feasting gang. The small busy bar makes for a perfect social pit stop while waiting for your table. And, if you smoke, be the Pasha and puff on a Hookah filled with Egyptian flavored tobacco: Apple, Apricot, Honey and Mixed Fruits are available.

A parade of fabrics and color provide an atmosphere that will slingshot your senses back to a 14th-century Moorish palace. Between the rich fabrics, terra-cotta wall finishing, pillow seating, Persian carpets, and burnished copper, the scene is set for modern-day Arabian Nights.

The menu is chock-full of delicacies just like mom's home cooking (if you had an Arabic mom, that is). Beef and chicken shish kebab go for $8.50, Dolmas are $3.25, and a Falafel sandwich is a worthwhile $3.75. If the call of hunger is yet to sound, land your tush on one of the throw pillows, and catch a belly dance performance while downing a jolt of Arabic coffee. *Kan Zaman* is where you might just might score a phone number for a future rendezvous in Cairo. Salaam...

Pasport: Free Hookah with the purchase of one entree.

13: Nightbreak   Live Music Bar

1821 Haight St. (at Stanyan). 415-221-9057. Upper Haight. **HOURS:** Daily, 1p.m.-2a.m. **ENTRANCE CHARGE:** $2.00-$7.00 depending on the act (Sundays are always free). **SPECIALS:** Presents 10 to 20 bands a week, up to 100 a month. **RESTRICTIONS:** NO dress code!.

In the city of San Francisco, when you say "kick-butt live music," you're saying *Nightbreak*. Let's make it simple for ya – if you want to know what is going on in Rock and Roll in the Bay Area, come here first. It's insane! This place has staged as many as *100 bands in one month,* and always puts up between 10 and 20 touring bands a week. Blastin' out seven days a week, you'll hear Alternative, Alternative Rock, Rockabilly, and practically anything else in the "Rock" category.

Nightbreak has 21 beers on tap, and specializes in northern California beer. You can also get wine – and saki "of course" – which is especially good on Sunday afternoons, when you can get 'good, low-cost sushi while taking in free live music. Yes, you heard us right, Sundays are free – as are Wednesday nights. This is not a big deal, considering that the price of entry is often as low as $2.00, *but hey,* free is free!

A San Francisco institution, the stage at *Nightbreak* has seen the likes of *No FX, Primus, 4 Non-Blondes, Chris Isaacs* and, of course, the *Grateful Dead.* Courtney Love has been known to drop in – not that you'd notice on a good day, when the scene is like sardines ... jumpin, dancin, Rockin sardines!

The clientele, often displaying brightly colored hair, tattoos, leather, and pierced ... *everything* ... meld into the decor, which is primarily black with some outrageously *savage* murals by local artist Kevin Woodson. Head into the back room, and step into the jaws of a B-52. But don't be afraid, *Nightbreak* welcomes everyone – even suburbanites and yuppies ... *as long as you like Rock,* that is!

14: Persian Aub Zam Zam   Bar

1633 Haight St. (at Clayton). 415-861-2545. Upper Haight. **HOURS:** Depends on the mood of the owner. **RESTRICTIONS:** Must purchase a Martini? (of course, you can take your chances!)

'Yes! I've successfully ordered!'

Only the rare newcomer to this quirky neighborhood bar will utter these words. It's known as *The Zam Zam Room* by insiders, and you almost have to be an insider to get served here. To keep out newcomers, Bruno – the ornery owner and bartender – has removed the sign that used to hang above his doorway. The address is not posted outside the entrance, either – and as you see in the pertinents above, we've chosen to make you look for it as well. But look for the Persian doorway and stainless steel doors with paisley portholes, directly to the right of Robert's Hardware. Don't bother asking if you are in the right place. He'll just say "No, you're looking for the other place, up the street on your right."

Finding *The Zam Zam Room*, however, is only half-the-battle. What the *Seinfeld's* Soup Nazi is to Manhattan, Bruno is to the Haight. To avoid being asked to leave, you must quickly grasp the unwritten Rules According to Bruno. First, never sit in the booths, unless invited. They are usually reserved for groups of four. And do not stand. You must be seated on a barstool to get served. Second, you are only allowed to order martinis. And don't tell him how to make them. You will be thrown out if you ask for anything else. *And don't ask for a 'Gin' martini – "what other kind is there?"* ... and you're out!

Bruno seems to have a bit of a soft spot for women. During our visit, female patrons successfully ordered both a Rob Roy and a vodka gimlet. Bruno was visibly irritated, didn't eject them. Regulars know how much drinks cost, so you give yourself away if you ask what you owe him (martinis cost $2.50 each). Have your money ready when he delivers your drinks. Tipping is apparently allowed.

The front room is dominated by the large, semi-circular bar – at which you *must* sit. A mythical forest scene is depicted in the mural behind the bar. A juke box, cigarette machine, and a single booth round out the room. The music in the juke box is the same stuff Bruno was playing on his Victrola back in the 40s – slow, horns-heavy Big Band. (By the way, he removed the pay phone in '43, so don't ask if he has one.) Through a second Persian arch towards the back is a second room full of small tables, at which you are not allowed to sit. The bathrooms are back this way, should you be afraid to ask.

I finish writing this review leaning against a light post on Haight street. Yes, you guessed it, I got thrown out. Another rule (one I've just learned the hard way): order a refill before your glass goes empty, and *never* nurse your drink.

The Publisher congratulates Mike for accomplishing this review ... yes, 'accomplishing.' Every other writer who tried to cover Zam Zam *got thrown out before you could say "Can I have a vodka martini, please?" GET OUT!!! (good luck).*

Lower Haight Scene

S tarting from **Market Street**, Lower Haight stretches like a ribbon up over rolling hills to Upper Haight, where it meets Golden Gate Park. Around Fillmore Street you'll find a cluster of cafes and bars that is locally known as the **Lower Haight scene**. Here you'll find large numbers of African Americans and thrift-store bohemians living together in poverty. Yet, between aging Victorians, you'll find one of San Francisco most unique collection of social-haunts.

Away from the tourist-clogged Upper Haight, this areas' disheveled appearance exudes a sense of struggle and adversity – the ingredients for a mouth watering soup of artistic inspiration. Struggling artists are a dime a dozen on this side of The Haight, and the watering holes are where they hold court.

If you like to sandwich your intimacy and intensity together, check-out **Nicki's** – the Lower Haight's answer to the SOMA club scene. Down half a block is the **International Cafe** – San Francisco's "United Nations of Loungers." Testament to the name, its patron-following resembles a bohemian roll call for a Beniton add. A few doors further you'll find **Mad Dog in the Fog,** a pub that offers a British style ruckus, where Guinness, pub-grub, and live music prevail. Across to the right sits **Noc Noc** which, while tiny, is the grand daddy of the Lower Haight scene. It's Dada decor is perhaps the most eccentric of all San Francisco's odd-ball haunts. Cutting back across the street, the **Horse Shoe Cafe** provides a surrogate living room for many of Lower Haight's out-of work artists. A game of chess while listening to Classical music

constitutes a night out for the stroll-in patrons of this cafe. Still further down sits the rough-edged **Midtown**. This "joint," with its large selection of liquid poisons and concoctions is a quaffer's dream.

While the area of the Lower Haight offers something for the ruckus-rascals or lounge-lizards in all of us, its is not without its criminal element. As darkness descends on this jagged neighborhood, the side streets can resemble Michael Jackson's Thriller video, so keep wise … and keep to Haight Street.

15: Cafe International   Cafe

508 Haight St. (at Fillmore). 415-552-7390. Lower Haight. **HOURS:** Mon-Thur, 7a.m.-11p.m.; Fri, 7a.m.-Midnight; Sat, 8a.m.- Midnight; Sun, 8a.m.-11p.m. **SPECIALS:** Tue & Thur, live Jazz; Wed, open-mike comedy; Fri, open-mike poetry; Sat, special event; Sun-open-mike music. **RESTRICTIONS:** Cash only.

Sitting as the social anchor of lower Haight, *Cafe International* was the 'first kid on the block' and, as such, remains King of the Hill among the lower Haight cafe scene. Its spaciously long room is separately decorated, yet you'll find all the trappings of a luring social haunt ring here with a truly global tone.

The spirit is found in the patrons – not on the walls. From inter-racial and inter-cultural young mothers stopping by for a coffee break with their children, to a Rastafarian penciling down a song, you'll always find mix reflective of the *Cafe's* name. The daytime crowed is treated to an amalgamation of music that is baffling, causing many to wonder from what countries or tribes the sounds originate.

The food is just as international, at times requiring an adventuresome taster.

Outside, the back patio awaits anyone in search of sanctuary. Its colorful wall-size mural can't be missed. It is so colorful and striking, in fact, that you're likely to feel its presence even before it registers into your visual awareness. We're told it took Kemit Amenophis 300 hours to paint this World Union masterpiece of song and dance. Kemit used National Geographic magazines to stylize the faces and images, then cleverly quilted them together. You have to see it for yourself. On a clear day, the outdoor patio – with its mishmash of furniture and the mural – is perfect for a gathering of either your thoughts or your friends.

At night, this cafe undulates to one creative vibe or another. Check at the counter, or call for the nightly performance, which kicks-off around 8 p.m.

16: The Horse Shoe Cafe   Chess Cafe

566 Haight St. (between Fillmore & Steiner). 415-626-8852. Lower Haight **HOURS:** Daily, 6:30a.m.-12:30a.m. **SPECIALS:** Chess Tournaments **RESTRICTIONS:** Cash only.

Entrenched in the social buzz of Lower Haight, *Horse Shoe* offers a pond for pondering ... a place to relax and down a fresh OJ while glancing over the paper. As late afternoon turns into early evening, the tables fill with pseudo intellectuals,

starving artists, and grungies who, in many cases, have just awakened, and are venturing in for their first-of-the-day cup-a-Joe.

This is not some loftily appointed haunt, and has only the lofty distinction of being a 'chess cafe.' Inside, many tables are topped with chessboard and clock, with two opponents locked into a life or death grip in pursuit of the other's king. When all boards are checked out, you can almost cut through the competitive tension with a knife. In anticipation of a stress-filled room, the owner plays the relaxing sounds of classical music, which delightfully interweaves between the activity and inactivity alike. So ... Pawn to King four ... *your move!*

17: Mad Dog In The Fog   Pub

530 Haight St. (between Fillmore & Steiner). 415-626-7279. Lower Haight. **HOURS:** Mon-Fri, 11:30a.m.-2a.m.; Sat-Sun, 9a.m.-2a.m. **SPECIALS:** Happy Hour 'till 7p.m., ¢75 reduction on all draft beer; Monday, free drink with meal, Tuesday, open mike, 8p.m.; Mon-Thur, pub quiz, 9p.m.; Sun, 9p.m., live music.

"Mad dogs and Englishmen go out in the mid-day sun." So said Noel Coward, and thus was the name of this worthy pub born. While *Mad Dog* resembles a bar, its character places it squarely as a pub. And, with its patrons claiming or rejecting allegiance to the Union Jack, you can expect a nightly fun-filled ruckus – British style.

For many a misplaced Brit, this pub offers a transplanted home-away-from-home, where televised soccer matches, dart boards, pub grub, stout lagers, and home-town gossip preside over a social feast of chattering and camaraderie. Since it opened (a week prior to the 879 quake), *Mad Dog* has established a firm foothold on the local scene by offering both a restaurant and pub with nightly entertainment.

The restaurant, with its provoking mural – that of one very unhappy bulldog – is first to greet your entrance, and offers a full menu. If you've already dispensed with the task of stuffing your face, however, shuffle your way into the pub, and fall into one of their pumped-up leather chairs ... as you fall into conversation with some 'bloke' from Liverpool?

As night descends, the 'micks' and amps turn-on to the sound of undiscovered – and discovered – musicians who, on occasion, return to their roots of being undiscovered. Adam Duritz from the Counting Crows has stopped in to test out some of his new material. The same goes for Linda Perry from 4 Non Blondes. We didn't know they were British!

18: Midtown   Bar

582 Haight St. (at Steiner). 415-558-8019. Lower Haight. **HOURS:** Daily, noon-2a.m. **SPECIALS:** Happy Hour daily, noon-7p.m., all beers $2.00. **RESTRICTIONS:** Cash only.

So you want something with a rougher edge. When you tire of the slew of sedate, casual 'mingle' locales, enter 'The *Midtown* Zone.' While geographically it may be located in the center of San Francisco, there is nothing 'mid' about it. Nor does it really fall on the fringes of any classification we can think of. Indisputably, *Midtown* is a drinking joint where (unless your body is garnished with piercings and tattoos) you may just as well order a glass of milk at the bar. Otherwise, you liquor connoisseurs will be happy to know this bar carries a bountiful selection that includes 15 types of tequila and 12 different vodkas.

Midtown's selection of liquid poisons is among the best in town – a point Tim, the owner, hastened to 'mention.' We suggest you go for the 'mad-mix mystery shot' – a James Addiction.

The interior is simply black: black walls; black booths; black tables; black chairs; black pillars; and black bar – all black! The room is brightened (scantily) by a few neon beer signs, and the light over the pool table in the back. The music is less consistent, but you should expect a mix with an alternative slant.

19: Nickie's BBQ   Dance Bar

460 Haight St. (between Fillmore & Webster). 415-621-6508. Lower Haight. **HOURS:** Daily, 9p.m.-2a.m. **ENTRANCE CHARGE:** $2.00-3.00. **SPECIALS:** Happy Hour, daily, 9p.m.-10p.m., tap beer $2.25; Daily Music Theme: Monday, Grateful Dead Jams; Tuesday, Africa-Asia-Arabia; Wednesday, Hip Hop; Thursday Groove, Jazz-Soul-Latin; Friday, Funk & Soul; Saturday, 70's Funk; Sunday, Live Music – Irish, Alternative.

This Lower Haight hot spot is affectionately known among our staff as San Francisco's most riotous hole-in-the-wall bar! With its worn-out dance floor and dim lighting, combined with dynamic DJ mixes and an eclectic funky set of groovesters, this tiny dive percolates with the ambiance of one of those BIG clubs (now all the owner needs to do is knock over some walls).

On the dance floor – which is pretty much *the entire floor* – you'll usually find articulate displays of dance styles from the shimmy-spin to dirty-dog-dancing. Just as a reminder ... *be sure to watch-out for those floor columns!* Nickie's rustic history goes back to the 50s and, from the looks of things, its seen many a day. But managing to keep fresh, at *Nickie's* every night offers a different musical theme – with a crowd to match. So they come. They come to frolic, and they come to rollick. And the sounds you'll hear range from Grateful Dead Jams to African Tribal slams.

The bar is the domain of busy-bodied bartenders who'll only serve beer and wine. On weekends, the basement room is open, with a second bar and some booths that hold court to a centrally placed pool table (thank God, we needed the breathing space). Come for the crush ... stay for the crush!

Pasport: Two for one entry or admit one free.

20: Noc Noc   Bar

557 Haight St. (between Fillmore & Steiner). 415-570-6340. Lower Haight. **HOURS:** Daily, 5p.m.-2a.m. **SPECIALS:** Happy Hour, 5p.m.-8p.m. Happy hour prices extended to 2a.m.

An Impressionistic version of an airplane's crash landing into the Lower Haight, *Noc Noc* is living, breathing modern art. Static-filled TVs perched on Roman columns greet you at streetside. Inside, the decor beckons your imagination to run wild. The brushed sheet metal shell of an old airplane has been incorporated into the bar. Chunks of the wings curve around the open ceiling, while the cockpit is hidden in the back corner. I use the term 'corner' loosely, because you'll find nary a traditional 90-degree corner in the place.

The crowd is mostly 20-something Haight dwellers on weeknights, with imports from the greater Bay Area on weekends. Seating is very limited, so the trend is to plop down and share a table with your neighbors. And what seating it is: the barstools recall the dining room chairs from Beetlejuice. Toward the back are jaggedly upholstered booths and a few low tables ringed with pillows. For good measure, a dash of Keith Haring-cum-African-tribal painting graces the bar and walls. The whole place basks in purple and green light. Think Flintstones meet the Jetsons (go figure), and you'll have a good idea of what to expect.

21: The Top   Dance Bar

424 Haight St. (between Webster & Fillmore). 415-864-7386. Lower Haight. **HOURS:** Daily, 5p.m.-2a.m. **SPECIALS:** Happy Hour from 5p.m.-10p.m. reduced price on two nightly liquor selections. **RESTRICTIONS:** Cash only.

To be among the few that occupy a place on San Francisco's highest peak of revelry is a hard-earned accomplishment. In this case, the talk of the town is not some blockbuster east-end club, but a small, lower-Haight dive bar. When the question "where are we going?" arises, a good answer for a downright good time is "to *The Top!*"

On Friday and Saturday nights, this place is on fire with a funky brew of groovers, ravers, grungers, and shaven-head fashion busters who sport that "I'm-so-cool" look – *and get away with it!* Within its humble space, you'll find getting to the dance floor can at times require a little side stepping here, and a little there, through a jungle-thick with bodies. *Hey,* take three short steps up, and jump into an arena of vibe and motion.

DJs have been known to cycle into a musical pallet-mix of House, Dub, Funk, Tribal, Jungle, Reggae, Rare-Groove, and Acid Jazz. If there is such a thing as musical mixed-breeds, you'll discover them here. After 'sati-San-Francisco-ying' your dancing appetite, quench your thirst with one of their specialty drinks – perhaps their Stompy ($2.50), or a choice from their large selection of beers and ciders. Then, get back on the dance floor. It's what you came *here* for!

Pasport: Buy one beer and get one free.

HAYES VALLEY

Hayes Valley rests solidly between *Heaven* and *Hell*.

Okay, that may be a bit extreme, but settled between San Francisco's Symphony Hall and buildings representing man's hypocrisy to man (the Projects), lies a small, somewhat sedate neighborhood that is free falling into its own. That's not to say the area's residents and business owners are not working actively in the slow process of gentrification. The fact that Hayes Street itself has managed to discretely present itself as a model neighborhood 'shopping street' speaks volumes.

Artsy-Funk are the best words to describe the store-bought offerings as you stroll down Hayes Street between Franklin and Laguna. In those short three blocks, you'll experience time-warp shifts. From the most modern cutting-edge fashion to the aged rusticity of other peoples used furniture, Hayes Street is San Francisco's promenade of odd offerings. With no particular rhyme or reason – except that there's usually enough of any one thing – it's hard to put this 'shopping' street into any specific category.

One resounding emphasis seems to be home furnishings. There's furniture (new and used), various types of art, such knick-knacks as glassware and pottery, and antiques. In fact, the variety of old stuff for sale at healthy prices abounds. There're also music shops beside cafes next to restaurants alongside a cool African 'boutique."

When it comes to fashion, whether new or 'vintage,' be prepared to see some funky stuff – much of what's offered seems to be hand made and very high quality. And, when it comes to shoes, forget Nordstroms, and head on down to Hayes Street. This is where you can 'step out in style' with some of the coolest shoes you can buy anywhere in The City.

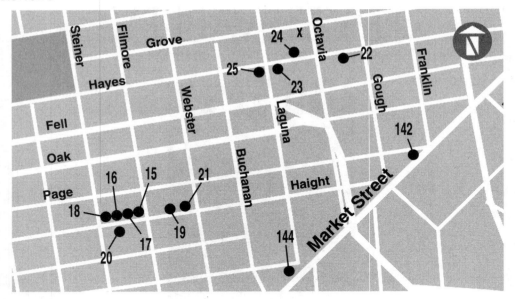

22: Hayes and Vine   Wine Bar

377 Hayes St. (at Gough). 415-626-5301. Hayes Valley. **HOURS:** Tue-Thur, 5p.m.-Midnight; Fri & Sat, 5p.m.-1a.m (food 'til 12:30a.m.).

Subdued, relaxing charm is the best way to describe this new Hayes Valley wine bar. Presenting an atmosphere fantastique, to coin our own phrase, Hayes & Vine presents an atmosphere that is subtly pleasing to the eye, comfortable in mood and presence, yet not overly sedate. Incorporating earthen colors, the white onyx bar is absolutely beautiful, and the custom furniture unique. There's a small room in back where you can escape the hectic goings on of the streets of San Francisco, and retreat into the seclusion of what may seem like your own private club.

Be sure to get there early to secure this seating ... or, better yet, introduce yourselves to the small room's occupants, and join with them in a human gesture of oneness.

Located in a 100-year-old structure who's last residents were lawyers, "The location chose us," state the proprietors, who enjoy the burgeoning vitality this small community provides. Hayes & Vine attracts a mixed clientele of professionals, wine enthusiasts, and theater goers "in the true spirit of San Francisco."

You could easily come to refer to *Hayes & Vine* as Hayes and *Wine* when you consider their *'very excessive'* selection of wines. Enough to make any wine aficionado happy, their goal "to make wine accessible to anyone" is evident when you ask for an opinion or recommendation. We suggest you go for their 'wine flights' – perfectly matched, taste-sized portions with "one thing in common." Ask for the perfect appetizer to match, and you're set for an evening's enjoyment.

23: Mad Magda's Russian Tea Room and Cafe!

579 Hayes St. (between Laguna & Octavia). 415-864-7654. Hayes Valley. **HOURS:** Sun, 9a.m.-7p.m.; Mon & Tue, 8a.m.-9p.m.; Wed-Fri, 8a.m.-Midnight; Sat, 9a.m.-Midnight. **SPECIALS:** Wednesday, Snap-Crackle-Pop; Thursdays, Visual Artist Night; Monthly Rotating Photo Gallery; Tarot, Palm, and Tea Leave Readings.

Perhaps *the heart* of the hidden, little refuge called Hayes Valley, *Mad Magda's* is "the only place in San Francisco where you can eat your favorite Russian dictator." While Yeltsen is still too tenuous to be on the menu, their Foccacia 'Pizzettas' and Blinis (Russian style crepes filled with meal or dessert-type fillings) rival their Borscht for our attention.

Starting with "nothing but a dream," the proprietor (who's grandfather was Russian) had *only an idea* where the money would come from to pull it off. But relying on *energy!!!* (and perhaps the incarnate spirit of St. Germain, aka *Mad Magda*, who was promised eternal life), he very successfully created something "very San Franciscan."

The space encompasses a corridor-like room leading back to a garden patio that literally radiates life – and also features a smallish gift shop. *Magda's* welcomes "an odd mix of people, a nice mix ... multi-cultural ... everything." How's that for eclectic?

The interior decor, by local artist Steven Hornbuckle, features symbolic metaphysical representations. It centers a universe for a monthly rotating photo wall, a visual artist night featuring "anything you can imagine in a box" (a window box, that is), and other special events. Be sure to check-out the chairs. The music can be "anything on the planet," from Baroque to 50s mixes, and if you bring a tape, it *may* just get played (but no guarantee).

When looking to imbibe, you can choose anything from beers, wines, champagnes ... and such tea concoctions as *Magda's* tears – black currant, or the Chernoble Disaster - orange and cherry.

A centerpieces of *Magda's*, however, is that you can have a reading of tarot, palm, and tea leaves, seven days a week ($13.00 for 15 minutes). So, when you're looking for a place to relax and sample the spirit of San Francisco, jaunt on down to *Mad Magda's*.

Pasport: Two for one lunch or dinner entrees. Mon-Fri only.

24: Place Pigalle   Live Music/Arts & Events Bar

520 Hayes St. (at Octavia). 415-552-2671. Hayes Valley. **HOURS:** Mon-Wed, 4p.m.-Midnight; Thur-Fri, 4p.m.-2a.m.; Sat , 11a.m.-2a.m.; Sun 11a.m.-Midnight. **ENTRANCE CHARGE:** $2.00-$3.00 for live music.

Situated in the center of the small, ever-changing neighborhood called Hayes Valley, sits a little taste of France. Not really a restaurant by our standards, *Place Pigalle* fits the French mold more in its eclectic personality. Like many of its Parisian counterparts, the decor is multi-faceted, a sort of antique store chic – yet without the Parisian attitude. And as the world-famous Parisian demeanor can make you uncomfortable *("Whaaat, jeu du not speegk Frrench? Whaat aere jou doingng hierre?")*, the scene at Place Pigalle is very comfortable – and could even pass for cozy. The loungy feel tempts you to sit back and put your feet up on the table, which seems to be no problem for the owners (who are probably your bartender and server).

This bar has become a center, of sorts, for area musicians and artists alike, and the substantial rotating art show, featuring painting, sculpture, and visual arts, has received quite a bit of attention. The iron work you see was commissioned from Peter Forakis, who's work has been seen in the Museum of Modern Art.

The food at Place Pigalle could be classified as light Mediterranean cuisine, featuring pastas, salads, 'tartines' (sliced baguettes), and soups in the winter months. Prices range from a reasonable $3.50 to $7.50 and the (mostly French) wine list features wines by the glass from $3.25 to $6.75. They also have up to 10 micro-brewed beers on tap for $3.25 a pint.

Thursday, Friday, and Saturday evenings are classified Jazz Nights, primarily featuring local Bay Area acts. Sundays through Wednesdays could be *'anything'* including acoustic guitar, performance theater, and the spoken word. Let's see ... *"There was a young man named Ted, a Frenchman who lived life in his head ..."*

Pasport: Two for one entry.

25: Suppenküche   German Restaurant

525 Laguna St. (at Hayes). 415-252-9289. Hayes Valley. **HOURS:** Daily, 5p.m.-10p.m., Bar 'til 10:30 (Check for future extended hours); Brunch: Sat and Sun, 10a.m.-3p.m. **SPECIALS:** The Beer! The Food!

Hold on to your gastronomic horses, and be prepared to discover German-style nirvana. While this is not a book of restaurant reviews, in the case of Suppenküche, it brought us rocketing back to our days researching *Let's Party! Europe,* Munich, Oktoberfest, Mädchens, and Bavarian beer.

When you step into Suppenküche, you leap out of San Francisco and into a country inn on the Bavarian countryside. Being very picky when it comes to the potables and fare of The Fatherland, we approached this restaurant of 'traditional German food' with a wry grin and expectations to be disappointed. What we discovered was *a taste of true Germany in the heart of San Francisco.*

As with any good German experience, we started with the beer – which is imported directly, authentic, and *exactly* the flavors that got us hating mass-produced American beers. To put it bluntly, the beer selection not only rivals, but kicks-butt on any selection of beer found anywhere in the city – if not the entire western hemisphere. (Have you gotten the idea we like this place, yet?) For a real treat, try their Schneider Hefe Weizen (wheat beer). It may take a little getting used to, but once you've developed the taste, you won't be able to get enough.

Other than that, you can choose from among their 20 varieties on tap, all served in the appropriate glass provided from the brewery. That, plus their bottled selection, will keep you sampling for some time.

Now, for the food – *it's all good!* – from an ample menu of primarily Bavarian delights of meats, and gravies, and dumplings, and sausages, and krauts ... and ... and ... and .... The soups 'hat gut geschmekt.'

We were especially impressed with their Nürnberger Bratwurst mit Sauerkraut, Rehsteak in Rotwein-Pflaumen Sauce (Grilled Venison in Red Wine-Plum Sauce), and you must sample their spätzle (Bavarian potato dumplings). The desserts were 'wunderschön.' All in all, try them all, and don't forget that they have daily specials that are truly special.

Wondering how we can stick this restaurant review in a book about partying. Well, they have a quaint little room tucked behind the bar where you can go and drink beer, talk, have some more beer, talk, have some more beer .... You get the picture. *Prost!*

Let's Party! Favorites
Coolest Clothes - New

- Ameba
- American Rag
- Banana Republic
- Bebe
- Behind the Post Office
- Backseat Betty
- Cignal
- Club Monaco
- Eddie Bauers
- Episode
- The Guild
- Innbar Matinique
- S.F. Center
- Urban Outfitters

Let's Party! Favorites
Coolest Clothes - Used

- Aardvark
- American Rag Co.
- Buffalo Exchange
- Captain Jacks
- Crossroads Trading
- Haight Street
- Urban Outfitters
- Wasteland

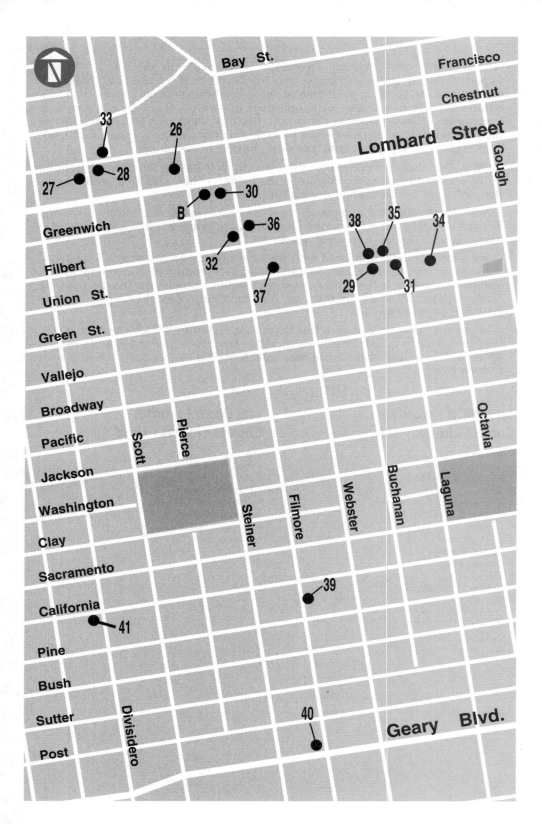

MARINA $-GREEN-$

P *ristinely wrapped* – like a perfect little package artfully topped with bow and ribbon – is one expression that comes to mind when describing the neighborhoods of the Marina, Cow Hollow, and Pacific Heights. From the right angles, the visual ingredients found in and around these areas is pulchritudinous ("very delightful, or pleasing to look at").

Standing atop Pacific Heights – San Francisco's most prime-cut real estate– you'll be treated to a panoramic view of Golden Gate Bridge to the North, and the hulking green grounds of the Presidio to the West. Looking out toward the bay, your eyes are guided down the sloping hills, through Cow Hollow, and onto the landfilled flats of the Marina, where concrete meets water at the northernmost tip of the peninsula.

In this area, San Francisco's class lines are drawn in this order:

- Young upscale professionals
- The wealthy
* The filthy rich.

Now you know why we call it Marina $-Green-$.

Bohemians in the area are rebellious, silver-spoon youths who have yet to find their way over the hill to the Haight (my, aren't we opinionated!).

We'll sidestep the residential thicket of Pacific Heights, where you'll find a sprinkle of private castles dressed with posh lawns and manicured bushes. This area is so placid that it *may* have been the inspiration for the Monkees' hit song, *Pleasant Valley Sunday*. Instead, we'll focus on the Marina and Cow Hollow areas.

Before there ever really was a neighborhood, the Marina area was the site of the 1915 Panama Pacific Exhibition. Before that, it was part of the bay (which came right up to the foot of Pacific Heights).

Coming as it did on the heels of the 1906 earthquake, the Panama Pacific Exhibition gave San Franciscans the perfect opportunity to show their newly rebuilt city to the world. Much of the rubble from the devastating quake was used to create the landfill that served as the Exhibition's site.

When the party closed, the landfill became a gold mine for realtors and speculators. Victorian- and Mediterranean-style houses and apartments popped on the scene like popcorn ... *and the Marina neighborhood was born.* Much later, an unfortunate twist of fate – the neighborhood constructed on the ruble of the 1906 quake was the hardest hit by the 1989 quake, caused by a quicksand-type effect on what was once a stream bed. Many TV shots flashed around the world showed the Marina's collapsed houses and torn-apart streets. Strangely, despite the area's precarious foundation, real-estate prices remain in six figures.

The Marina

The Marina is home to two of San Francisco's prime-time hangouts – *The Palace of Fine Arts, and Marina Green.*

The Palace of Fine Arts is located on the northwest corner of the Marina. Neither a palace nor an exhibitor of arts, this 10-story classic rotunda is the only structure surviving from the 1915 Exhibition. This monumental-sized piece of eye-candy serves no purpose other then to just *be.* At its base, a small park surrounds a pastoral duck and swan pond that captures the rotunda's breathtaking reflection. Watch out for hungry beaks, and – more importantly – *fowl feces,* which is scattered throughout the walkways. Bird-'do' notwithstanding, this fairy-tale setting can transport you back to a classic, romantic age (explaining why so many wedding photos feature the rotunda in the background).

The Palace of Fine Arts offers the quintessential setting for a sun-splash picnic ... *or for crashing a springtime wedding reception.* The area's enchanting lure also serves nicely for popping "the big question" to your significant other.

Marina Green (the park) occupies the northernmost edge of San Francisco, where land meets water. There she sits, directly facing the Yacht Club *(oh yes, my dear ...),* and within Kodak distance of Golden Gate Bridge – *offering one of San Francisco most revered post-card views.* For the lucky few who live in the surrounding area, this is their back yard ... or, more appropriately, the front yard of some San Francisco's of most expensive real estate. Marina Green is one of those austere San Francisco locations in and out of focus in countless movies.

On weekends, this rectangular spread of green resembles a park on steroids:

- Sun worshipers marking their ground, as cyclists and roller bladers scoot by
- Somewhere music fills your ears, as Frisbees vie with stunt kites for control of the air
- A young man celebrates a touchdown, as a young Irish lass scores a goal (much to the consternation of her male rivals)
- And ... over there ... the dog that's chasing a stick just startled a young girl, who dropped her ice cream on the pages of someone's journal ....

If you're looking for a luring distraction from your busy itinerary (or a reason to be late for your next appointment), fall into the leisure zone – and under the spell of San Francisco's playground. Just remember, this is The City's most earthquake-sensitive area ... but at least there's nothing that can fall on you. *All in all, it would probably be one hell of a ride!*

Chestnut Street lies within the sprawling neighborhood that constitutes the Marina, where you do not merely walk around ... *you stroll!* And the strip to stroll in this area is Chestnut Street. This neighborly road – at least the part that lies between Fillmore and Divisadero Street – is sprinkled with trendy shops, *chi chi* boutiques, delis with exotic imports, 'see and be seen' cafes, and numerous very good restaurants.

As you walk – *oops, sorry!... stroll* – you'll have no trouble finding a bank teller machine. As an indication of the sort of money circulating in this area, you can find a bank branch on nearly every corner, so don't bring cash – *bring your cash card!*

Starving writers that we are, we skipped the high price tags, and went straight for the area's few social haunts where our money would buy us at least a few good memories – specifically, places where our business cards got us a free beer – or two (those that plied us with liquor, of course, are the ones with the *good* reviews). What we found was a cluster of lively happenings near the intersection of **Scott and Chestnut Streets**. *Pluto's* is a popular stop-off for a light snack and, opposite, is the *Paragon* – a popular stop-off for live music, where those who have it, come to flaunt it. Or, if you're hoping to let your guard down, check out the unassuming ambiance of **The Grove**, a small cafe where you can enjoy a relaxing time-out with *Let's Party!* while you ponder your next area to plunder.

Shift your gears into *urban drive*, if you take our meaning, and you're confronted by **Lombard Street** (also Hwy. 101), which serves as one of The City's main thoroughfares. The street's fast-paced traffic to and from the Golden Gate Bridge brings you to San Francisco's foyer. Along Lombard Street (also known as motel row), you'll find 24-hour gas stations, fast and not-so-fast food places, and the not so pleasant odor of auto exhaust. With the exception of **Mel's Drive In,** featured so prominently in American Graffiti (a fact they won't let you forget), there's not much here worth mentioning.

On Lombard near **Fillmore Street**, however, is one of San Francisco's best live-music haunts. So, after waiting for the light to change from red to yellow to green, cross Lombard and make straight for the blue neon sign of **Blues**. No mystery here folks – this is a bar that lives up to, and beyond, its name. As a bonus, the nightly feast of southern-style R & B comes without the melancholy vibe usually associated with Blues music.

After enjoying a good jam session, it's time to do some jamming of your own – so turn the corner on Fillmore, and prepare to lose yourself in one of San Francisco's prime-time singles scenes. Here, in what locals call **"The Bermuda Triangle,"** you'll find a rambunctious mix of clean-cut All-Americans who belong to either the Fraternity & Sorority Gang or the Burbs-R-Us Crew. It's 'off to the triangle' they go on weekends – to flip, slip, and *let-it-rip*. While the scene has waned lately (due to changing ownership and the closing of some popular watering holes), old legends never die. So be warned – there have been numerous reports of wandering party-ers (and newly acquainted friends) vanishing inside 'the triangle.' It seems they were (happily) lured off course, only to awaken the next morning wearing that "what-the-hell-did-I-do-last-night" look.

As you'd expect, we dug up a few 'triangle' haunts that offer a lively gathering of the rollick and frolic variety. We hate to beat a dead horse, but if we don't say it, who will? So, before you get on to the main event, prepare your stomach for the coming alcoholic onslaught and try out the Mexican menu at the **Baja Cantina**. The food is that *messy kind of great,* and they're famous for their drop-dead Margaritas – ask for one 'Top Shelf.' Next door sits the **Pierce Street Annex,** a venerable 'triangle' anchor , where you'll find inebriated minds showing off their dance-floor grinds. Down a bit, the scene at **Desert Moon** is dominated by drinking games (and, lest we forget, your garden variety bar-side flirtations). But there's more, so explore.

26: Flying Kamakazi's Rock 'n' Roll Sushi   Fun Sushi Bar

3339 Steiner (between Lombard and Chestnut). 415-567-4900. Marina. **HOURS:** Mon-Thur, 5:30p.m.-10:30p.m.; Fri-Sat, 5:30p.m.-11p.m.; Sun, 5p.m.-10p.m. **SPECIALS:** Saki Bar with 13 varieties of Saki; 22 unique and exotic *specialty rolls.*

Okay, you're in San Francisco, and everyone has said you simply *must* have the sushi. But you have a problem ... you're looking to have fun ... and everyone knows

sushi restaurants are no fun at all! (Excepting that feeling you get in your sinuses when you eat to much wasabe.) So you have a dilemma – *what to do?* Thankfully, the insightful staff at *Let's Party!* has anticipated your predicament, and come to the rescue.

Kamakazi Sushi, perhaps San Francisco's only *real* bar/sushi bar, is just the ticket. Strategically placed off the Marina's Chestnut street loop, a visit will bring you not only that top-quality sushi you crave, but also a front bar area where you might just meet that person with whom you can share their trademark Kamakazi Roll ($9.95, but worth it!).

Unique to *Kamakazi Sushi* is a Japanese menu laced with hybrid delicacies not available in most traditional Japanese restaurants. Tapas style dishes like Pot Stickers with Ahi Tuna and Hamachi with a chili-soy-vinegar dipping sauce ($5.95), and Hawaiian Poke-style Ahi ($8.95) will make you want to return until you sample the entire menu.

Get the idea we were impressed with this place? You're right. New in the highly competitive sushi business, *Kamakazi Sushi* passes the *Let's Party!* Ambient-Gastronomic Test, offering great food in a cool scene.

Forget that we wrote this review after sucking down a few pitchers of saki. We're usually a little touched when we review *every* place, so why should this be an exception? Whatever, when you're ready, raise your cup and repeat after me: "Kompai!"

(Remember, you're not supposed to fill your own glass ... and you can eat the sushi with your fingers ... and saying "thank you" in Japanese ("Arigato") doesn't get you a discount ... and fried prawn heads are actually pretty good (as long as you have beer to help wash it down ... and ... and ...)

27: Paragon   Bar & Grill

3251 Scott St. (at Chestnut). 415-922-2456. Marina. **HOURS:** Daily, Bar, 4p.m.-2a.m.; Dinner, 5:30p.m.-10p.m. **SPECIALS:** Live Music Sun-Wed starting 9:30p.m. (Rock, Jazz, Funk, R&B, Blues).

Packed to the brim on weekends, this East Coast-style bar dishes out a healthy dose of revelry and merrymaking. To its realm of followers, this bar may very well be the paragon of the Marina-area scene. Hosting a healthy array of 'regulars,' the *Paragon* caters primarily to the sleek and fashionable single-set, who venture in seeking like-minded patrons. Earth tone colors and ceiling fans prevail over the front half of the establishment, where the long bar is graced with 12 micro brews on tap. Whether it's Anchor Steam or Wyders Cider, Red Nectar Ale or Pyramid Porter, you'll find something to tickle your tonsils.

A small dance floor fronts a squat square stage, where you'll find an eclectic repertoire of musical acts, and a kingly fireplace demarcates the boundary between the social happenings and the restaurant. In back, the dining room is accented by a omnipresent 3-D mural of the cubist genre created by local artist Michael Brennan. (geez, we *love* to play with big words!) The American cuisine is worth a few stars, and the big hits are their Shrimp and Red Snapper Taco Salad, Red Curry Lamb dish, and Herbed Skirt Steak. Come for dinner, and stay for 'dessert.'

28: Pluto's   Supper Cafe

3258 Scott St. (at Chestnut). 415-775-8867. Marina. **HOURS:** Mon-Thur, 11:30a.m.-10p.m.; Fri, 11:30a.m.-11p.m.; Sat, 9:30a.m.-11p.m.; Sun, 9:30a.m.-10p.m.

On the corner of Scott and Chestnut sit the Marina District's latest entries. *Pluto's* sits somewhere on the fringes, between a full-fledged cafe and short-menu restaurant. The stylish 'yupified' patrons sit wrapped in a planetary (i.e., spacey), yet simplistic nook-like setting. A high, blue, ameba-shaped ceiling, maple wood tables, and a loud orange backrest (spanning the length of the cafe) are all whipped-up into the scheme. Oh, looking for an adjective? Hmmm, looking for an adjective? Look no further (the writing's on the wall!).

While the decor is engaging and happy, *Pluto's* specialty – carved meats and poultry sandwiches – packs both the lunch and the supper crowds in. *Pluto's* really American-style fresh food is served from walk-up food stations, where you can watch as your food is cooked and prepared. The big hit here is the Turkey Delight. To quantify, *Pluto's* carves through 25 20-pound, herb-roasted turkeys each day, and that's a hell-of-alotta feathers in their cap!

Cow Hollow

Head up Fillmore from the Marina and hang a left onto **Union Street**, and you'll come to the heart of **Cow Hollow**. No – no hollowed-out cows! This district earned its name during the post-Gold Rush days, when dairy farms dotted the landscape. Answering the call for advancement, the peaceful grazing fields once marked by the sound of cow bells *(and maids-a-milking)*, eventually gave way to a shoppers' feeding frenzy marked by the sound of cash registers ringing.

Quenching the genteel thirsts of San Francisco's most refined gentry, Union Street sports a virtual gallery of restored Victorian mansions. Garnished with flower-filled windows and color trim, many are home to fashionable boutiques, art galleries, antique shops, Danish bakeries, Italian deli's, French restaurants, gift shops, *fu fu* manicurists, hair salons, jewelers, florists and (of course), high-maintenance fashions the likes of Armani and Lornenzini. You'll also find European-style cafes that provide a quick pit stop for the *time-is-money* schedules of so many who live and shop here.

The only loungers you're likely come across are tourists – *perhaps like yourself!* Lest our commentary seem harsh, be aware that, despite Union Street's undulating sophistication and spit-and-polish appearance, the community feeling here is comfortable and down to earth. *If there's 'hob-nobbing' to be done, it's in neighboring Pacific Heights.* Okay, enough already (sometimes we almost feel as if we're writing one of those Vagabond Publishing books about shopping!).

With its nocturnal side studded with singles bars that cater to a motley mix of weekend-warrior's on leave from their 9-to-5 song-and-dance, Union Street adds a colorful feather to San Francisco's party cap. So, let's get our feathers ruffled (sorry – we couldn't resist) by starting off at **Perry's**, where you can drink or dine with a (slightly older) crowd that *networks*, not *socializes!* Half a block east, at **Pasand**, you can listen to the sounds of live Jazz as you dine on cuisine of southern India.

A half a block back – popular among armchair jocks and sports enthusiasts – you'll find the **Bus Stop**. With it's two satellite feeds and 15 TVs, this 96-year-old establishment is San Francisco's quintessential sports bar. Moving on to the rowdy half of Union Street, you'll come to the **Union Ale House** where, a few steps below street level, you'll find a buzz of social camaraderie (much of it the 'boy-meets-girl' variety). Across the street, the stylish **Blue Light** is also popular among San Francisco's late 20's and 30-something singles set. Down a couple blocks, you'll find **Tarr & Feathers**, but – be warned – this is one of those 'on again, off again' places (what can you expect when revelry meets Jäegermeister?).

29: The Blue Light   Sports Bar/Restaurant

1979 Union St. (at Buchanan). 415-922-5510. Cow Hollow. **HOURS:** Mon-Sat , 4p.m.-2a.m.; Sun, 10:30a.m.-2a.m. **SPECIALS:** Fat Tuesdays is girls night with women bartenders, $1.50 discount on all beers, and dinner menu is half price.

Formally owned by Boz Scaggs, this 'sport' bar is a delightful departure from the numerous meat-and-potato, paraphernalia-cluttered bars scattered throughout The City. In fact, you won't find a more elegantly designed 'sport' bar in this book, or in San Francisco as a whole.

Along with the avant-guarde decor of galvanized metal walls, etched glass panels and, for good measure, a 45-foot bar, you'll find TV's mounted in every corner – poised and ready for a daily diet of sporting events. If the slick maneuvers of Monday Night Football provide little stimulation, however, on most nights you'll find an engaging singles crowd with whom to exercise some of your own maneuvers.

The menu is from the school of Cajun cuisine, and features spicy flatbread sandwiches. If the energetic goings-on the bar provides make you ravenous, sink your hunger into the red meat of their Skirt Steak ($8.25).

30: Blues   Live Music Bar

2125 Lombard St. (at Fillmore). (415) 771-2583. Cow Hollow. **HOURS:** Daily, 8p.m.-2a.m. **ENTRANCE CHARGE:** Thur-Sun, $5.00 **SPECIALS:** Monday, walk-in Jam Session, Daily, Live Music starts 9:30p.m. Two for one entry.

If there is one bar that lives up to its name, it's *Blues*. In fact, this Cow Hollow haunt is one of San Francisco's little darlings of Blues. A nightly mix of revelers comes here for a happy workout of dancin'-'n'-prancin,' orchestrated by some of San Francisco best live Blues talent.

On Friday and Saturday nights, the dancing and grinding is non-stop and, at full capacity, table-tops are often confused for the dance floor. The interior is warmly lit, and the stage and dance floor are surrounded by a not-so-grand viewing area. But hey! cozy can be good – especially if you're looking to lay-on that primal charm of yours.

Six nights a week you can expect a stage performance of good-ol' Southern Blues, but as if to make a point, on Sundays *Blues* becomes the *Leopard Lounge*. 'Intimate' leopard-patterned booths lining the wall opposite the bar lend the name to this Sunday night happening. On that night, R&B sounds more like Acid Jazz and House, as live acts and DJs spin to the club cats of SoMa and beyond. For the house special, try their Absolute Blues ($3.00).

Passport: Two for one entry.

31: Bus Stop   Sports Bar

1901 Union St. (at Laguna). 415-567-6905. Cow Hollow. **HOURS:** Mon-Fri, 10a.m.-2a.m.; Sat & Sun, 9a.m.-2a.m. **SPECIALS:** Daily, 5p.m.-6p.m. free hors-d'oeuvre.

It may not be obvious (with its burnished wood and brass interior), but as 'watering holes' go, the *Bus Stop* saloon is this area's patriarch. First opened in 1900, it pioneered the 20th century at a time when horse-drawn trolleys served remote, cobblestoned Union Street. But as always, the times have changed, the trolleys have given way to 'Beemers,' and what was once a cowboy saloon has become one of San Francisco's premier sports bars.

Okay ... *its time for a little math.* With 15 TVs stemming from two satellite dishes, each of their three rooms can have up to five different sporting events on at any time. So, in the time it takes you to move between rooms with three beers, you can expose your sports-info-craving to everything from acrobatics to volleyball – and everything in-between.

The bartenders, in-between concocting one of their famous Rum drinks, sit at the helm of the star-ship 'remote,' and will take requests. If hanging on every play isn't your thing, and you're left wanting for a participatory sport, hang a few shots on one of their pool tables.

The bar features 21 different brews, and their CD jukebox doses-out classic tunes with a cramped neck *(you figure it out)*. The *Bus Stop* is, perhaps, the best bar in San Francisco where you can root for ... or *with* ... your favorite sports stars. On occasion, one of the many 49ers who live in this area will stop in for a brew (so keep that autograph book handy). That tall guy with large hands sitting in the corner ... perhaps, maybe ... is it possible ... could it *really* be ...???

32: Desert Moon   Bar

3111 Fillmore St. (at Filbert) 415-567-5589. Cow Hollow. **HOURS:** Mon-Thur & Sat, 6p.m.-2a.m.; Fri, 5p.m.-2a.m.; Sun, noon-2a.m. **SPECIALS:** Happy Hour, Mon-Sat, 6p.m.-9p.m. – $2.00 draft beers.

Desert Moon is popular among the 21- to 35- year-old bunch (self proclaimed as the 'Bridge and Tunnel Crowd') who, on weekends, journey over the hills, through the tunnel, and across the bridge to land in this – one of Cow Hollow's beloved drinking holes. There's nothing glossy about this social haunt and, while garnished with a Southwestern look, the interior is nearly as sparse as a desert.

While trend-junkies and 'fashion gurus' are busy cat-walking through SOMA venues on weekends, *Desert Moon* hosts a rambunctious gathering that swells into a virtual beer orgy. As with all good drinking holes, the bar is the center of a social eddy, where buoyant flirtations run high. The wooden benches and tables fall prey to an occasional slew of drinking games reminiscent of college days past (or present).

In the back, a well used pool table stands beneath a mural of the Marlboro Man on his trusted horse. Not known as one of The City's swankier haunts, the *Moon's* faithful patrons nevertheless present a high-energy atmosphere. If he hasn't moved on, as yet, you'll be lucky to get Tony behind the bar, preparing his fare with a casual flair. Tell him we said "hi."

Passport: Two For one, any beer.

33: The Grove   Cafe

2250 Chestnut St. (between Pierce & Scott). 415-474-4843. Cow Hollow. **HOURS:** Mon-Tue, 7a.m.-11p.m.; Wed-Fri, 7a.m.-Midnight; Sat, 8a.m.-Midnight; Sun, 8a.m.-11p.m.

On the 'spit & polish' street of Chestnut, *The Grove* presents cafe-life's more refined face. From the tables and chairs to the wooden plank floors (which, curiously, first served as the side of a Connecticut barn), this little locale beams with antiquated comfort. It offers to the Marina, a trendy spot with an American Gothic slant.

Throughout the day, don't be surprised to see local writers and poets tanking-up on espresso while banging out the next Great American Novel on their laptop ... as they check out the inspiration that just walked in the door (yes, the people watching is *that* good!). You can also expect a constant influx of *TREND-ies* dropping in for a shot at the end (or beginning) of their daily jogging or Roller Blading routine.

As evening descends, *The Grove* begins to *hummm* with GAP-clad students interfacing, between groups of mild-mannered young professionals trading office stories or comical banter. For your solitary pleasure, you'll find a selection of newspapers to browse and, if you're looking for a one-on-one chess or backgammon match, ask at the counter for one of their boards ... p-K4 ... *anyone?!?*

On the menu, the main attraction is the Caesar Salad ($6.00). Also popular, in this, The City's most 'ya gotta watch your weight' area, are healthy soups and sandwiches. At lunch time, you can expect a line – composed of employees from the many area boutiques – leading out the door. When you get your chance, grab your gourmet treat and venture to their outdoor cafe tables, where you can get a dose of sun and conversation (if you're alone, it's easy to eavesdrop on the table next to you).

34: Pasand   Indian Restaurant/Live Jazz

1875 Union St. (at Laguna). 415-922-4498. Cow Hollow. **HOURS:** Tue-Sun, 11:30a.m.-1:30a.m.; Mon, closed. **SPECIALS:** Daily, live music-Jazz and R&B, 8p.m.-1:30a.m. **RESTRICTIONS:** During live music, two beverages per set per person.

In Hindu, "Pasand" means beautiful and delicious – and that's exactly what you can expect from the food here (that is, if you have the palate for spicy, curried foods). The setting is not quite as worn as an old shoe, but it *has* seen better days (like sometime back in the early 70s, to be precise).

In the front section of this Indian restaurant, you'll be treated to somewhat out-of-place, but pleasing, live Jazz tunes. The interior is choked with plastic plants stretching back to the glass-enclosed patio.

Adding to the exotic surroundings, most menu items are written in their original Hindu name and, if it weren't for the 'subtitles,' you'd need a Hindu translator at your table. Tops on the vegetable curry menu is their Palak Mutter Paneer Curry (spinach, green peas and homemade cheese cubes) served with Rice Pilaf ($10.50).

35: Perry's   Bar/Restaurant

1944 Union St. (between Laguna & Buchanan). 415-922-9022. Cow Hollow. **HOURS:** Daily, Bar, 9a.m.-2a.m.; Restaurant, 9a.m.-Midnight.

You'll find this 26 year-old-bar and restaurant tucked under the bay window of an old Victorian. Over the years, *Perry's* has matured into the up-scale scene that an up-scale neighborhood like this requires. Modeled after New York's famed *PS Clarks, Perry's* is one of San Francisco's who's-who haunts. Among the frequent drop-ins are John Travolta, Nicolas Cage, and Steve Young.

Between the celeb-parade, *'good old boys'* and aging jocks come to this classic bar to bend elbows and trade fish stories, while shoppers play show-and-tell and tourists check their list of 'must things to see.' The decor is a mixture of polished woods, checkered table cloths, embossed ceiling tiles, and a collage of historical pictures and memorabilia.

As if that isn't enough, Perry's full menu is among San Francisco's most acclaimed. Tops on the sandwiches list is the Reuben ($8.25) or, for an entree delight, try the Grilled Swordfish ($16.95).

36: Pierce Street Annex   Dance Bar

3138 Fillmore St. (between Filbert & Greenwich). 415-567-1400. Cow Hollow. **HOURS:** Daily, noon-2a.m. **ENTRANCE CHARGE:** Thur-Sat, $3.00 after 10p.m. **SPECIALS:** Karaoke on Monday, 9p.m.-1a.m.; Tuesday, Long Island Ice Tea Night starting at 8p.m.; Wednesday, one dollar draft beer night; Friday, 7:30p.m.-10p.m., Live Jazz. **RESTRICTIONS:** Cash only.

Deep within the nocturnal thick of Cow Hollow's singles scene, is *T-h-e A-n-n-e-x.* At 35-years-old and still counting, this rollicking spot has seen the rise and fall ... and rise ... and fall ... of the notorious Bermuda Triangle. After a recent change of ownership at both Golden Gate Grill and Balboa Cafe, this founding member of the Triangle has become the sole original survivor.

Okay, enough with its celebrated past, it's time to celebrate the present – and there's no better present *here* than Thursday through Saturday. If you're not one of those lame-o's who comes early (and we *know* you're not), as you enter this 'love-shack,' you'll be hit by a mob of shiny happy people dancing singing and drinking. Immediately in front, on your right, is a Jägermeister bar with, believe it or not, Jäeger on tap (*hooray* for good-ol' German ingenuity!).

A wide mix of cultural Americans come here to throw-down and shake-it-up with a young bridge-and-tunnel bunch who love to flash their designer jeans and flannel fashions. Among the ever-undulating mob, you'll see wide-eyed newbees who've just reached the cut-loose age of 21. With a license to kill (pardon the double entendre), no one holds back.

On the dance floor, a DJ-mix of Top-40 music captures any moving body into a thumping, pumping, dirty-dancing routine. Along the side line, one-liners and sexual innuendoes are exchanged with sophomoric wit ... but eventually, someone blinks, takes a heavy drag of their cigarette, and dives in. At the bar, be brave, and order their characteristic concoction – the Jones Town for $3.50 (Kool-aid never tasted this good!).

37: Tarr & Feathers   Live Music/Sports Bar

2140 Union St. (between Webster & Fillmore). 415-563-2612. Cow Hollow. **HOURS:** Mon-Fri, 1 p.m.-2a.m.; Sat-Sun, 10a.m.- 2a.m. **SPECIALS:** Happy Hour, Mon-Fri, 4 p.m.- 7 p.m., beer is $2.50; Tuesday all day, Beer is $2.00, Jagermeister shots only $2.00.

The name *Tarr & Feathers* may suggest visions of medieval torture, but – on weekends – rest assured the only torture here is the wait you'll endure trying to capture the bartender's attention. While waiting, pay attention to a couple of legacies left from the previous owner – they hang behind the bar. One is stuffed, and makes a perfect hat holder; the other can either be a watchful wooden eye or a companion bar fly ... you figure it out!

This popular Union Street haunt has just turned drinking age and, by the looks of it, *Tarr & Feathers* is here to stay – at least for another 21 years. Its brand of down-to-earth revelry sets it apart from the many haughty-taughty pick-up bars found throughout the area (but that's not to say you won't find your share of social-intercourse). Much as *Tarr & Feathers* is known as a sports bar, you will be hard-pressed to pin it down. It offers such a mix of genre's, it's as schizophrenic as any bar in San Francisco.

While featuring quiz nights and televised sporting event, *Tarr & Feathers* brandishes rave-tribal art in what manages to resemble a cowboy saloon. Loyal patrons are as eclectic as the ambiance, ranging from the 'what's-up-serf's-up' type to the 'hello-how-do-you-do' variety. If you're looking for diversion from the bars social arena, head over to the pool tables and pinball games. The jukebox is chock-full of classic Rock goodies, and (to pamper your hunger), in the back, on the side, is a pizzeria offering tasty slices.

Passport: Shot of Jägermeister for $2.00.

38: Union Ale House   Ale House Bar

1980 Union St. (at Buchanan). 415-921-0300. Cow Hollow. **HOURS:** Mon-Thur, 3:30p.m.-2a.m.; Fri-Sun, 11:30a.m.-2a.m.; Serving food daily until 9:45p.m. **SPECIALS:** Handicap access, Happy Hour, Mon-Fri, 3:30p.m.-6:30p.m., $1.00 off all drinks.

Looking to whet your whistle? Twenty 'brewskies' on tap (including a cask ale), plus a full bar is the selection you'll find once you venture down the stairs and into this supremely social spot. You'll also find that the all the ingredients are there for an evening with *all-the-right-stuff*. Lotsa dark wood, a large atrium, a little brass here – a couple of dart boards there, a pool table and shuffle board ... then add-in a mad-mix of college students and young locals, serve hot, and you have this *House's* recipe for an American style pub.

For a side-order, the Buffalo Wings ($4.95) or Baja Nachos with chicken ($5.50) are tops on their appetizer menu. Coming back to their liquid selection, for all you wheat lovers, we recommend their Widmer Hefeweizen or the Thomas Kemper Weizen Berry. Better yet, for just 20-bills you can sample the whole lot in 5-oz sample glasses (which go for only $1.00 each).

Pacific Heights

39: Harry's on Fillmore

Coctail Bar

2020 Fillmore St. (at Pine). 415-921-1000. Pacific Heights. **HOURS:** Daily, 3:30p.m.–2a.m. (sometimes 1a.m. on Sundays and Mondays). **SPECIALS:** No Cover Charge for music.

Mirror, mirror, on the wall, who's the *grooviest* of them all ...?

Long established as a Fillmore entertainment institution, *Harry's on Fillmore* persists to this day as a favorite social gathering spot of both San Francisco's young professionals and bridge-and-tunnel weekenders. And although Harry may be gone – having moved on in his quest to become a City entertainment institution in himself – this club maintains its status as one of the classier San Francisco joints.

The scene inside *Harry's* is one of resplendent beauty catering to *late-20 boom-fringe not really generation X-ers, through 40s-hipsters*. The entirety of its decor is richly appointed with dark woods and ornate lighting set against a backdrop of subdued green that sets the tone. Behind the fine bar, you find a ceiling-high mirror that reflects on the nebulous connections and rendezvous that enter its all-encompassing gaze.

The patrons never seem to age, as *Harry's* holds a spirited grip as one of The City's 'mature' clubs. The live music that flows six days a week from the small street-backed stage is the musings of local Jazz and Rhythm and Blues artists. A springboard for rising stars, the beat pumping out of the state-of-the-art BOSE system picks up on weekends, when your feet are sure to get-a-movin'.

For some odd reason, a TV in the back corner by the full-bar can often be found mouthing the banter of Jay Leno. While his words don't exactly match those coming from your new acquaintance, its presence is surreal enough and, if you're not

careful, may foretell of things to come, a la Johnny Carson.

40: Jacks Bar   Live Music Bar

1601 Fillmore St. (at Geary). 415-567-3227. Lower Pacific Heights. **HOURS:** Daily, 2p.m.-2a.m. **ENTRANCE CHARGE:** $5.00 for Fri-Sat only.

Suffering "a 20-year facelift," *Jack's Bar* has *opened up* its location on lower Pacific Heights. Gone is the dark moodiness that gave *Jack's* interior the shady feel of a South-Side-Chicago dive bar. The 70s era fixtures are gone too, and the raised seating area, and the stage ... "*What ... The stage!?!*"

Don't worry, we know 'the bedraggled feel' was one thing you knew and loved about *Jack's*, but the music is the same as it's always been. "How can that be without a stage," you ask? Well, the powers that be at this austere R&B institution have rearranged the place, adding length (and corners) to the long, curved bar. Along the way they've devised a way to transform this 'night club in a neighborhood' into just that – a nightclub Wednesday through Saturday evenings, and a neighborhood bar the rest of the week.

They do this by rolling the pool table in back, clearing the way for the band to set up. By the time you read this, they may even have their portable stage finished. At the end of the day, once they turn down the lights and get that classic R&B jammin', you'll forget completely about the *Jack's* of old, and get those feet-a movin'.

As for the music, it's still what you'd expect from "the oldest continually operating Blues bar west of the Mississippi" – and, since 1932, their stages have seen the likes of Van Morrison, Merle Saunders, and James Brown. "Overseen" by John Lee Hooker (Mr. Lucky himself), you *know* they ain't gonna mess with the groove – at least not Wednesday through Saturday evenings between 9:00 p.m. to 1:30 a.m.

Tuesdays are 'open mike' Comedy Night, and that's okay. We're told a booking connection at the Punch Line has given *Jack's* the inside scoop on established comedians trying out new stuff. Other than that, weren't *you* always thinking about gettin' up there? *C'mon, give it a go ....*

If you're hungry, forget it – unless 'just chips' is enough to satisfy your munchies. With 100 beers at your disposal ($3.00 for a pint) and a full bar, however, you'll never be at a loss when it comes to something to drink – especially for scotch drinkers, who are presented a line-up of 15 to 20 top-of-the-line, single-malt Scotches.

This is a club where 'people dance,' and the owners invite you to "come here to have fun" in an atmosphere that "is *not* a meat market." We're sure you get the idea.

Now, before we let you go, remember that your ticket or ticket stub from the Kabuki Theater is good for free entry (except during special engagements). So head on over after your show or, when you find your show sold out, bring your ticket over and catch some live music ... you may just decide to stay!

41: Rasellas   Jazz Bar/Restaurant

2801 California St. (at Divisidero). 415-567-5010. Pacific Heights. **HOURS:** Sun-Thur, 5p.m.-12:30a.m.; Fri-Sat, 5p.m.-2a.m. **RESTRICTIONS:** Dress Code.

This thriving club delivers an unusual blend of jazz and Ethiopian food in a classic, high-ceilinged, spacious environment. The main room is ringed with cozy brown leather couches. Floor to ceiling windows on two sides, plus clouded-sky-motif wall coverings, combine to give this small local nightspot the feel of a large, open space. Brass accents, stained glass interior windows, and period light fixtures lend an early 20th-Century feel to the place. Tiny lounge tables cluster in the center of the main room, which is divided from the 'stage' by only a baby grand piano. The club features live R&B and Jazz nightly, from 8:00 p.m. to midnight Sunday to Thursday, and 9:00 p.m. to 1:00 a.m. Fridays and Saturdays. The musical offerings rely heavily on various incarnations of *Rasella's* quite-talented house band, interspersed with appearances by local Jazz and Blues groups.

The white canvas-draped dining room seems like an afterthought. Its eight humble tables are placed down a few stairs, out of the way and completely in the back of the club. Regardless, the simple, small menu is reasonably well managed and fairly priced. The *tibs wat* ($10.50) – sautéed beef strips cooked in a zesty berbere sauce – is the favorite dish among Ethiopian regulars. The Vegetarian Combination ($10.50) is an assortment of four interesting meatless entrees that is great for sampling different tastes.

Meals are served family style, on an immense platter covered in traditional *injera* bread, so the custom is to share. Another custom involves eating with your hands – just tear off a bite-sized piece of injera, grab a bit of the food item of your choice with it, and pop it in your mouth. Your snobby friends may disapprove, but it makes for a fun meal. *Tej*, an Ethiopian nectar concocted of honey and white wine, is the ideal accompaniment to spicy food. But remember that the spices are toned down quite a bit to suit American tastes, so if you want your meal to have a genuine kick to it, you'll have to ask. Friday through Sunday, reservations are suggested.

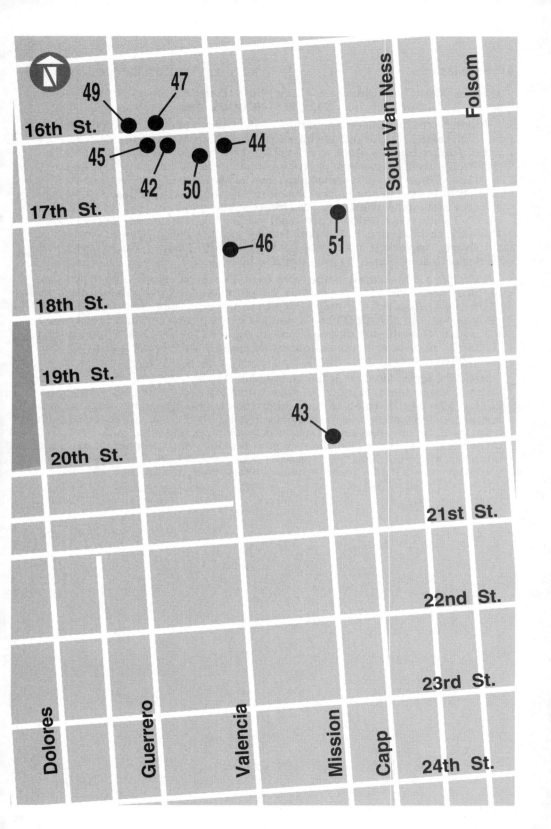

THE MISSION

Among the many neighborhoods of San Francisco, the **Mission** offers an experi-ence layered with perhaps the most chaotic mishmash of sights and sounds:

- Its streets are pregnant with an orderly/disordered buzz.
- On weekends, residents seem poised and ready to erupt into a neighborhood-wide fiesta.
- Traffic is more congested than other parts of the city and, adding to the confusion, is the *orchestra* of car-horns exchanged with a determined weight (often heard just to be heard).
- You'll see the occasional gang member 'peacocking' his air-brushed low rider through the streets.

Along **Mission and 24th Street**, taquerias sit waiting to ambush pedestrians with their spicy aromatic allures; amigos stand beside doorways vying to drive-home their point on the argument of the hour; and mothers clad in colorful South American dress (many used as a may-pole for their children to orbit) walk from one fruit stand to the next hunting down daily bargains. Yes, the Mission marches to its own beat, and as for its rhythm ... this neighborhood's boisterous nature is only equaled by the ever-present Mariachi music that blares into the open – sometimes from all directions.

The manicured bushes and private castles common to the Marina and Pacific Heights neighborhoods may be located on the other side of the city, but – in char-acter – the Mission seems more like it's a continent away. While most tourists opt for the quintessential sure-hits of the Wharf, North Beach, and the Union Square area, take a chance – *a giant leap* – away from parade-rout routine and into the hid-den discoveries of the Mission. You'll find nothing like it!

And, with the exception of bohemian pockets-of-life found elsewhere in The City, the Mission district provides a banner example of a street culture's pursuit of leisure and merry-making. Sure, you'll find some streets trashed to third-world propor-tions, but don't sweat it – it's all part of the ambiance.

THE MISSION
Intro

With its predominately Hispanic and Chicano communities, the Mission is a neighborhood embroidered with a social and festive fabric all its own. Yet, its character is deeply founded in the rich soil of San Francisco's spirit. The Mission is so deeply founded, in fact, that *this* is the 'grand-daddy' of all San Francisco districts. And, being the cradle of The City's birth, it was the Mission area where Western civilization made its grand entrance.

You see, it was on one eventful November afternoon in 1769 – while busily doing … well, whatever the local tribe of Native Americans called the Ohlones did – that a silver-armored Spanish cappy by the name of Gaspar de Portolá (with his compadre of soldiers, muleteers, and a few jelly-bellied Franciscan Friars) entered the bay on an overland reconnaissance in quest of new souls to offer The Church.

For the indigenous Ohlone Indians, nothing could have been more life changing. Never before had the Ohlones seen such oddities as the elaborately dressed soldiers, weapons, or, for that matter – horses. They must have been overwhelmed! It was

probably comparable to our having an encounter with an alien space ship. All we can say for certain is that it was the beginning of the end of traditional life for the Ohlones.

We don't know whether the Mission ultimately acquired its name from Gaspar's mission to carry-out the church's mission to build a Mission. We do know, however, that it was a mission of a mission to establish a Mission. Ultimately, a Mission was built – *and it's the oldest structure in San Francisco*. It was named Mission Dolores, and was the sixth Mission in the Spanish mission to build Missions – and gain submission of all west-coast tribes under Mission rule.

We can only speculate that it was some dumfounded Ohlone tribesman who was first in the Bay Area to cry the four words have been repeated uncountable times: "Not another bible lesson…!"

The Ohlones gave way to the colonial Spanish, who eventually relinquished control to the []Californios – basically, wealthy Mexicans who had amassed large land claim. And they, too, in time, gave way to an increasing number of American pioneers. The latter came armed with an idea of Manifest Destiny.

After the turn of the 20th century, the Mission teeter-tottered between immigrants from Scandinavia, Germany, and Ireland before returning to its original Spanish character.

So, now that we've established the Mission as the *oldest* neighborhood in San Francisco, we'd like to add a few other superlatives:

- The Mission is the *largest* neighborhood in San Francisco and, due to the sheltering hill of Twin Peaks, is also the *most-fog-free* stretch of land on the peninsula. Sunnyside-up, anyone?

- It is, therefore, no coincidence that the Mission is The City's most-populous neighborhood.

- Its plentiful housing and affordable rent offer a welcome mat for newly arrived immigrants; cheap living translates into an economic sanctuary. Recently, this affordability has also attracted students and bohemians, who have put *fun* back into *funky*. While many of San Francisco's neighborhoods have gone through a wash cycle of gentrification, the Mission and its Pan-American families are witnessing a steady churning of "bohemianization."

If variety is the spice of life, the Mission is one hot tamale – and the hot and spicy relaxation and revelry zones can be found on **Valencia and 16th Streets**. So, without delay, we'll skitter along to this not-really-Hispanic side to see what all the fuss is all about.

Clad in a politically-opinionated T-shirt, fashionable shades, and a rasta-style doo, stands a newborn hipster who's jumped up to participate in an open mike reading. His lyrical tail is expressed with the tonality of a 'made' man. "Howl" it is not, but who cares when you can sit in a cafe for four hours without spending a penny. Enrichment through words of poetry and philosophy is once again hip, and the collection of folksy cafes and smoky bars found near the intersection of Valencia and 16th Streets has been adopted as the new home and command-center of a revived "beat" movement.

Yes, Kerouac is back. But where is the City Lights Bookstore, the anchor of the 50's beat movement in North Beach. Don't look too far. The **Roxie Theater**, with its bizarre and shocking films, has taken up the banner as the cornerstone for the alternative scene. Its screen is home to a range of political-activist, gay-lesbian, and artsy-fartsy movies. And what better venue for expression? The Roxie is deeply entrenched as the oldest, longest running independent theater in San Francisco So pay homage (and get "shocked").

If you're looking for a time-out session, enter **Cafe Macondo**, where you'll find the defining pose of pondering patrons snug with book in hand and feet resting on the furniture. Across the street, **New Dawn** has taken 'art-deco-funky' to outlandish extremes. We *think* it's a cafe.

If you let your nose direct you, you'll probably find yourself taking in the delectable aroma of gourmet omelets cooking next door at **Mission Grounds**. At their street-side tables, you can enjoy a pedestrian parade sure to reveal a few alien sightings.

We've heard of a newly legislated Mission mandate that requires visitors to sample at least one Hispanic taqueria before leaving. And, just in case you get any funny ideas, be warned that strict penalties are handed down to anyone caught cheating at Taco Bell. We consider **Pancho Villa** to be the area's 'prima Taqueria.' It's located on Valencia near 16th.

For the anarchists who insist on bucking the system – cross the street to **Cafe Istanbul**, a tiny haunt where falafel sandwiches and "pillow talk" set the tone.

Now that you're all fed and burped, its time to check out the **Albion**. This dive bar is an *anti-scene scene*, where the owner scoffs at scoffers, and barflies are busy ignoring other barflies. Across the street is the **Kilowatt**, 16th Street's "amplifier" featuring loud and alternative live music.

For a glimpse of daily Hispanic culture and life, venture down **24th Street**. The 14 block stretch between **Portrero Avenue & Valencia Street** reveals a congested melange of Cuban Delis, Salvadoran restaurants, Brazilian taquerias, and Puerto Rican bakeries. Without listing the full selection of Latino countries, we think you get the picture!

Complete with language barriers and storefront signs in Spanish, this area is, in essence, a slice of land that seems to have happily gone adrift before being washed ashore on the banks of 24th Street. It has currently matured into a self-reliant island neighborhood, featuring the San Padro flower shop, Rodriques appliance store, meat and fruit markets, an optometrist, dentists, lawyers, travel agencies, barber shops, barber shops, and more barber shops.

For some odd reason, 24th Street is a hair-cutters Mecca. On one street block after another sit traditional small shops (with their spinning candy-cane icon), next to glossy fashionable salons. Why so many barbers and stylists are needed here defies the laws of supply-and-demand and hair growth but, after loosely investigating this peculiar phenomena, we believe the obsession with hair grooming has something to do with the neighborhood's ongoing preoccupation with festivals, weddings, and birthdays.

Ah, but there's more (you didn't think we'd leave you hanging with barber shops, did you?). For a more visual attraction, the Mission, and particularly 24th Street, boasts a colorful parade of wall paintings known as the **Mission Murals**. These eye-candy depictions of Latin struggle and celebration have gained international acclaim as 'the largest open-air gallery,' and conducted walking tours are very popular. These much-photographed and written-about motifs testify to this community's spirit. As many as 40 murals are sprinkled along 24th Street alone, with the largest concentration running down Balmay Alley.

The neighborly ambiance of 24th Street shifts into urban drive as you turn onto palm-tree-lined **Mission Street**. While holding the distinction as San Francisco's longest thoroughfare, Mission Street is also this neighborhoods main artery, and an eight-block stretch between **24th and 16th Streets** is its economic heart.

Brimming with commercial activity of the anything-goes variety, nudged side by side are discount stores crammed to the ceiling with an endless variety of affordable (read 'cheap') merchandise. Window shopping is easy – they've dispensed with the windows, so "stumbling onto a bargain" should be taken very literally (if not cautiously). This is due to what we call a shops S.O.D., or "Spill-Over Display." Chances are you'll find that special no-name product you're looking for hanging outside on hooks and racks that are strategically placed for stumbling into. So, skip the blue-light specials – you'll find all the dancing flowers and fuzzy dice you need here – at bargain prices.

Fact is, between the kitsch stores, clothing shops, furniture outlets, and a few restaurants and taquerias, Mission Street marches to a shopping jingle made up of three words – *bargains, markdowns, and close-outs.* If you missed the cheap-shop tour bus to Tijuana, Mission bargains are a close second (lacking only Paso price tags).

42: Albion   Dive Bar

3139 16th St. (between Valencia & Guerrero). 415-552-8558. Mission. **HOURS:** Daily, 2p.m.-2a.m. **SPECIALS:** Happy Hour: Mon-Thur, 5p.m.- 8p.m.; Fri-Sun, 5p.m.-7p.m. ($2.00-pint of beer). **RESTRICTIONS:** Cash only.

The *Albion* is San Francisco's anti-scene scene. If you're betting on finding a particular look or clientele, you'd have better luck playing Russian Roulette than looking for them here. From yuppies to hippies, conventionals to transsexuals, like a varied-beat, the mix just goes on and on. As for the music, you can expect anything from Zepplin to Zappa.

The long bar offers a medicine chest of cures, and features, finely-lit in neon print: "Service For The Sick." So if you're among the sodded lot, be brave and ask for a their specialty – a Pink Lemon Drop ($4.00). On weekends, this multi-room bar and its pool tables are packed with mingle junkies jousting for discrete corners and free microwave snacks. Pizza, anyone?

43: Bruno's   Live Music/Bar/Restaurant

2389 Mission St. (at 20th). 415-550-7455. Mission. **HOURS:** Mon-Sun, 6p.m.-2a.m.; Dinner, Tue-Sun, 6:30p.m.-Midnight. **ENTRANCE CHARGE:** Starts at $2.00 during live music performance.

Step back into the future, and find yourself socializing with your parents – *Eeeeuuuwww!!!* This may seem a bit obscure, but to understand the phenomenon that is *Bruno's* is to go back into the Freudian mind, where Id, Ego, and Super Ego wreak havoc through your childhood, preparing you to be adults in a time of insecurity.

That's right, here comes the 21st century – a time when the cartoons (e.g., the Jetsons) told us we'll be living in floating homes, driving flying cars, and eating pill-sized meals ... but they never told us we'd have to do it *as adults!*

So where do we find refuge? Where else than a dinner club, flush with filet mignon, martini's, and evening-wear-attired hostesses – but it doesn't stop there. How familiar, those thickly cushioned red Naugahyde booths that feel so rich (and wiped so clean when we, as children, dripped our ice-cream cones).

Okay, we're adults now, so get used to it. Forget the fact that we're not only facing a new decade, or even a new century – but a *new millennium!* Forget the fact that we're frightened at what lies ahead, beyond that arbitrary barrier ... into the unknown. What does that tell you? Probably that *Bruno's* will be hip with 20- and 30-year-old visionaries who frequent this old/new (or is it new/old) *'din-aah – club'* seeking solace in the fact that at least *something* familiar to their youthful mind still exists in this ever-changing world.

Forget your fears – the multiple bars and restaurant at *Bruno's* will remind you, "There's no place like home," so come and socialize with your future friends and business associates. If you didn't know it all along, your parents, and their parents, and their parents before them, developed their contacts, and thus, their power base, from contacts made at social spots just like this. So, you can just do your job and hang out with your buds – or you "can get out there" and meet the people with whom you're going to change the world, have a martini, and have a whole lot of fun along the way.

Bruno's recent expansion features a stage that was just getting rockin' at the time · of the deadline for this book, so call to learn the evening's entertainment. But before you go, don't forget to don your favorite 20th-Century attire (remember, Dick Tracy wouldn't be caught naked without a hat) – and be ready for an evening of "Puttin' on the Ritz."

44: Cafe Istanbul   Middle Eastern Cafe/Restaurnt

525 Valencia St. (at 16th). 415-863-8854. Mission. **HOURS:** Daily, 11a.m.-Midnight. **ENTRANCE CHARGE:** $1.00 cover charge for the show. **SPECIALS:** Saturday, 8:30p.m. & 9:30p.m., live show, 'Fat Chance Belly Dance.'

Western-style social merrymaking meets Eastern coffee-house culture in this intimate, casual setting. At *Cafe Istanbul*, you can lounge beneath colorful drapery while downing a wake-up-call blend of rich coffee. Due to *Cafe Istanbul's* size, privacy is a rarity, so cozy-up to a Turkish pillow while joining the happy flow of conversation.

The background music is, of course, the gyrating rhythms of Arabic music. On Saturdays, the belly-dancing shows are *most* entertaining ... but more amazing is the show's exercise in space utilization.

Try the menu topper – House Plate: a small Falafel sandwich plus Dolma, Tabuli, Hummos & Babaganoj ($5.75).

Pasport: A Chai tea with the purchase of a Mid-Eastern plate.

45: Cafe Macondo   Cafe

3159 16th St. (between Guerrero & Albion). 415-863-6517. Mission. **HOURS:** Daily, 11a.m.-10:30p.m. **RESTRICTIONS:** Cash only.

This Mission haunt provides a *great* escape from the usual chit-chat buzz found in most of The City's cafes and bars. In fact, *Cafe Macondo* offers a charming setting, perfect for a rare gathering of the "me-myself-&-I" variety. Upon walking in, you'll immediately notice a sense of the 'solitaire' among the pondering patrons, most occupying tables accompanied only by their books, journals, lap-tops, and thoughts.

This cafe rates high on our R&C (relaxed and cozy) scale, and the staff actually encourages patrons to kick-up their feet on the furniture and lounge. The ambiance is comprised of aged wood, health food, and non-alcoholic drinks. From the wooden floorboards and a thrown-together mix of kitchen tables and chairs, to the soft Jazz and Latin music playing in the background, you'll find it difficult not to relax in such surroundings. We recommend the Vegetarian Lasagna ($5.00) or Spinach-Artichoke Delight ($4.25).

46: Elbo Room   Bar/Live Music Venue

647 Valencia St. (between 17th & 18th). 415-252-7788. Mission. **HOURS:** Daily, 5p.m.-2a.m. **ENTRANCE CHARGE:** $3.00-$5.00 during live music performance. **SPECIALS:** Happy Hour, daily, 5 p.m.-8 p.m. ($0.50-off all beer). **RESTRICTIONS:** Cash only.

This two-story party house is a transplant from the 16th Street scene and, with its strong local following, is also the Mission's *in-your-face* entry into San Francisco's social scene pageant. Unlike the see-and-be-seen *clique* of many of SoMa's hot spots, the *Elbo Room* is a place to simply hang out – *or Jam ...!*

While it may not be *precisely* correct (and you know how we're such sticklers for clarity), you could easily imagine that the party bunch you find here prefers to arrive by foot or motorcycle – rather then by auto. Weekdays, the place is to the brim with a funky mix of local Bohemians who set, not follow, trends. Many of those you'll find will be wearing 'signature' headwear and self-made cloths.

On weekends, the Elbo Room plays host to many from among the Bridge & Tunnel crowd. After 10:00 p.m., the crowd is so thick that the bar is hardly visible. As for the pool tables, just put your name on the board and move into the social arena while you await your turn.

After you clean up on the billiards table, pay the cover charge and venture upstairs, where a second bar, dance floor, and stage are home to a nightly feast of an avant garde jazz, and funk, and 'whatever.' At the time of this writing, and for some time, Tuesdays have featured the Broun Fellinis, a three piece band that first put the *acid* into *Acid Jazz*. But, whether you come on Tuesday, or any other day of the week, the *Elbo Room* is one of San Francisco's lead contenders for the elite Seven-Day Sure Hit! award. Before you go, visit the photo booth downstairs, where you can capture (or create) a memory... *so don't be shy!*

47: Kilowatt   Bar

3160 16th St. (between Guerrero & Valencia). 415-861-2595. Mission. **HOURS:** Mon-Fri, 4p.m.-2a.m.; Sat, 1p.m.-2a.m.; Sun,10a.m.-2a.m. **ENTRANCE CHARGE:** Live Music Cover, $4.00-$8.00. **SPECIALS:** Happy Hour, 4p.m.-7p.m., all pints $2.50, pitchers $8.00; Pool Tournament, Wednesday 7:30p.m., $5.00 entry fee, winner takes the pot; Live Music, Sat & Sun, 8p.m.-11p.m. **RESTRICTIONS:** Cash only.

It has been just over a year since *Kilowatt's* brand of revelry was splashed on the 16th Street scene. During the week, you can expect a composed giant. On the weekends, however, a thumpin'-pumpin' jolt of live music sparks this venue to life. While at times your eardrums may be pushed to overload, you'll be treated to a

variety of raw and powerful alternative rock. Many out-of-town – and beyond bands (from Japan, to be exact), find *Kilowatt* one of the West Coast's top springboards.

Peter Athanas, Kilowatts owner, felt The City needed a showcase for Bay Area new comers, and that's just what you get – four to six San Francisco debuts every Saturday and Sunday. The intimate (200-plus person) space features high ceilings, an art deco bar, pool table and, as a final touch, suspended aquatic sculptures. Packed on weekends, you can easily find the *Kilowatt* by locating the crowd milling around outside chatting and smoking cigarettes. But you'd better come early (or don't plan on getting in!).

48: Mop Tops   Restaurant/Bar

538 Valencia St. (at 16th) 415-436-9415. Mission. **HOURS:** Tue-Thur, 5:30p.m.-Midnight; Fri-Sat, 5:30p.m.-2a.m.

Owner Kaz Tashiro is leading the British Invasion of the Mission from his post at the helm of this campy Beatles pub and restaurant. His Union Jack sign sticks out like a Redcoat in the forest amid the burrito parlors of the Mission. Inside, plenty of Beatles memorabilia on the walls suggests that this is no ordinary British Pub. Here, attention is focused almost obsessively on Scouse food and music. For the uninitiated, 'Scouse' refers to the people from the Liverpool side of the Mersey River, the working class city where the Mersey Sound (probably now thought of as the Beatles sound) was born.

'Scouse' is also the name of a hearty sailor's stew perfect for The City's foggy nights. *MopTops* kitchen also offers such pub staples as fish and chips, as well as shrimp and crab cocktails, deep-fried bar food, and burgers. Entrees average about $7.00. All night long, Tuesday through Friday, oysters are half price (normally running $6.50 for a plate of six.)

The smurf-blue walls and floors of the front area are in marked contrast to the black walls and red tables of the back room. A dark, low-ceilinged table in the back is reminiscent of The Cavern, the Liverpool dive bar where the post-Hamburg Beatles played before they became famous.

Kaz considers *MopTop's* to be mostly a restaurant but, with 15 beers on tap and obscure Scouse vinyl playing in the background, it's also a great place to down a few pints. Friday nights, the DJ focuses on more accessible British Rock (and even a few American artists), spinning records from the Hollys, the Stones, the Kinks and the Animal, as well as the Swinging Blue Jeans and the Searchers.

49: New Dawn   Low Tech Greasy Spoon Cafe

3174 16th St. (between Guerrero & Albion). Mission. **HOURS:** Mon-Tue, 9a.m.-2:30a.m.; Wed-Sun, 9a.m.-8p.m.

Sanford & Son meet Santa Claus in this outlandish, yet friendly, setting. The 'mustard' is so thick, upon entering you'll find it hard to resist looking for price tags. There's absolutely *nothing* like *New Dawn*. Among the strategically positioned clutter of masks, statues, pillars, mannequins, religious icons, lit-up candy canes, and the partridge-in-a pear-tree camouflage of stuff you can identify, you may find something remotely resembling your table settings.

Capture a seat and chase away that Sunday morning drone by chasing down their menu topper – Veggie Homefries ($6.95). One heaping serving is good for five people! Many of the 'drop-ins' you'll encounter belong to the stylish counterculture fashion brigade. They carry, or more appropriately, 'juggle,' an air of sarcasm while plucking their Jam off a Hot Wheels service center. Lurking in the background are the sounds of Industrial Ambient and Retro Punk.

50: Pancho Villa   Taqueria

3071 16th St. (between Valencia & Mission). 415-864-8840. Mission. **HOURS:** Daily, 10a.m.-Midnight. **SPECIALS:** Art Gallery.

In the Mission, the hot bed for hot food is *Pancho Villa* where, besides getting a big taste of the Mexican munch, you'll get a taste of the Bohemian circus resident in this, San Francisco's oldest district. On weekends, the line leading to the food bar may have you standing outside – a-h-h-h, but it's worth it!

The menu is found on the wall in big print, so you can browse through their many south-of-the-boarder delights while waiting your turn. Tables toped with bowls of chips and salsa are set in rows down a hallway-shaped interior. Among The City's houses of art, *Pancho Villa* is listed as an official gallery. Curtly framed within its Mexican motif, you'll find five wall-sized 'canvases' pregnant with color and images that give-way to new exhibitions monthly.

51: The Uptown   Dive Bar

200 Capp St. (at 17th). 415-861-8231. Mission. **HOURS:** Sat-Tue, 4p.m.-2a.m.; Wed-Fri, 2p.m.-2a.m. **RESTRICTIONS:** Cash only.

A faithful regular wearing a cynical smirk pointed out to us that there is no better place then a dive neighborhood to open a dive bar named *The Uptown*. With a cheerfully wicked ring, this concept holds true. Along with one or two ladies of the night, *The Uptown* occupies one of the 'off the beaten path' corners of Capp and 17th Streets.

Inside, you're likely to find a paint-splattered artist shooting the jive with a member of the unofficial Urban-Hell-On-Wheels Skate Boarder Association. A smoke-filled room where being cute is – just – not – enough … and emptying the ashtrays is the least of the bartender's concern. *The Uptown* is just what you should expect – it's not about breaking the rules, it's about creating new ones! And, with wall-size paintings, a white 'L' shaped lounge couch, cream-green diner-style booths, and an eclectic crowd, it remains a dive minus the ding – and easily one of our San Francisco favorites.

Let's Party! **Favorites**
FOOD:

Pizza

- Blondies (by the slice)
- Brothers Pizza
- Diamond
- Giorgio's
- Golden Boy
- Hay Stack
- Milano's
- Mr. Pizza
- Noe Valley Pizza
- North Beach Pizza
- Pizza Inferno
- Roma's
- Uncle Vito's
- Uno Pizzeria
- Victor's
- Village Pizzeria
- Za Pizza

Hamburger

- Barney's
- Burger Joint
- Clown Alley
- Hamburger Mary's
- Irving Street Cafe
- Little Joe's
- Mels
- Moe's
- Nations
- The Ramp
- Red Robin
- Smoke House

Chinese

- Brandy Ho
- Chan's
- China Village
- Empress Garden
- Excelsior
- Great Hunan
- Ha's
- Henry's Hunan
- House of Nan King
- Narai's
- Pot & Pan
- Tong Palace

Mexican

- Baja Cantina
- Cadillac Bar & Grill
- Chevy's
- La Barca's
- La Canasta
- La Rondalla
- La Taqueria
- Pablito's
- Pepito's
- Taqueria San José
- The Mission
- Veecha
- Victoria's
- WA-HA-KA
- Zaparillia

Thai

- Khun Phoa
- Lemon Grass
- Little Thai
- Marni Thai
- Minora's
- Mitapab
- Neecha
- Royal Thai
- Suko Thai

Japanese

- Aya
- Benihana
- Ebisu
- Fuku Sushi
- Godzilla Sushi
- Hamano Sushi
- Isobune
- Flying Kamakazees
- Mifune
- Nanbantai
- Oishii
- Shimo's
- Sushi Bune
- Tempura House
- Tenichi
- Yoshida-Ya

Vegetarian

- Amazing Grace
- Good Karma
- Green's

Brunch

- All You Knead
- Bechelli's
- Cafe for All Seasons
- Chloe's
- Courtyard Cafe
- Ella's
- Green's
- Il Fronaio
- Judy's
- Seal Rock Inn
- Sam's (in Tiburon)
- The Patio
- Tong Palace (on Clement Street)

NOE VALLEY

S nuggled against the high slopes of Twin Peaks up on 24th street is the squeaky-clean, yet hip, little neighborhood of Noe Valley. Because it sits away from the three-ring circus many call "The City," Noe Valley is one of San Francisco's best kept secrets.

Unfortunately for this little community, we here at *Let's Party!* command central are bad at keeping secrets. Why should we? There are too many cafe's and bars to overlook. So, to cut to the chase, here's what we found for you.

52: Diamond Corner Cafe   Cafe

751 Diamond St. (at 24th). 415-282-9551. Noe Valley. **HOURS:** Mon-Sat, 6:30a.m.-9p.m.; Sun, 8a.m.-8p.m. **SPECIALS:** Full weekend Breakfast. **RESTRICTIONS:** Cash only.

"A quiet little cafe, for a quiet little neighborhood" is the rhythm and rhyme you'll find at this laid-back scene. While this cafe rates low on our hype and glamour scale, it radiates with repose as it sits perched on upper 24th Street. The mostly-local patrons make the short jaunt to *Diamond Corner* with the ease of a person shuffling from their bedroom to the living room. From the cafe's outside tables, you can soak in the panoramic view below while enjoying a few moments (or hours) of leisure accompanied by a Roma Coffee, a friend, or a book.

On Saturdays and Sundays, between 9 a.m. and 1 p.m., enjoy an omelet breakfast with pancakes and trimmings. On weekdays ... during the early morning hours ... this cafe erupts with the sound and energy of a commuter train. Here, in the midst of the hustle for the American Dream, one has little time to fret over white shirt coffee stains and rainy days.

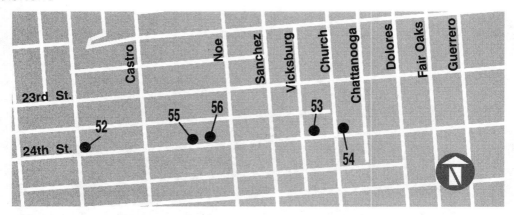

53: The Dubliner   Pub/Bar

3838 24th St. (at Church). 415-826-2279. Noe Valley. **HOURS:** Mon-Fri, 1p.m.-2a.m.;
Sat-Sun,10a.m.-2a.m. **RESTRICTIONS:** Cash only.

Here's a twist – an Irish pub with the feel of an *American* bar! Walk into *The
Dubliner*, and the sound of Irish accents will clearly be heard between the play-by-
play of European soccer matches displaying on the bars five screens. Everywhere,
you'll see *lads* and *lasses* imbibing that pure Emerald-Isle dark brew (Guinness)
against a backdrop of peach-oak wood, green wall lamps, and the large leather
booths that dominate the setting.

As night falls, the buzz of conversation takes over with a patronage of all ages.
With 33 beers on tap and a good selection of 'Hot Shots,' you can easily find challenge in an elbow bending marathon with some laddie from Cork. *The Dubliner's*
juke box has much more to offer than a Morrison or U2 tune, so think eclectic –
because all around, *that's what you'll find* at The Dubliner.

54: Lovejoy's   English Tea Room

1195 Church St. (at 24th). 415-648-5895. Noe Valley. **HOURS:** Daily, 10:30a.m.-7p.m.
RESTRICTIONS: Cash only.

While in Noe Valley, take a virtual leap over the great pond to capture a slice of
English culture. This tea room (with a catch) is so authentic you might as well bring
your passport. From the antique furniture and table settings, a collage of flowers
and painted landscapes, right down to the 100-year-old wood-plank floors, this tiny
leisure zone exudes the traditional radiance of an English country cottage. To further the point, the English owners, Martin and Marianne Spicknell, have worked
hard to import nearly every ingredient and condiment from the motherland.

In addition to the finest selection of Taylor's & Harrogate's English teas, the menu
offers an assortment of Scones & Crumpets, Finnan Haddock, English sausage rolls
w/pickles, and English sandwiches – (soft, white, crustless triangles topped with
alfalfa sprouts and a selection of poultry and meats). It may appear to be a peculiar way for a sandwich to be, but they're *very* tasty. Rare treats (e.g., Piccalilli mustard, Chutney, and Stilton Sage Derby) are also available.

Okay, so what's the catch? You say the chair you're sitting on is so comfy you'd
like to take it home? Well ... you can! In fact every antique – from the cups and
saucers to the tables, chairs, and paintings – are for sale. The owners replenish the
tea room weekly with bygone furniture and trim from their antique shop located

on 23rd and Sanchez. This only leads us to one conclusion: *every* seat in the house is best. After all, it may be yours!

Passport: A free pot of English Tea with meal

55: Rat & Raven   Bar

4054 24th St. (between Noe & Castro). 415-285-0674. Noe Valley. **HOURS:** Daily, noon-2a.m. **SPECIALS:** Happy Hour, Mon-Fri, 4p.m.-6p.m., $.50 off all beer. **RESTRIC-TIONS:** Cash only.

In the sedate, pristine setting of Noe Valley, The *Rat & Raven* stands out as the 'rebellious son.' Open for over 10 years, it is Noe Valley's grand-daddy bar. As for the interior scheme of things, this bar radiates a *dive-style* tavern ambiance. As for the regulars – a mix of refined frat boys and dive dwellers – the *Rat* is their home-away-from-home.

Named after a haunt made famous in the tales of Sherlock Holmes, with a selection of 19 micros and 35 international brews, this bar is a quaffers heaven. If you're so inclined, this is your perfect opportunity to partake in that *'round-the-world-beer-tasting-game* you've always wanted to play.

Traditionally, on Sunday's between 7:30 and 8:30 p.m., their wide-screen TV holds the attention of a captive audience to that wacky and notorious world of ... *The Simpson's.* For the showing, all pints are $1.00 off *(... thanks Bart!).* In back is a pool table, and *one step beyond* sits a door that leads to the beer garden... *Sprechts du auch Deutsch? PROST!*

56: The Rovers Inn   Bar/Pub

4026 24th St. (between Noe & Castro). 415-821-7861. Noe Valley. **HOURS:** Mon, noon-2a.m.; Tue-Fri, 1p.m.-2a.m.; Sat-Sun, 10a.m.-2a.m. **SPECIALS:** Occasional Live Music.

If the Dubliner is an Irish pub with the feel of an American bar, then *The Rover* is an American bar with the feel of an Irish pub! Take it from us – *the difference lies beyond mere syntax.* The American part prefers to watch college football over a soccer match *any day!* With four TV's connected to two satellites, this is Noe Valley's sports bar.

If being a spectator isn't your 'bag,' turn on you competitive drive with a round of darts or a game of pool around back (why are the pool tables always "... around back?"). On weekdays, the happy 30/40-something regulars pile-in after work, joining in a brew of social chit-chat that doesn't die until last call. The bar offers a selection of 25 beers, with Guinness and Harp topping their list ... *and* – for all baseball enthusiasts – the wall facing the bar is a shrine displaying classic photos of baseball's greatest players and moments.

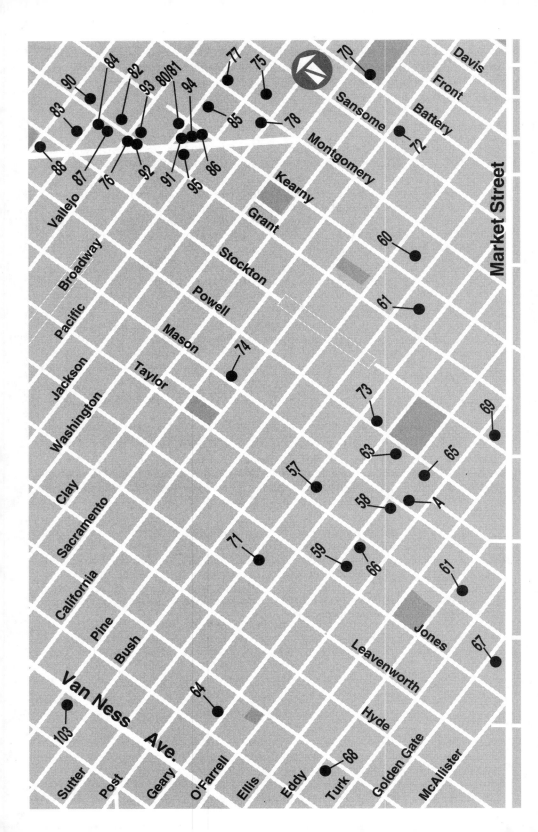

NOMA

I n our never-ending 'quest for quietude,' we're going to break a bunch of rules, and erase a few lines from the map by combining a neighborhood, an area, a district, and a town under one name: **NoMa**. It stands for **North of Market Street**. Besides, what good is a *SoMa* if there's no *NoMa?*

North of Market Street – which will forever be known herein as NoMa – is sandwiched between **Van Ness Street** to the west; the waterfront to the east; and California to th north. Unlike SoMa, however, NoMa is a *group* of areas, and comprises the **Tenderloin** neighborhood; the **Union Square** area, the **Financial District**, and **China Town**.

Although San Francisco is a surprisingly *small* city, NoMa's door-to-door shopping, big-name hotels, and towering skyscrapers are a few of the reasons The City rates among America's top urban centers. And, as with any urban center, you'll find the good, the bad, the poor, and the rich all joined together in a disparate dance that lacks tempo ... *but such is life in the not-so-big city.*

Throughout NoMa, you'll find shoppers hustling to reach a Macy's sale; bankers hustling back to work from lunch; tourist hustling to catch a cable car; and street tramps just hustling for handouts. Even the pigeons don't stop for breath as they hustle for crumbs.

Amidst the madness, we've found both 'mainstream' and 'not-so-mainstream' spots where you can break away from the day's humdrum activities, and get lost in that special time between dusk and dawn that we call *"the Party Zone."*

The Tenderloin

San Francisco's 'problem child,' the Tenderloin, is a scruffy patchwork of triple-X movie houses, massage parlors, and low-rent buildings – all providing the backdrop for a dubious collection of pimps, prostitutes, drug dealers, and drunks. Mixed in are honest, working-class families struggling to survive while eking out a living among dreams of better times – and better neighborhoods. You'll also find a harmless collection of runaways (and 'throw-always') simply looking for charity. In fact, due to a Tenderloin's ten-der-*less* reputation, many so-called 'comprehensive' travel guides have completely sidestepped this neighborhood in their editorial coverage of San Francisco.

Despite the bad rap, however, a busy police station and a recent influx of Asian immigrants has taken strides towards taming this – San Francisco's most ornery inner-city neighborhood. During daylight hours, pedestrians and cars no longer find it necessary to bypass this area en-route to their destinations.

As the sun sets, however, the streets fill with all sorts of freaks and foibles, flirts and fakers. With no clear boundaries, it's all too easy to stumble into the Tenderloin from neighboring Union Square. Our recommendation – especially for women – is to make a point of avoiding this area alone at night.

Please study the *No Mas Zone* on our map carefully. This doesn't mean you should avoid the area completely; it means you should take pains to know (and park close to) your destination if you must go there after dark.

Oh – that 'attitude' walk you've been working on? Now's the time to use it! Look like you belong, and *know* where you're going. A better suggestion is to take a taxi to and from your destination (no fuss, no muss – at least it'll keep you from having to yell *"no mas, no mas"*).

But never fear – its not all doom and gloom. For one, the Tenderloin is not exclusive to a shady collection of riff-raff. Among the locals out for a night out, you'll find a more mainstream crowd coming to the area for a concert or play at the historic **Warfield Concert Hall**. The Tenderloin is also home to **Hollywood Billiards**, the largest and most acclaimed pool hall in The City – *and hey,* it never shuts down. Never! Another popular stop is **Club 181** where, on varying nights, you'll find hard core local clubbers, or the weekend bridge-and-tunnel crowd, who venture to this locale for a dose of live music and DJ spins. So, grab a cab … *and go!*

The Union Square Area

Serving as the roof of an underground parking garage is a square patch of land garnished with palm trees and manicured bushes. In the center towers a pseudo-Corinthian column crowned with the statue of Winged Victory. Appropriately, there's usually a swarm of pigeons, in perched position, worshipping this Winged Goddess. The column celebrates the triumph of some admiral or another – if you really need to know, read the plaque. Although Union Square is not more centrally located than the spout of a whale, many consider it San Francisco's ground-zero.

One thing Union Square is, is the heart of downtown; and if there's serious shopping to be done, it's done here, in the many temples of consumption sitting shoulder to shoulder, framing the square. Here's where dreams are granted by the demigods of fashion and style – *as long as you have the cash, Visa, MasterCard, Diner's, or American Express!*

Who's here? Gucci, Cartier, Tiffany, Saks, Neiman Marcus, and Macy's ... to name a few. All shamelessly flaunt their flaunt-*ables* in extravagant window showcases. Here, also, are many of San Francisco's high-maintenance fashion elite, clad in designer brands – high-heeled ladies stepping-out on the street, and from limousines and Royces, with leather-clad hands. Adding to this landscape of posh shops are the surrogate homes of kings and queens – luxurious hotels, resplendent with the grandest foyers in the country. **The Sir Francis Drake** and **The St. Francis** hotels are definitely worth a few gawks.

As the wealthy few, with beeline accuracy, criss-cross the area, the rest of us (he, she, him, and her) wander aimlessly – and the lucky ones stumble on the many amusements and discoveries to be found in ... "t o u r i s t - c e n t r a l." From camera-toting travelers, comparing price tags with those back home in Tokyo, to wide-eyed passengers departing on a bus excursion of The City, the flow diffuses in all directions. As you see a cab recklessly flying down the street, you're apt to hear a citizen testifying to a visiting friend how San Francisco cabbies are indisputably the worst in the world.

Not unlike London's Piccadilly Circus, the energy of Union Square is charged at night. As the festive rhythms of street musicians play beneath a wash of light emanating from billboards and store fronts, a group of pedestrians huddles around a sketch artist across the street. In the center of the square, daring acrobats careen by on skateboards to a resident audience of aging homeless seen sharing a corner bench ... and bottle of Gin.

Union Square and the surrounding area may be San Francisco's *shopping central command,* but we've sifted out some social destinations to facilitate your escape. Read on – we'll point you to where you can exchange the street-side hubbub for some bar-side hubbub.

We start in the morning, and there's nothing like a good cup of java to launch your day. At **Yakety Yak** there's an early stream of fresh-eyed regulars paying a visit before heading to the neighboring art school. You, on the other hand, can just sit and enjoy the 'street-side art' passing on the sidewalk.

Once you've made the rounds, treat yourself to lunch in the opulent, trendy setting of the **Grand Cafe**. But be warned – the menu prices reflect the overhead!

A s the day progresses (your feet *must* be hurting), the **Gold Dust Lounge** – conveniently located just off Union Square – is a shopper's time-out. In this historic setting, enjoy a cold brew while live Dixieland band plays in the background. But if its live Blues you want, the newly opened **Biscuits & Blues** and the historically 'divish' **Blue Lamp** won't disappoint you.

If you're ready to be *"puttin' on the Ritz"* with that glamorous evening dress or sporty blazer you just bought, its time to engage in some of that dance-floor dialect. Try **The Starlight Room** on the top floor of the Sir Francis Drake where, among the posh surroundings, the sophisticated (and those seeking sophistication) are busily looking *mahvolous* while hob-nobbing on one side of The City's most stunning social viewpoint.

Kitty-corner and down the block, inside and just off the lobby of the St. Francis, **The Compass Rose** is alive with jazz and romance. Take the elevator to the top, and the yellow brick road will bring you to the land of Oz ... well ... **Club OZ**, where you can stress out your well-worn feet to a more classic beat.

The Financial District

B illed by many as the "Wall Street of the West," this appropriately named district is San Francisco's cash cow. It has been so since way back in the days of the Barbary Coast, when The City answered to the name of Yerba Buena – and all roads from northern California seemed paved with gold.

It was at that time that the high rollers of business and trade found Montgomery Street's proximity to the bustling harbor a perfect site to keep a shrewd and watchful eye on their merchandise. As miners came rushing into town with their gold and silver, traders and shopkeepers had the only scales for weighing – and safes for storing. They were to become the areas first bankers and, as the gold and silver mines spewed up their fortunes, the back rooms of many corner shops matured into banks.

The seeds were planted for what developed into the West Coast's largest finance center and, despite some financial droughts and the Earthquake of 1906, this fertile growth eventually gave birth to a blooming field of skyscrapers.

If the Financial District is San Francisco's cash cow, the intersection of **Montgomery and California Streets** is where the cow is milked. Here, the Bank of America's world headquarters, Security Pacific Bank, and the Merchants Exchange command their own squares on a grand-scale Monopoly board. From the lounge on the top floor of the *B of A Building*, there's an unsurpassed view of the bay – from the Golden Gate Bridge to the Oakland Hills (but beware, you've probably never paid *that* much for a glass of cola before!).

Heading North on Montgomery, you'll run smack-dab into the San Francisco skyline's most famed signature – the Trans America Pyramid. Reaching 885 feet skyward, it offers the most distinctive marker on which new arrivals can set their bearings. On the 27th floor there's a free observatory (that's right – we said *free*).

Deep in the Financial District's narrow valleys of marble, garnet, steel, and glass, bike messengers blaze by a lunch-time traffic of sharply dressed bankers, brokers, lawyers, secretaries, and retail workers. If you close your eyes and listen, you'll hear a New York-like sound-pollution of taxi horns and construction noises. Unless you have a deal to cut, make, or wield, we strongly urge you to shuffle over to neighboring North Beach or China Town. But, if you insist on hanging around, we found a few delightful and fun getaways from the urban quagmire.

For relaxing dose of French cafe life, check out **Cafe Bastille** and **Cafe Claude** – two Parisian haunts located within 30 seconds of each other, tucked into two of San Francisco's most quaint alleyways. In a playful mood? Jump on the cutting edge of technology, and into the cockpit of a Virtual Jet at **Virtuality**, at **One Embarcadero Center**. Around the corner on **Embarcadero**, you can enjoy tasty appetizers while laughing yourself to tears at the acclaimed **Punch Line**. If you're looking to *mix it up,* however, discover your Latin side at the stylish, multi-level **Sol Y Luna** supper club, where you can eat, drink, and be very, very merry.

China Town

Tightly wedged between the Financial District, Union Square, and North Beach is a quarter-mile-square enclave holding the largest Chinese community this side of Taiwan. San Francisco's most populous neighborhood, it's also the smallest, most self-contained microcosmic neighborhood – perhaps in the country. To visitors who don't understand the contribution Chinese made to *the taming of the West*, this neighborhood may seem quite an oddity – a misplaced presence among San Francisco's neighborhoods. *Not so* – it's a key that opens the door to another world.

At the intersection of **Grant Avenue and Bush Street** is a dragon-crested, lion-flanked, gate that marks the entrance to China town. Here, San Francisco ends abruptly, and dragon-entwined lampposts, street signs with calligraphic script, and the Guangzhou dialect begin.

Up Grant Street lives a bazaar-like atmosphere, with shops selling all types of Oriental goods. Strangely, Middle Eastern-owned electronic shops also survive, selling such items as sunglasses and refurbished watches, cameras, and boom boxes. Perhaps it's a 'marriage of culture' thing.

Along the many alleyways, especially up **Stocton Street**, coexist food market after food market – all displaying exotic delicacies. The ambiance is rich with []bazaar-like goings-on. Riotous chickens scramble in their crates, awaiting their fates next to whole-drawn pigs, freshly caught fish and, most notably, golden-glazed ducks hanging in the windows by the neck – looking like a boomtown after a lynching fest.

China Town offers a dizzying array of gastronomical delights. From top-notch gourmet restaurants with lavish decor reminiscent of the Ming Dynasty, to back-alleyway teahouses specializing in dim sum, there's much to be had.

Our suggestion? Try one of the small, upper-floor restaurants filled exclusively with Chinese people – the kind without an English-language menu. Persuade your server that you want the chefs-special, which will usually be a delicious concoction of meat and vegetables. You may not know exactly what you're eating, but odds are it'll be delectable. If you're afraid to eat what you ordered, don't worry – every meal comes amply supplied with sticky rice.

Oh, that dish of chopped-up meat in sauce being eaten by the old Chinese gentleman next to you? We call that *RunOver Chicken* – runover, because it looks like it's been run-over like a Mack truck. Chicken, well, because it's chicken! *Ah,* and that fish ... the one that looks like it's still breathing? That's *FlashFry Fish* – and a little too under-cooked for our tastes.

Oh, before you go, be sure to check out the Chinese-speaking McDonald's at the corner of **Grant and California Streets**.

When it came to finding social haunts of the cafe-bar-club variety, we at *Let's Party!* command central have to admit we were stumped. You can find traditional Chinese night-club activity and some bars, but with the congested street-side chaos of San Francisco's China Town, the party is on the streets – *that is, if you're not claustrophobic!*

57: Beer Cellar   Dance Bar

685 Sutter St. (at Taylor). 415-441-5678. NOMA (Sutter Street Tube). **HOURS:** Daily, 6p.m.-2a.m. **ENTRANCE CHARGE:** Up to $5.00 depending on night.

It used to be called the Heart of Europe, an *out-of-sorts* sort of dive bar two blocks up from Union Square ... in The City's theater district. Joseph, a jovial young man from the Czech Republic, was the owner, and ran a bar 'plain and simple' in the basement of a building. A hand-painted sign led you down the stairs to a watering hole where locals, Czech expatriates, and drunken characters convened. Wooden tables, a pool table, and a jukebox – that's all there was for years.

Then came Matt, who started bartending there about a year ago. He probably thought to himself, "Now here's *primo* space in the heart of the city. It's just a bar ... it's not making any money... so why not turn it into a club? I've always wanted to run my own club ... I've got ideas ... and ..." Keep Joseph, but change the image – new sign ... new logo ... hmmmm ... the *Beer Cellar*! *Voila!*

One of the guys who re-did 1015 Folsom helped prepare this joint for a facelift. Now there are magenta walls, silver roman columns, and a huge disco ball that throws glimmering shimmers against the walls. What a transformation! On weekends the DJ- spins really get things happening. Matt invites you to come and shoot pool, kick-back, or dance to Acid Jazz, Alternative, House, Techno and Funk grooves. There's a good range of tap beers, and always daily drink specials. Happy Hour (4:00 to 8:00 p.m. Wednesday through Saturday) features $2.00 Jaeger shots ... *get it?!?* This place has potential, you know ... great locale, and all it takes is "word-of-mouth." Tell Matt we sent you!

58: Biscuits & Blues   Live Blues Bar/Restaurant

401 Mason St. (between Post & Geary) 415-292-2583. NOMA (Union Square). **HOURS:** Tue-Sat, 6p.m.-2a.m.; Sun, 6p.m.-Midnight, Mon closed. **ENTRANCE CHARGE:** Tue-Thur & Sun $5.00-7.00; Fri & Sat $10.00-15.00. **SPECIALS:** Happy Hour, 6p.m.-8p.m., $1.00 off all drinks; Live Music, 9p.m.-1a.m.

Sitting on a corner, in the middle of San Francisco's inner city buzz, is "the house that vibrates with blues." If there ever was any question, their biscuits are as good for the stomach to digest as their blues is for the soul. Living true to their Magna-Carta-type oath – Biscuits & Blues is "dedicated to the preservation of the blues."

This new venue has featured some of the best local and national talents, and draws a predominately international crowed indulging in the made-to-order delights. If you drop in to eat, their Midnight Breakfast menu is so bad it's good; if you drop in for a blues-boogie session, a dance floor awaits; if you drop in just to enjoy the music, the low-ceilinged, traditional half-circle room and candlelight ambiance will envelop you in 'comfy-ness.' But if you if you choose all the above, you win the prize – so skeedaddle over to the bar and celebrate what ever you feel like celebrating with the rest of the happy and lively bunch. As for your prize, we offer one advance and a piece of advice – good memories and two aspirins.

Pasport: 50% off entrance charge.

59: The Blue Lamp   Dive Blues Bar

561 Geary St. (between Taylor & Jones). 415-885-1464. NOMA (Union Square). **HOURS:** Daily, 11a.m.-2a.m. **SPECIALS:** Happy Hour daily, 4p.m.-7p.m., Bud beer for $1.50 (pint); Live Blues. **RESTRICTIONS:** Cash only.

Located on the fringe of the Tenderloin, San Francisco's trouble-child district, sits the *Blue Lamp*. If dive and dinge were served as a main entree, this locale would be a five-star chow house – and live Blues would be their magic sauce. Leaving metaphors aside (and moving on to stereotypes), the *Blue Lamp* is where you'll find a cop talking to a turban over the virtues of a hooker ... or was it Johnny Lee Hooker?!?

Neighborhood 'eclectics' have turned this Blues house into a stable (read: s-a-f-e) night out. A bartender explains: In the spirit of 19th-century preservation, when this venue was a brothel, red brocade and chandeliers have been left untouched. So untouched, in fact, that even the dust has settled down in its old age. As for the music, we're happy to say the sorrowful tears of a Blues note has found a home under this dim Lamp. Not to be missed is Sunday's 8 p.m. standing-room-only performance of The Blue Reptiles Jam.

60: Café Bastille   French Bistro/Bar

22 Belden Place (between Pine & Bush). 415-986-5673. NOMA (Financial District). **HOURS:** Mon-Fri, 11:30a.m.-11p.m.; Sat 11:30a.m.-2a.m.; Kitchen closes at10:30p.m. **ENTRANCE CHARGE:** Saturday after 11p.m., $5.00. **SPECIALS:** Tue-Sat, 7p.m.-11p.m., live Jazz & Blues; Sat 11p.m.-2a.m., Acid-Jazz with DJ;

Cafe Bastille's French owner, Eric Klein, sees his role in San Francisco as that of a missionary intent on spreading the Parisian call-for-the-good-life. Taking no chances, he designed *Café Bastille* to resemble a Parisian's true-blue everyday encounter – an underground metro station. From the street lamps and metro signs, to rivets painted on walls – that's right, *Café Bastille* is decorated after the French icon of mass transit: the Metro.

Café Bastille sits on Balden Place, a narrow alleyway that conjures up images of Parisian street life. With its outdoor tables, it is the perfect choice for a lunch-time appointment, or an intimate encounter on one of those hot, balmy, summer nights. Downstairs is a slightly cramped dining room featuring Castellane Champagne ads. Evenings, *Café Bastille* is a somewhat discrete gathering place, while downstairs Saturdays, DJ music spins Acid Jazz to a more rambunctious crowd.

Not unlike its counterpart, Café Claude, *Bastille* caters to the many young French professionals and bohemian expats who reside and travel through San Francisco. In a roundabout-cuisine way, the food is just like 'mom's' (that's French for 'mothers') home cooking. Topping the menu is Hachis Parmentier with salad ($8.95). If you're American, and can properly pronounce this entre, you may get a discount. Their mussels and crepes are also very popular selections.

Pasport: Free coffee drink with purchase of an entree.

61: Café Claude   Cafe/Restaurnt

7 Claude Lane (off Bush & Kearny). 415-392-3505. NOMA (Financial District). **HOURS:** Mon-Sat, 8a.m.-11p.m.; Sun, closed. **SPECIALS:** Tue & Thur 7-10p.m., Fri & Sat 8-11p.m., Live Jazz & Blues.

If you can't afford Paris this year, let Paris come to you via this tasty morsel of café culture. From the zinc bar right down to the salt and pepper shakers, *Café Claude* has been transplanted, stock-and-barrel, from its old home, Porte d'Orleans in Paris, to its new home on Claude Lane. The nuances of the secluded little alley-lane are uncannily reminiscent of a Parisian setting.

During weekday lunch hours, you'll find the action – both inside and at their street-side tables – undulating with a distinct French buzz. Testament to its authenticity, many of the frequent faithful are a mix of French consulate employees and Parisian bohemians. In fact, if San Francisco adopted a French writer, it would be here, at *Café Claude*, that he or she would hold court.

At night, particularly on Fridays, live jazz and romantic lighting offer a charged experience to all who partake. Be warned, however – late arrivals find themselves removed from the standing-room crowd, listening to the music from the alley.

The menu is a treasure chest of Parisian cuisine – from Soupe à L'oignon ($4.25) to the Entéer Cassoulet w/garlic sausage ($11.75), you get the great tastes of Paris, without the Paresian prices. As for the attitude, you'll just have to find out for yourself.

62: Club 181   Dance Club/Restaurant

181 Eddy St. (at Taylor). 415-673-8181. NOMA (Tenderloin). **HOURS:** Thur, 9p.m.-2a.m.; Fri-Sat, 9p.m.-3a.m. **ENTRANCE CHARGE:** Varies depending on night

A Tenderloin version of the Speakeasy, *Club 181* is a geometrically intriguing space, where broad curves and unorthodox angles are accented by candlelit tables and ceiling tapestries. The novel winding bar writhes like a snake through the crowded lounge area, enveloping patrons in its folds, and facilitating conversation. The raised bar area looks out over a dozen intimate tables, and a large dance floor and stage. Overlapping floor shapes, each placed at a slightly different level than the next, create the illusion of multiple rooms where there is really only one, large main space.

Further back is a second bar area with a pair of coin-operated pool tables. The back room is slightly quieter, so more conducive to conversation. On one wall, a bold, colorful mural by Lamont portrays a three-piece jazz band wailing away as hip couples sway to the beat. Across the room, artist Marcia V. Marsh has installed a double shelf of backlit bottles, which from a distance appear to be covered in cob-webs. On closer inspection, the bottles prove to be covered with magazine cutouts of advertising models, a statement bemoaning the entrapment of women by media-perpetuated images of superficial beauty. And you thought you just came here to dance ...

Entrance to the new, semi-industrial VIP lounge behind the mural room is highly selective, based on who you know and how you're dressed. If you make it in, you'll find a dimly lit space with its own DJ, two more pool tables, a wall full of couches, and yet another bar.

The highly eclectic, multi-ethnic crowds on Fridays give way to a Yuppie-ish 20-something crowd Saturdays. The DJs spin disco and funk classics, taking occasional breaks to allow 70s cover bands to take the stage.

Pasport: Two for one entry (not valid for special events).

63: Club Oz   Nightclub

St. Francis Hotel, 335 Powell St. (across from Union Square). 415-397-7000. NOMA (Union Square). **HOURS:** Sun-Thur, 9p.m.-1:30a.m.; Fri-Sat, 9a.m.-2:30a.m. **ENTRANCE CHARGE:** Sunday, $5.00; Mon-Thur, $8.00; Fri-Sat, $15.00. Hotel guests are complimentary Sunday and Monday. **SPECIALS:** *Cool elevator rides!* **RESTRICTIONS:** Dress code Friday and Saturdays.

HYPE • HYPE • HYPE • HYPE • HYPE • HYPE • HYPE

• *OZ in OZ!?! it may seem paridoxical, but it's here. So, for your benefit, here is the* official version, *written for Club OZ by some P.R. maven at some big P.R. firm.*

STEP INTO THE FANTASY OF CLUB OZ AT THE ST. FRANCIS HOTEL

Thirty-two stories above Union Square stands Club Oz, the city's most elegant dance club. With its spectacular views, unique interiors, state-of-the-art audio/visual and lighting systems, and an international mix of music and videos, the club attracts all types of music aficionados, who come for non-stop dancing or just for the sights of the club and the city outside.

Juliana's of London, known throughout the world as "purveyors of disco to roy-alty", has installed a lighting system in Club OZ which creates the atmosphere of a clear night sky with twinkling stars. What transpires throughout the evening is a dramatic separation of the ceiling into four quadrants and a myriad of lighting effects that produces a dazzling "galaxy of stars" with white light and vivid colors or soft neon washes. At the same time the "San Francisco fog" creeps in, with the help of a fog machine, and fiber optic effects creating a moving web of multi-colored lightbeams.

In addition to the latest electronic wizardry of Club OZ, Juliana's disc jockeys manage the console and coordinate the musical audio, video and lighting effects, with uplifting house music heard on the outstanding sound system, and videos flashed on unique screens around the club.

63: Compass Rose   Piano Bar & Lounge

The Westin St. Francis Hotel (Powell) on Union Square. 415-774-0324. NOMA (Union Square). **HOURS:** Daily, Lunch, 11:30a.m.-2:30 p.m.; High Tea, 3 p.m.-5 p.m.; Dinner, 6 p.m.-10 p.m. ; Lounge open til Midnight, Fri & Sat 'til 1a.m.

The location of today's *Compass Rose* has been 'the place' to rendezvous since the St. Francis Hotel opened in 1904. Legend has it that Ernest Hemingway asked Ingrid Bergman to star in *For Whom the Bell Tolls* here over lunch in 1943. It's no wonder, because the St. Francis has hosted many famous guests over the years, including Queen Elizabeth II, Ronald Reagan, and Grace Kelly.

Its name comes from the multi-pointed design, known as the "compass rose," that appears on the background of all compasses. It also alludes to the restaurant's exotic elegance of custom artwork, sculptures, and museum-quality objects brought in from all points on the compass. The room is also rich in San Francisco history.

Among the magnificent black and gold lacquered tables, velvet couches, and gold-tasseled chaise lounges, are 19th-century Korean cloisonné vases, an early 18th-Century Chinese bamboo screen, cobra lamps from the art-deco period, and an antique Burmese carved wooden Buddha. These all surround a patent-leather bar purchased by Templeton Crocker – one of the owners of the St. Francis in the 1940s.

The bar was nicknamed the "the bar sinister" and "coffin corner" due to the sinister padding of the black patent leather. Ansel Adams captured the innate beauty of the leather bar in a series of black-and-white photographs which he, in turn, gave to the St. Francis as a gift.

Enjoy lunch at *The Compass Rose,* or an evening tasting of brie and crab cakes in this very ornate lounge. In the evening, you can listen or dance to the sounds of the Abe Battat Trio, a blend of Samba and serenade ... *The girl from Ipanema goes walking ... and ... ahhhh ... this is the life!*

But the highlight of *The Compass Rose* is afternoon tea. While classical tunes play on the baby grand, enjoy a rendezvous over an afternoon of high tea. Begin with a fresh homemade scone, finger sandwiches, berries with Grand Marnier cream, and a selection of assorted petit fours along with a dreamy exotic tea. This is all part of what this book is all about – the good life.

64: Edinburgh Castle   Bar/Live Music

950 Geary St. (between Larkin & Polk). 415-885-4074. NOMA. **HOURS:** Daily, 5p.m.-2a.m. **ENTRANCE CHARGE:** Varies depending on performance.

You'll know you're in the right place when you see the word "Pub" in three-foot-high letters in the front window. Inside this traditional Scottish pub are rough wooden tables and church-pew-like booths, from which patrons sample 35 single malt Scotch whiskeys and 18 beers on tap. How traditional is this pub? Check out the huge wooden shaft on the wall above the regulation dart boards, near the pool table. It's called a caber, and is the essential piece of equipment for the traditional Scottish sport known as 'tossing the caber.' Black and white photos on the wall show actual caber tossers heaving the miniature telephone poles skyward. The phallic implications boggle the mind (and many other senses) ....

The Castle attracts a young (80 percent 20-something), slightly pierced crowd, many of whom live within walking distance. The only neckties are worn by the bartenders. In addition to live music Wednesday through Saturday at 10:00 p.m., the venue stages occasional plays.

Food is limited to fish and chips, which run $4.50 per serving, and cooked off site. Your waiter runs through a very rough neighborhood to pick up your order from 'The Old Chelsea' restaurant, so make sure you tip well to compensate for the risk. The fish and chips are authentically British, down to the old newspaper wrappings. Billed as 'Scotland in San Francisco' and open since 1958, *The Castle* is worth checking out.

65: Gold Dust Lounge   Jazz Bar & Lounge

247 Powell St. (at Geary). 415-397-1695. NOMA (Union Square). **HOURS:** Daily, 6a.m.-2a.m. **SPECIALS:** Live Dixieland Jazz, nightly, 8:30p.m.-1a.m. **RESTRICTIONS:** Cash only.

Somewhere between your sessions of devour and combat within the commercial madness found around Union Square, you may choose to fit-in a stop at the *Gold Dust Lounge*. This retreat of social merrymaking is a virtual mind-tumble back to the Victorian era, when settings of red floral carpeting, neo-Rococo wall paper, plush red lounges, chandeliers, and ceiling murals of winged cherubs reigned over the world of chic. The decor has not been revamped since the early 50s, when it's previous owner, Bing Crosby, bestowed a hefty cash infusion into this congenial site.

Finding a perplexed bartender is a rarity here, and if there's any question of your 'poisons' amalgamation, feel free to flip through their hefty Bartenders workbook. Expect a crowd of international vacation hoppers who provide a true cacophony of dialects and tongues that only stop when the music starts. And the music here is strait Dixieland Jazz, offering the occasional throw-in of 'Honeysuckle.'

66: Grand Cafe   Cafe/Bar/Resturant

Hotel Monaco, 501 Geary St. (at Taylor). 415-292-0101. NOMA. **HOURS:** Breakfast, 7a.m.-10:30a.m.; Lunch, 11:30a.m.-3p.m.; Dinner, 5p.m.-10p.m.; Bar, 11a.m.-Midnight.

Set in an architecturally restored turn-of-the-century ballroom, the *Grand Cafe* is richly blanketed with a brocade of aesthetics (and so was that sentence). Here, high tribute is paid to the charm and opulence of Old Europe. The *Grand Cafe* sits as a modern-day patron of the arts, and among the many commissioned works you'll find Guibara's larger-then-life sculptures. From luminous murals to faux finishes, 'no expense was spared' in creating the Grand's art nouveau-deco theme. Adding to the show is their open-kitchen design, with its suspended mirror reflecting the busy cook line.

Okay, enough with the interior titillations. At the risk of artistic overdose, make your way to the bar quickly. There you can down a brew, or daintily sip a fine Sauvignon in an atmosphere where 'refined-elegance' is an appropriate buzz word (and completely optional). And, while deals are struck by the captains of industry, casual jean-wearers mingle with Euro-fad flaunts as telephone numbers are just a napkins pass away.

Among the hot picks on their dinner menu is the grilled Delmonico steak Au Poivre Vert with Pommes Frites ($16.95), Don't worry, it's just a fancy way of saying 'meat and potatoes' – but delicious!

67: Hollywood Billiards   Billiards Club/Bar/Resturant

61 Golden Gate Ave. (between Taylor & Jones). 415-252-9643. NOMA (Tenderloin). **HOURS:** Non-Stop. **SPECIALS:** Happy Hour, Mon-Fri 4-7p.m., $1.00-off beer. Single elimination w/handicap pool tournament on Sunday & Wednesday beginning at 6:30 with $15.00 entry fee. Pool time specials – Mon, Student Night, $5.00 for five hours; Tue & Thur, Customer Appreciation, $10.00 for five hours; Wednesday is Ladies Night, Ladies play free for three hours. All specials run from 6p.m. to 3a.m.

If it didn't exist, it would simply have to be invented. Thankfully, it exists – a 24/7 billiards club! That's right ... it never closes! This rack 'em-up Mecca is frequented by top-notch, eye-of-the-tiger players the caliber of (rest his soul) Minnesota Fats, right down to leisure-seeking casuals who think that massé is a French term for a shoulder rub. The mix ranges from after-noon visits by business men, to early morning drop-in-stragglers made up of insomniacs, tweekers, and party girls.

Internationally known for being the oldest – *and best* – pool hall on the West Coast, it provides a stage for pool sharks and hustlers. So, unless you're looking to get whipped like a red headed stepchild, with stakes ranging up to $10,000, our advice is to watch out for anyone who tells you they're blind in one eye and "can't see outta the next."

When it *is* time *for* those big games, or perhaps just an intimate pool party, visit the three-table private room. It may set you back $50 per hour, but it features a $40,000, eight-legged, 6/12 twin of the pool table in the Hearst Castle.

When you decide to take a break from breaking, carom over for a Purple Hooter ($2.00) at their 110 ft bar – the longest in the city. If you're looking for an amusing diversion while sitting out a game, check-out the rotating art gallery that appropriately features paintings of a more risqué nature. They also have four video games, two pinball tables, and a juke box offering a fantastic selection.

Okay, let's get down to some real stats. For you *real* players, *Hollywood Billiards* is furnished with two full-on billiards tables, two 5/10s, and one 6/12 Snooker table. The 32 remaining surfaces are 4-6/ 9s. All tables are antique Brunswicks, topped with an 8/60 double-wrested felt. Light measurements provide a perfect shade line, and carpet padding provides the final touch ... and the rails are sweet to the touch! *Rack-em!*

Pasport: Pay for one hour and get one free.

68: Miss Pearl's Jam House   Live Music/Restaurant

601 Eddy St. (at Larkin). 415-775-4992. NOMA (Tenderloin). **HOURS:** Wed-Thur, 6p.m.-1:30a.m.; Fri-Sat, 7p.m.-11p.m.; Sun, 5p.m.-9:30p.m. **ENTRANCE CHARGE:** $3.00-$5.00 depending on the night.

This self-described Caribbean restaurant and "party palace" is another of the bright spots in the troubled Tenderloin. The restaurant uses tropical print table cloths, wicker chairs, and bright colors to create a festive, Caribbean atmosphere.

The menu is full of Jamaican, Cuban, and Creole influences, although not even the infamous jerk chicken ($11.00) is spicy enough to draw tears. Appetizers you won't find anywhere else in town include grilled corn arepas with caviar and creme fraiche ($8.00), and wild mushroom empanadas with goat cheese and herb mojo ($7.00). Entrees average about $11.00.

A full 25 percent of the menu is dedicated to tropical specialty drinks. Our recommendations include the huge strawberry daiquiris ($6.00), served in a pint glass and blended until a perfect peak forms above the rim, and the Sunburn ($4.50), a blend of Malibu rum, cranberry, and pineapple juices that give Cosmopolitans a run for best fruity drink served in a martini glass. Flamenco fusion guitarists occasionally play in the dining room. The restaurant will soon be rolling out its Soul Food Sunday brunch, from 11:00 a.m. to 2:00 p.m..

A long hallway leads to the dimly lit, low-ceilinged bar area, which turns into a humid cave when the live bands come on. (Don't worry – if it gets too hot, you can always sneak out to the Hotel Phoenix's swimming pool nearby.) Neophytes will be surprised to find that the ladies room is literally backstage *(hmmm ...)*.

Fridays and Saturdays, live bands take the stage, playing a mix of Reggae, Soca, Calypso, and World Beat. DJ music is the bill most other nights; the highlight is the deep house mix on Thursdays. Covers range from $3.00 to $5.00.

69: Planet Hollywood   Tourist Restaurant

2 Stockton St. (at O'Farrell). 415-421-7827. NOMA (Financial District). **HOURS:** Daily, 11a.m.-1a.m.

A wide, curving staircase leads past a life-size replica of *Ahnaald* Schwarzenegger into this popular 'museum of movies.' Radio-toting security personnel monitor the flow of tourists (85 percent of the clientele) in order to maintain a respectable line out the door onto Stockton Street. A wait of one to two hours on weekends is not uncommon, while Mondays through Thursdays the wait is minimal. On holidays, they do accept a few reservations.

Planet Hollywood is a joint venture by major investors Demi Moore, Bruce Willis, Sylvester Stallone, and Schwarzenegger. A multitude of major sports and entertainment figures hold smaller stakes in the business. Celebrity appearances are a weekly occurrence.

Visually stimulating to the extreme, this place is very, well, *Hollywood*. Let the theme song from *The Beverly Hillbillies* run through your head, and be on the lookout for "Swimming pools ... Movie stars..." In fact, the design highlight is the false swimming pool forming the background for the cocktail lounge. This pool isn't built into the ground – it curves from wall to ceiling like a Salvadore Dali clock. Plumes of bubbles oscillate from the liquor shelves skyward. While you wait for a table, the bar staff will happily ply you with thematic specialty drinks: the '007 Margarita' is made with all-top-shelf liquors; the 'Comet' is a fruit punch made with a potent blend of five different types of alcohol; the 'Home Alone' is popular with kids (and those recovering from one too many Comets) – it's the house version of a virgin strawberry/banana daiquiri.

Elsewhere in the restaurant, cardboard cutouts of stars literally pop out of the walls. And you'll be comforted to know memorabilia-laden lucite display cases are continuously within arms reach, no matter where you are in the club. Big-screen TVs emit a constant flow of movie clips, celebrity appearances, and music videos.

Overall, the food is decent for a restaurant with so many tables (remember, though, that people come here as much for the entertainment as for the food). Pasta dishes we sampled were made with fresh ingredients; crispy thin-crust pizzas are better than average; burgers are the subject of boastful management claims and, by and large live up to their reputation. A house specialty is Chicken Crunch, a concoction in which chicken is rolled in crushed Cap'n Crunch and corn flakes, then deep-fried. If your meal fails to mesmerize you, shift your attention to the 'Name That Celebrity' placemat under your plate, featuring amusing high-school-yearbook photos of dozens of famous actors.

Planet Hollywood is located just outside the Powell Street BART Station, just off Market Street, and a block from Union Square. It's easily accessible from the Muni Metro, the Market trolleys, and just about any bus serving Market Street.

70: The Punch Line Comedy Club   Comedy Club

444 Battery St. (between Washington & Clay). 415-397-7573. NOMA (Financial District). **HOURS:** Daily, Door opens at 7p.m.; Show, 9p.m.-11p.m. **ENTRANCE CHARGE:** Mon-Thur, $8.00; Fri-Sat, $10.00; Sun, $5.00. **SPECIALS:** Sunday shows features local talent.

Punch Line is not only the biggest comedy club, it is rated the 'best in San Francisco' – a city known for being the stand-up comic capital of the world (at least so says the *Bay Guardian* newspaper). Okay, enough with the superlatives, but if you're looking to overdose on laughter, you can't go wrong with this house of madness.

Featured often on the Comedy and A&E cable networks, rising stars find performing at *Punch Line* means they're a mere spit-take away from the likes of Letterman and Leno But be warned – the three featured national talents (plus host) may put your stomach and facial muscles through a two-hour workout of non-stop laughter ... so choose from the menu wisely.

While we're on the topic, try their irresistible Buffalo Chicken Wings ($7.25). And, remember – there's a drink minimum, so you don't have to come pre-tanked.

Passport: Two for one entry valid only Sun-Thur (except special events – call to verify).

71: The Red Room   Bar

827 Sutter St. (at Leavenworth & Jones). 415-346-7666. NOMA (Sutter Street Tube). **HOURS:** Daily, 5p.m.-2a.m.

Appropriately awash in overwhelming waves of deep, lipstick red, a stop at the sensuous *Red Room* is a uniquely pleasurable experience. The sheer variety of red textures is astounding. The sweeping Formica bar, ball-peen hammered columns, cloth sashes, matte painted walls, supple leather seats, and even the beechwood floors all scream out red. Near the doorway, a wall of red liquid-filled bottles curves it way into this chic but small cocktail lounge. The bar is efficiently managed by the charming Michelle, a redhead (of course.)

The Red Room caters to the 25- to 35-year-old set, who come to sample the extensive martini bar. The staff mixes the classic cocktails, including Manhattans, sidecars, and the signature red cosmopolitans. If it can be served in a martini glass, the bartenders will be happy to make it for you. The only food is the olive in the bottom of your glass. In the background, you'll hear strange modern cocktail music and Acid Jazz. Attire is dressy, seductive, maybe a bit Italian. The more retro, the better.

In a matter of what seemed moments, this smallish cocktail bar found immediate popularity. So much so that, on weekends, you may have quite a wait trying to get into this bar that can seem like a sardine can when it's too crowded. Weekdays, however – and every day, if you manage to find seating on one of the stylish, yet comfortable couch/lounges – you'll be set for an evening where the color seems to get your red blood pumpin'.

Oh, and we have it on the highest authority, they have the best drinks in town (shhhh!).

72: Sol Y Luna   Spanish Supper Club

475 Sacramento St. (between Battery & Sansome). 415-296-8696. NOMA (Financial District). **HOURS:** Lunch: Mon-Fri, 11:30a.m.-2:30p.m.; Dinner: Mon-Sat, 5:30p.m.-10p.m.; bar is open until 2a.m. **ENTRANCE CHARGE:** Varies depending on performance & night.

Sol y Luna opened in the financial district in 1991 as an eclectic Spanish Tapas restaurant. When they added live music and dancing, *Sol y Luna* became San Francisco's only Latin Supper Club. Showcasing fine artists performing everything from Flamenco to Salsa, we advise that you come early for a table and a bite to eat (which is exactly what Tapas are – little Spanish appetizers). Try some gazpacho (chilled tomato soup first created in Seville), the empanadas (fresh hot pastry stuffed with chicken, shiitake mushrooms and capers), or tiger prawns sautéed in garlic white wine and butter.

To wash it down, maybe you'll like a chilled white wine, a small glass of dry sherry, or a pitcher of Sangria-Sol y Luna (their own original recipe, made with Torres orange liqueur and brandy). Have enough, and you won't only see the sun and the moon ... but also the stars!

If you're looking for *action,* Wednesdays and Saturdays are the best nights. At 8:00 p.m. there's a live flamenco dinner show and, at 10:30 p.m., the *Sol y Luna* Band kicks-out the Salsa, Rumba, and Flamenco. By that time, they've moved the tables to make room for a dance floor, leaving a few candlelit tables on small raised section by the stage. On warm nights, a DJ sets up outside in the courtyard right along Sacramento Street – and the conga line proceeds in the same direction.

Thursdays feature live Flamenco from 8:00 p.m.-10:00 p.m., and Fridays feature live Latin Jazz from 9:00 p.m. to Midnight. DJ music always follows live sets. There's a $5.00 cover charge per person added to your dinner bill, or a $10.00 cover charge at the door if you come just for dancing. (As far as that dancing is concerned, be aware that there are some phenomenal Salsa and Flamenco dancers that 'perform' here – so you'd better hit a class or two, and then *get out there with your dancin' shoes.)*

The restaurant is quite small, but the atmosphere is pumpin'. Come with a group of friends, and you're guaranteed to meet other people and have a great time. *Sol y Luna* is popular among the after-work crowd, Latinos, and the late 20s *clique* that wants a change of music. On occasion, you might meet Giovanni, *aka the Margarita King,* passing out flyers to special events he hosts at *Sol y Luna.* He's also Rico Suave (he just loves women). This is a touch of Spain in the middle of the financial district. Buen provecho!

Pasport: Two for one dance cover. After 10 p.m. only.

73: Starlite Room   Nightclub/Live Music

450 Powell St. (at Sutter). 415-395-8595. NOMA (Financial District). **HOURS:** Mon-Sat, 4:30p.m.-2a.m. **ENTRANCE CHARGE:** $6.00-$12.00 depending on time and day. **SPECIALS:** Penthouse, 360 degree view of San Francisco. **RESTRICTIONS:** Dress Code.

San Francisco's most glamorous nightclub sits 21 stories above Union Square. Perched atop the Sir Francis Drake Hotel. The Starlight Room offers a dazzling, panoramic view of The City. Well-heeled, well-dressed San Franciscans congregate in this plush environment to see and be seen. Inside, chandeliers and extravagant furnishings make the beautiful people look even better, with women mostly in their 20s, and men, interestingly enough, seeming to range 20 to 50. Featuring "1930s glamour with a certain 1990s swing ..." the Starlight Room is *the place* to show off your best, classiest, threads.

Your host is the unflappable Mr. Harry Denton, who previously brought San Francisco both *Harry's* on Fillmore, and, of course, *Harry Denton's,* South of Market. Let the truth be known, this club is also often referred to as *Harry Denton's Starlight Room.*

And why not, while the doorman is checking to make sure you are appropriately dressed, Harry is often found checking on the doorman – to ensure that the The City's elite are treated with the appropriate regard. He is also often the larger well-dressed *flash* who zips by you on one restaurateur quest or another.

Unlike Harry's SOMA dinner club, your only choices for *repast* is a choice from the Starlight's "Lite Fare Menu" which features *hoddy-toddy* appetizers like the (highly recommended) Beluga Caviar, and Oysters on the Half-shell. The menu is served from 5:00 p.m. to 12:30 a.m.. You can also get desert, *ala: "Dahling, why don't we scoot on up to the Starlight for desert ...."*

Tuesdays through Saturdays, the music starts at 6:00 p.m.. At 9:00 p.m., Harry Denton's Starlight Orchestra lets loose with its wide range of Swing, Blues, and Big Band sounds. There is no live music on Sunday or Monday.

Remember – the view from the dance floor, set in the middle of the city and literally surrounded by the famous skyline, is simply incredible.

74: Tonga Room   Polynesian Restaurant/ Hurricane Bar

Fairmont Hotel, 950 Mason St. (between California & Sacramento). 415-772-5278. NOMA (Nob Hill). **HOURS:** Happy Hour, Mon-Fri, 5 p.m.-7 p.m.; Dancing Nightly, 8 p.m.-1a.m. **ENTRANCE CHARGE:** $3.00 per person. **RESTRICTIONS:** One drink minimum.

Located in the historic Fairmont Hotel, who's facade was used as the St. Gregory in the 80s TV show *Hotel*, the *Tonga Room* has one of the best Happy Hours in town. You'll also want to check-out the pseudo Polynesian riki-tiki-atmosphere. What once served as the hotel's swimming pool, now resides as a lagoon around which you sit on bamboo chairs, at bamboo tables, amidst a tropical rain forest.

Waitresses dressed in oriental satin kimonos serve up Fantasy Island-type tropical drinks, complete with those cute little umbrellas and fruit that might tip the glass over. For $5.00 per person during Happy Hour (5:00 p.m.-7:00 p.m., Monday through Friday), you can feast on a limitless Chinese/Polynesian buffet featuring dim sum, chow mein, and short ribs. Now that's a good deal!

At 8:00 p.m. every evening, a band floats out to the audience through the lagoon, featuring everything from Englebert to Michael Bolton. There's a $3.00 cover, and room to dance on a small dance floor. The highlight ... the sporadic hurricanes that light up the ceiling with sounds of torrential rain. And, as you wait for the storm to pass, it's time for another drink.

57: Yakety Yak   Cafe

679 Sutter St. (at Taylor). 415-885-6908. NOMA (Sutter Street Tube). **HOURS:** Daily, 7a.m.-10p.m. **SPECIALS:** Poetry Readings, Fridays, 7p.m.-9p.m. **RESTRICTIONS:** Cash only.

It's 7:30 a.m. and, as the sun begins its busy ascent, the cheerful staff is busy turning out gallons of their dark bean brew to a pilgrimage of zombie-eyed walk-ins who (despite themselves, given the time of day) are quickly transformed into a boisterous, jovial crowd. After years of work as a cafe supplier, the owner took the next step, or two, and decided to launch his own coffee house ~ and *Yakety Yak* was born. The cafe's devotees claim it is their morning-Mecca. Be it strength through numbers or mighty coffee beans, or both, *Yakety Yak* makes for a social morning pit-stop.

Moving into the evening hours, this cafe takes on a more-relaxed clientele who are perfectly content reading a Burroughs or Ginsberg novel, battling over a game of chess, or enjoying deep conversation. From paint-splattered wooden floors, to paint-splattered canvases (courtesy of neighboring art students), the setting is inviting and unpretentious. For a more intimate gathering, trot on up to their spacious loft, where you'll only find two tables.

As if its day-to-day appeal is not enough, on Fridays between 7 and 9 p.m., *Yakety Yak* features a can't-miss poetry reading we can only describe as a poetic liturgy, or a slam session of poignant pros – you decide! If you're hungry, skip the usual and try their famous salads, pastas, and sandwiches. You'll also find SF-Net here, but why plug-in to the virtual chat box when you're sitting in a real one?

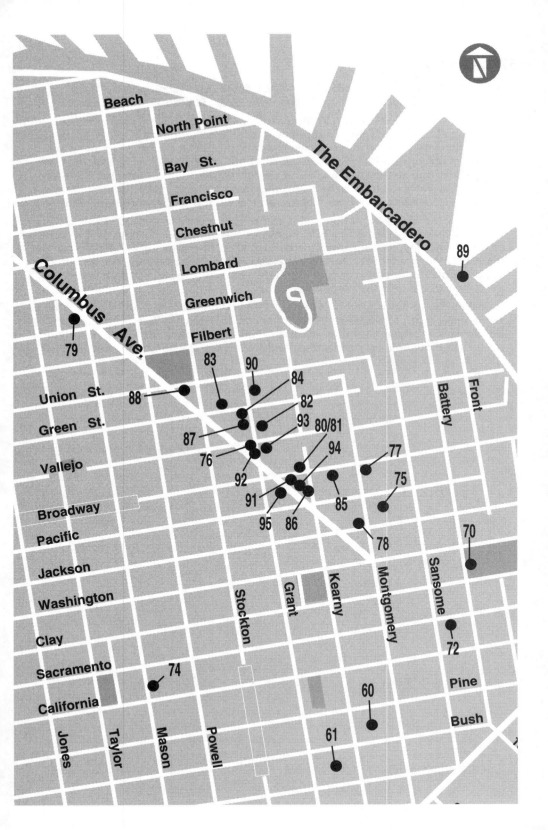

NORTH BEACH

I f San Francisco were a mother, and its many neighborhoods its children, North Beach would be The City's proud little darling. But, before you get all excited, lose the towel and beach ball – North Beach was 'de-beached' in the early 1800's. As the result of a small landfill, in true California tradition, North Beach now sits *casually lounging* between Telegraph Hill on the east and Russian Hill on the west. As for the beach – *it* changed residence, and moved down Columbus Avenue to the Wharf.

Although North Beach is popularly known as "Little Italy," the area historically has seen its ethnic makeup change hands like exquisite furniture in a swap meet. In the beginning (the 1850's to be precise), Chilean prostitutes were the first to call this neighborhood home. Catering to the needs of the bearded Forty Niners, they came to make their fortunes off the fortune-hunters during those fortune-making Gold Rush days. As time passed, they were pushed out by the Irish, who were later outnumbered by Latin Americans, who were in turn replaced by the current 'residents' – the Italians. Now, North Beach actually finds itself San Francisco's most eclectic neighborhood, populated by persons of many cultures – many of whom call North Beach their first home in the U.S.

The attraction of North Beach has far transcended ethnicity and, as one culture replaced the next, so did cultural revolutions. Ever since it was known as the Barbary Coast (after the marauding North African pirate haven), the streets of North Beach have provided a hot bed for hot heads of the times. From Bohemians to modernists, beatniks to hippies, punkers to grungies, they've all left their mark – often in the form of art or political awareness. True recognition didn't settle here until the mid '50's, however, when the groovy cats of the beat generation flung North Beach onto the *national* map.

D isillusioned by the Eisenhower era, the beatniks rejected the mediocrity of their *Zeitgeist* (look it up!). Around the tables of Vesuvio and Cafe Trieste, they brewed their magic lives-potion, filling their cup of fervor to the brim with Eastern philos-

ophy, poetry, jazz, and – for good measure – a dash of decadence. Despite (or due to) media hype, Jack Kerouac emerged as king cat after publishing *On the Road*. He was soon followed by Allen Ginsberg, who lit the proverbial fuse of social unrest with the public reading of his inflammatory poem, *"Howl."*

As the 'beatnik bunch' ran amok on the streets of North Beach, their exploits made conservatives run for cover. A federal court deemed *Howl's* contents graphically obscene, leading to its banning, and the subsequent arrest of its publisher, Ferlinghetti, the owner of City Lights Bookstore, on obscenity charges. The ensuing legal battle ended with an historic ruling in favor of Ginsberg and City Lights. With Ginsberg's reading, the cat did not merely jump out of the bag – *it tore it to shreds!*

On The Road and *Howl* became catalysts for the beat generation, and Kerouac and Ginsberg became overnight literary icons. As the media circus and tourist parade came marching in, was North Beach suddenly sitting among the avant-garde ranks of Paris and its existential-laden Left Bank.

As time passed, the volatility of North Beach's past has given birth to the vitality of its present. If the Golden-Gate Bridge sits at the edge of the Western frontier, then North Beach is the gateway to infinite frontiers of thought and lifestyles (not to mention an occasional slant of wackiness). Italian *cultura* and its Mediterranean charm have served as the dominant *and affectionate* custodian of North Beach. Many newcomers from all corners of the globe are pulled by this neighborhood's alluring landscape of cafes, bars, restaurants, boutiques, and the *strip clubs* lining the shimmer-

ing avenues of **Columbus and Broadway**, and their many side streets. It is, in fact, the intersection of Columbus and Broadway that designates this neighborhood's ground zero – *and around this area, you're more likely to find an outdoor cafe table than a parking spot.*

It's easy to understand why many Europeans who visit or live here consider this San Francisco's most European-*like* neighborhood. Upon arriving at their new home in the new world – short of packing their quaint piazzas and the Coliseum – Italians brought with them a grab bag of goodies, reminiscent of Italian *vita,* to share with the other kids in this leisure playground.

Indulging in 'active' sessions of lingering, while enjoying the sun-drenched days and moonlit nights with friends, is not an activity ... *it's a way of life!* And *here* is where North Beach ceases to be *'just a neighborhood,'* and becomes a state of mind. Strolling the avenues – you'll enjoy enough distraction to melt the day away with the ease of a sweet-dripping Italian *gelato.*

As you stroll, notice the strained foreheads of writers busy chiseling out their labor of love in the historic, poignant setting of Vesuvio, and the sharply-dressed professionals enjoying a time-out power-lunch at the outdoor tables of **Enrico's**. A rooting hullabaloo of Italian soccer fans will likely be huddled around the tables of **Steps of Rome** (fixated on the satellite feed of Italy's favorite past-time), as other aficionados enjoy the high pitched sounds of *live classical opera* performed by the owner at **Caffe Trieste**.

As you wander aimlessly, you'll a beat that accompanies you from one discovery to the next. If there's any *hustling* and *bustling* to be found, it's only because the locals are in a *hurry* to *relax* at their favorite cafe or restaurant. Given the abundance of each found in North Beach, pedestrians (to the annoyance of street traffic) busily make traffic of their own ping-ponging and criss-crossing the streets en route to their desired chill zone. So, let the street-side aroma of dark brewed coffee and ambiance capture you into its web of diversion, and plop yourself down at one of the many table-side chairs. The 'rest' is up to you.

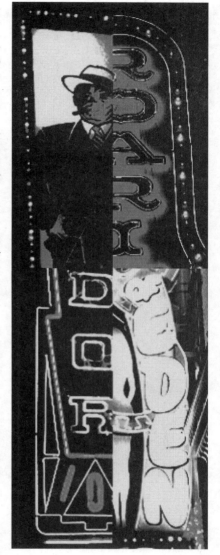

A s the sun sets over The City by the Bay, North Beach awakens with a notable buzz. It was not long ago that the descending sun was accompanied by hordes of tattoo-tailored sailors, themselves descending on The City in search of cheap whisky and women. Sailors – replete with cash and hormones – rollicked through a rich jungle of saloons, tattoo parlors, strip joints, and one-hour hotels. It was then that North Beach undulated with Popeye-white uniforms amid an erotic bonanza of neon lights, while tartly dressed women prowled up an down the streets – baring their brand of 'fast-food-love.'

Well, the hustlers have moved on to the Tenderloin, but faint remnants of that robust period can be found down **Broadway and Kearny Streets** near Columbus. There, the night is still illuminated by a canopy of neon light radiating from establishments featuring an electrical dance on the outside ... and erotic table dancing within. The **Hungary i**, and **Roaring 20's** are among the last of a dying era. A few doors down Broadway sits **Finocchio's**, offering a less-raunchy, more-family-style cabaret.

At the corner of **Broadway and Columbus** is the **Condor Bistro**, a spiffied-up sports bar (and not really a bistro at all). Today, it's a mere shadow of its notorious days as the area's first strip club – once featuring a topless Carol Doda. Today, the two-story-high flashing-nipple sign (made famous in the Streets of San Francisco TV show) is gone. The Condor name, however, lives on in the fond (and not so fond) memories of many locals as a reminder of those dubious, electrifying days when San Francisco sat as the most desired port of call for thousands of sailors.

Washington Square Park

If Columbus Avenue is North Beach's artery of life, its soul lies within the grassy confines of **Washington Square Park**. Sitting snugly at the bottom of Telegraph Hill, with its crowning Coit Tower, and across from the spires of the Church of Sts. Peter and Paul (famous for hosting the marriage of baseball great Joe DiMaggio and Marilyn Monroe) – and pressed all around by ever-present traffic – many consider this park a haven for escape.

In fact, this idyllic slice of land can easily be mistaken for an Italian piazza ... and for good reason. Washington Square Park is the neighborhood's center of open-air *activity* and *inactivity* alike. Lovers populate tree-covered hideaways, with picnic baskets of goodies from **Molinari's Deli** (XXX); buskers perform a strum-jam-diddy the ever present congregation of friends chat the day away; soccer players nimbly 'air-dribble'; and sunbathers pursue the rigorous art of sunworshipping.

Many benches are occupied by the elderly, lounging the day away while reminiscing and swapping stories of their memorable youth back in the old days of Italy or China. If you're there immediately after school hours, you'll catch children criss-crossing the park, schlepping their homework and cartoon-adorned lunch pails, some stopping off at the park's corner playground before racing home for dinner.

On weekends, the park is visited by artists who come to bare their canvases, *and their souls,* in the open-air gallery. And, if you manage to make it through Saturday night, on Sunday mornings you can watch the Chinese at work on their Tai Chi routines.

We found a couple of peculiarities you may find interesting:

- First, good-old George is nowhere to be found. No bust, no equestrian statue ... nothing but the name.

- To further the confusion, a statue of Ben Franklin occupies the center of the park – half-encircled by a cathedral of trees.

The enigma has defied resolution, to the point that a local newspaper, the North Beach *Now*, conducted a contest in pursuit of the answer. Adding to the confusion is the fact that Washington Square is, in fact, an irregular pentagon (but let's not nit-pick).

No matter your itinerary, there's no question that a visit to San Francisco is not complete without a visit to North Beach – easily one of The City's most interesting neighborhoods. And, when you're looking for night life on those relatively barren early weekdays, you can rest assured that in North Beach you'll find *something* to hold your interest. *Ci vediamo.*

Your Mission

Okay, first thing's first! Before you gallivant your way through the nocturnal jungle of North Beach's many social haunts and drinking holes, heed this warning: Do *not* beer-drench yourself on an empty stomach. Go feed yourself!

'Tis time to dine and, with a choice of 150 restaurants, you *may* be overwhelmed by the dizzying selection. So, unless you're armed with one of the many restaurant guidebooks, you'll have a tough time deciding. *Let's Party!* is here to help, and we've devised a game plan to aid your search for 'gastronomic-nirvana.'

Here's the beef! Your point of attack starts on Columbus Avenue at Broadway. As you walk north, your senses will most likely be accosted by an atomic barrage of garlic, onions, spice, *and everything nice.* Many of the restaurants have cleverly made use of wall-sized street-side windows, exposing the warmth and atmosphere of each interior. This also provides you a visual menu of their artfully orchestrated dishes, being devoured atop their smartly arranged tables. *As for* the ambiance, North Beach provides *a lot* of something for everyone.

If you're up for a blend of dining, camaraderie and garlic rich foods, check-out the flashy **Stinking Rose** (at 325 Columbus Ave) or **Little City** (on the corner of Union and Powell). If you prefer your dinner accompanied by live Jazz, choose a savory plate of 'home-cookin' ribs' in the aged comfort of **Jazz at Pearl's**, or enjoy the more avant-garde and pricy California/Mediterranean cuisine at **Enrico's** .

If an elegant yet spartan decor is more to your liking, accompanied by a critically acclaimed cuisine where the chef holds celebrity status, enter **Moose's** (1652 Stockton). But, if you aim to please with something simple and sweet, with a bar/cafe setting, venture into **Mario's** at 566 Columbus Avenue. Here, your taste buds will be treated to the best focaccia sandwiches this side of Genova.

The essential element to remember in our game plan is to not let your nose fall prey to the first pleasing scent that crosses your path. Temptations are a dime a dozen – *so don't be a Pavlovian-dog.* Besides, with the exception of the occasional, mostly harmless beggar, North Beach is a stroller-friendly neighborhood full of colorful findings. So, whether you're just out to stuff your face, or looking to create a dining event of historic proportions, we suggest you whet your appetite while shopping around.

Night Tracks

Moving on to the night's main event, let us guide you into the realm of revelry along a short narrow stretch of upper **Grant Avenue**. Following the true tradition of those rowdy Barbary Coast days, the level of revelry here almost appears to be busting at the seams with a happy-mingling mob, busy at play with he, she, they, and the rest of the international hodgepodge of *20-* and *30-something's*. For many, their time spent in North Beach is but a small dose of merriment – perhaps only one weekend in time – before it's off to their next vacation destination.

This fresh, ongoing wave of wide-eyed visitors is a vigorous infusion to the already madcap scene. While North Beach is the only neighborhood where you'll find action every day of the week, it's no surprise that the days that *rule* are Thursday through Saturday, when the bars and venues of Grant Avenue are most charged with live music, dancing, laughter and coy flirtations.

75: Bix   Jazz Supper Club

56 Gold St. (lane off Montgomery, between Jackson & Pacific). 415-433-6300. North Beach. **HOURS:** Mon-Thur, 11:30a.m.-11p.m.; Fri, 11:30a.m.-Midnight; Sat, 5:30p.m.-Midnight; Sun, 5p.m.-10p.m.

This classic spot to drink classic cocktails is tucked away on a narrow Barbary Coast alley in the shadow of the Transamerica Pyramid. Dark, dramatic, Deco and decadent, *Bix* reminds us that not everyone was relegated to soup lines during the Depression. *Bix* is a favorite among The City's upscale 25-and-over crowd, who recreate the glamour of high society 30s life nightly.

Ornate marble columns support 30-foot ceilings crowned by an immense, opaque skylight. A sweeping staircase leads up to the second-floor dining area, from which diners can observe the sharply-dressed crowd below.

Bix's outdoor tables, set amid picturesque Gold Alley's Goldrush-era brick buildings, are a great cocktail spot for parties of two. The narrow sidewalk puts third persons at risk of being toppled by taxis trying to squeeze through the tiny alley.

Formal, white-jacketed waiters shake your martinis at table side, and pour them with a flourish. Connoisseurs will appreciate the bar's use of special Miss Scarlett's vermouth-marinated jumbo olives – "the perfect garnish to the perfect martini."

The menu changes daily, but is always impressive, with excellent appetizers and salads ranging from $5.00 to $15.00. We enjoyed the crispy, delicate potato-leek pancake with house-smoked salmon and caviar, as well as the cornmeal breaded calamari with aioli. The pate de fois gras, served hot over pear bread pudding, was outrageously rich. Entrees, priced from $12.00 to $26.00, included a crisp duck confit with wild rice, grilled orange and escarole, and a molasses-grilled pork chop dish.

During the cocktail hour, *Bix* features recorded Prohibition-era Jazz. Later every evening, they have live Jazz. Mary Stellings mellow Jazz vocals begin Monday to Thursday nights at 8:30 p.m.. Friday and Saturday nights, a sax/bass/piano trio belts out more swingy Jazz tunes. Sunday night features a solo pianist.

76: Caffé Trieste   Cafe

601 Vallejo St. (at Grant). 415-392-6739. North Beach. **HOURS:** Sun-Thur, 6:30a.m.-11:30p.m.; Fri-Sat, 6:30a.m.-12:30a.m. **RESTRICTIONS:** Cash only.

Under the watchful eye and smile of Poppa Gianni, *Caffé Trieste* provides its peculiarly alert-looking patrons with "the best cup of Espresso this side of Rome." Practice makes perfect, and at *Caffé Trieste* they've been roasting and grinding their Java for over 39 years. The pictures on the wall speak historically of Poppa Gianni's

marketing efforts, and celebrity pictures from Bill Cosby to Francis Ford Coppola adorn the walls. *Caffé Trieste*, in fact, is where Coppola ironed-out his rough draft of The Godfather.

Whether you fancy a session of sun worshipping at one of their street-side tables, or prefer the European ambiance inside, the staff proudly claims *Caffé Trieste* to be the 'eye' of North Beach's carnival-like hurricane. Its a place where a wide mix of people comes to relax. On Sundays from 1:00 p.m. to 5:30 p.m., you can catch live opera performed by Pappa Gianni and family. Don't forget to try their highly acclaimed Caffé Fantasia, made with Almond Torani.

77: Centerfolds   Gentleman's Club & Restaurant

932 Montgomery (at Broadway). 415-834-0661. North Beach. **HOURS:** Mon-Fri, 11:30a.m.-2a.m.; Sat-Sun, 5:30p.m.-2a.m., Dinning Hours: Lunch, Mon-Fri, 11:30a.m.-6p.m.; Dinner, Daily, 6p.m.-1:30a.m. **ENTRANCE CHARGE:** $15.00 Befor 6p.m., $20.00 After 6p.m. **SPECIALS:** Limousine Pick-Up Service, Four Course Dinning Package, $65.00/person; Occasional Playboy & Penthouse Dance Features; Show Girls, Minimum Tipping, Private Table Dances, $10.00; Privat Room Dances, $20.00; Stage Tips, Your Option. **RESTRICTIONS:** Dress Code.

Located on upper Broadway, this 'gentleman's Club' keeps a lofty distance from the more *sleazy* strip joints found in the up the street or in the Tenderloin. Due to its stylish and elegant surroundings, *Centerfolds* is The City's most respectful offer-

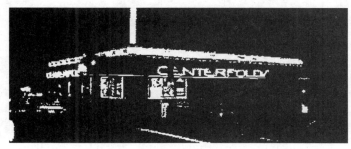

ing of 'the flesh' – but it doesn't come cheap! A night out here can easily set you back a hundred Captain Georges.

Single men dressed in power suites, fashionable looking couples, and tourists all sit back to enjoy a non-stop performance by a wide selection of drop-dead-gorgeous showgirls who keep their panties on, and take their Pasties off only at the end. The elevated dance floor offers a new performance by two girls every five minutes, and this is where you can play that guessing game with your friend on whether either of the two girls is busting with silicone.

Some girls obviously prefer to view the stage as their blank canvas, just waiting to be filled with erotic lure by their artful poses and gyrations. While the showgirls do their thing on stage, scantily clad dancers circulate through the place and, as your blood circulates through your veins, you'll be treated to a visual parade of all sizes, shapes, and colors.

And there's more! *Centerfolds* offers a pricey lunch and dinner menu that has been critically acclaimed as a cuisine experience that is good enough to divert your attention from the stage. Our hot tip is their Grilled New York Steak ($28.00). We won't talk about the *private dance* rooms. If you're wondering, you probably know already ... *hands-off!*

78: Cypress Club   Elegant Dining/Jazz Bar

500 Jackson St. (at Montgomery). 415-296-8555. North Beach. **HOURS:** Daily, Bar 4:30 p.m.-Midnight.

So what's all the buzz about at this Jackson Square Haunt?

A night out for drinks and live musical at this very elegantly designed restaurant makes for a spectacular evening. A night out at *Cypress Club*, and you feel you've lived in style.

John Cunin opened it up back in 1990 with investor Bill Kimpton. We all know from the successes of Harry Denton's, Kuleto's and Masa's, that Kimpton doesn't take any venture lightly.

Cypress Club is wildly popular among many of San Francisco's intimate circles. The decor is *absolutely* the draw. Designer Jordan Mozer of Chicago says, "A restaurant should have a personality. Every time you go there you should see something new." And *Cypress Club* expresses just such a statement.

The design represents the spirited optimism of America in the 40s ... rich red velvet curtains ... bronze and copper metal work ... tile floors. What Mozer did, however, was incorporate those elements, but bring them into the 90s. Here's some of the cool stuff he did: the entry door is puffed up like an airplane wing; a funky coat

cabinet is shaped like an old TV set with bronze cartoon frogs for pulls; there are cigar-shaped marble beams and parachuting donut chandeliers.

A mural inspired by WPA paintings of the 30s wraps the room in images of Monterey Cypress trees and Napa Vineyards. The bar stools are shaped like wine casks with corks for seats, and mohair dining chairs look like curves of a Hudson fender. It is a fantasia-like setting that keeps you in awe.

Rhythm & Blues and Jazz musicians perform Monday through Saturday evenings in the lounge area. Along with that is plenty of eating and drinking decadence you can bury yourself into. Try eggplant caviar, cypress fries with mushroom ketchup, cypress spicy chicken wings, and breads cooked in tandoori ovens. *Cypress Club* has two temperature-controlled wine cellars that house over 14,000 bottles. It also features Martini Night every Wednesday from 4:30 p.m. to 7:30 p.m., and Champagne decadence every Thursday from 4:30 p.m. to 7:30 p.m..

79: Doo Wash Cafe   Laundromat/Cafe/Amusement Room

817 Columbus Ave. (at Mason). 415-885-1222. North Beach. **HOURS:** Daily, 7a.m.-11p.m. (last load 9:30p.m.). **ENTRANCE CHARGE:** Washing, $1.25, Drying, $1.00 (one hour).

Ah, bachelors and bachelorettes, it's never been this good! If there is such a god, it would seem the god of Laundromats has smiled down on this wash-and-dry venue. And, it's probably high time for the rebirth of your clothes, so ... Okay, enough with spiritual mumbo-jumbo!

As you walk into the *Doo Wash*, you're greeted by a cafe with just four tables. It's there, while you wait for your laundry to spin, that you can order a sandwich (Pastrami – $3.75, Bagel Club – $1.95), or check-out some of their yum-yum sweets – brownies with milk ($1.50); muffins ($1.25). Or, you can just kick-back with a good book over a cappuccino ($1.85).

As you walk further in (much to a media-babies delight), you'll find the TV room, lined with comfy couches. Posted next to the TV, the movie schedule announces your upcoming entertainment (it's not so bad ... is it?). So, chase away those folding-blues with a movie (or two), or make use of the pool table, pinball machine, or any of the video games there for your amusement. Oh yeah, lest we forget – you'll find washers, dryers, and professional dry-cleaning available. But don't get to carried away ... you're here to do your laundry ... remember?!!

80: Enrico's   Jazz-Blues Restaurant/Bar/Outdoor Cafe

504 Broadway (at Kearny). 415-982-6223. North Beach. **HOURS:** Sun-Thur, food, noon-11p.m.; bar, noon-2a.m.; Fri & Sat, food, noon-Midnight, bar, noon-2a.m. **SPECIALS:** Wine Dinner starts 7p.m. the last Sunday every month, Four-courses including wine, $40.00; Occasional poetry readings & operas; Live Jazz: Mon-Thur, 8p.m.-Midnight; Fri & Sat, 9p.m.-1a.m.; Sun, 7p.m.-11p.m. (no cover charge).

In a city that prides itself on fine dining and cafe culture, *Enrico's* stands tall among the heavyweights. So, whether you're on a hunt for North Beach's cafe society, or looking for a Mediterranean/California-style taste bud explosion, you won't be disappointed at *Enrico's*. Replete with such trimmings as a rotating art gallery, grand piano, live jazz, first-class wine list, and a beautifully carved bar, the ambiance is engaging.

Outside, under the warmth of heaters, you'll find a spaciously arranged patio where you can enjoy Broadway's circus parade of city lights.

Enrico's Dinner menu takes on a new face monthly, but you'll find the prices always range from $9.00 to $14.00, and an extensive list of hot and cold Tapas runs from $1.25 to $8.00. Check-out their most popular beer – Full Sail Amber Ale on tap ($3.75).

81: Finocchio's   Transvestite Cabaret

506 Broadway (at Kearny). 415-982-9388. Dragboss@aol.com. North Beach. **HOURS:** Summer, Wed-Sat, 8:30p.m., 10p.m., 11:30p.m. Winter, same show times, but only on Friday and Saturday **ENTRANCE CHARGE:** $14.50, no drink minimum.

This variety comedy-driven cabaret is not a showcase for eroticism, nor is it a coat-and-tie Paris-style cabaret. It is a night *full* of laughs and surprises. With the aid of smoke, mirrors, laser lights – and dress and hair styles that jumped out of Peg Bundy's closet – the nine performers wipe-up the one-and-a-quarter hour show with the ease and pace of a Madam on steroids. The show is laced with comedy, dance, song, and production numbers, and the mixed audience is encouraged to interact with the performers.

Although the performers are billed as female impersonators, look-out for the wild-card in this 'drag' show (there's real female in the cast). In operation for over 55 years, this family-run show is one of the oldest running cabarets in the world and, as such, is a North Beach landmark. As the saying goes ... "The prettiest girl that was a guy that you ever saw?" Well ... we'll leave that for you to decide.

82: The Gathering Caffé   Cafe

1326 Grant Ave. (between Vallejo & Green). 415-433-4247. North Beach. **HOURS:**
Mon-Fri, 5p.m.-2a.m.; Sat-Sun, 11a.m.-2a.m. **ENTRANCE CHARGE: SPECIALS:** Live
Jazz, Sun-Thur, 9p.m.-11:30p.m.; Fri-Sat, 9p.m.-1:30a.m.; rotating art exhibition.
RESTRICTIONS: Cash only.

If you're looking to hear live jazz, this is one of North Beach's
unpretentious jazz houses. Among the neighborhood's social
haunts, *The Gathering Caffé* is the new kid on the block. Inside, you
won't find the rustic charm common with the many aged-out
(read 'rustic') cafes of this area. What you *will* find, is an intimate
gathering of locals and tourist alike. The setting is accented with
a pictorial frieze depicting the art of merrymaking and, in the
back, a rotating gallery features jazz notables.

During the day, this cafe offers a relaxing time-out, where you
just may run into an eccentric refugee from the Beat generation.
At night, however, *The Gathering Caffé* is filled to the brim with
Jazz enthusiasts. Come early if you hope to find a seat (or even get
a glimpse of the tiny stage). *The Gathering Caffé* can often be spot-
ted easily as you walk up Grant street by the gathering of semi-
patrons milling around on the sidewalk waiting to get in – or just enjoying the
'back-beat' while viewing the musicians hind-quarters on the stage (which is situated in the cafe's front window).

83: Gino & Carlo   Italian Neighborhood Bar

548 Green St. (between Columbus & Grant). 415-421-0896. North Beach. **HOURS:**
Daily, 6a.m.-2a.m. **RESTRICTIONS:** Cash only.

Charles McCabe, the famed (and deceased) *Chronicle* colum-
nist, loved to write his column while at *Gino & Carlo*, but to pre-
serve his carefully secluded hideaway, he always referred to the
bar as "The Bank of Italy." We know North Beach is dotted
with an ample selection of celebrated Italian cafés and restaurants ... But an Italian bar!?! Yes, and here it is.

This Sicilian-family owned bar, where a Campari Cocktail is
known as a Comperion, and a Bloody Mary (not coffee) is the
morning drink, is an 'oldie-but-goodie' Italian original.

Opened daily at 6:00 a.m., *Gino & Carlo* is among North
Beach's few early risers to cater to The City's just-released
grave-yard-shift workers (and occasional all-night party-ers).
As the day progresses, the scene begins to 'normalize' (that is,
until night falls). In the evenings, the rooms begin to vibrate
with the buzz of engaged conversation, laughter, and the
sound of a perfect break coming from one of the two pool
tables that sit wrapped by "the walls of fame." Unless a major
sporting event is televised, the social merriment relegates the
two TV screens to a mere light-show.

Every bar has its devoted regulars, and *Gino and Carlo* is no
exception. Rest assured, however, that tourist and casual walk-
ins are happily welcomed (rather then scoffed at). Be sure and
ask for *Frank* at the bar!

84: Grant & Green
Live Blues Bar

1371 Grant Ave. (at Green). 415-693-9565. North Beach. **HOURS:** Daily, 6a.m.-2a.m. **ENTRANCE CHARGE:** Fri & Sat $2.00-3.00 for live music. **SPECIALS:** Daily, live music starting 9p.m. **RESTRICTIONS:** Cash only.

While along your Grant Avenue shuffle, you'll most likely first hear G & G before you see it. As if the music and goings-on aren't enough, the front offers a wall mural of a $50 bill – it can't be missed.

Dominated by nothing but black walls, small stage, and a dance floor, the interior of this veteran venue offers no visual treat. However, as night descends, a wing-ding raucousness prevails over a scene that can, at times, swell to riotous proportions. *Grant & Green* dishes out a daily serving of live Rhythm and Blues to a friendly mix of locals and tourists who come armed with their get-down dancing shoes.

Two years ago, when it was discovered that G & G had never had a dancing license, city officials attempted to enforced a most bird-brained restriction: No Dancing! But that was *not* to last, as a mob of happy faithfuls marched into court, petition in hand, to voice their opinion on the matter. Dancing was quickly reinstated.

Wednesday features the seasoned music of Syklopps, comprised of former band members from Journey, Santana, and Sly Stone – they are not to be missed. Thursdays and Saturdays G&G brings to its stage The City's favorite sons – the Johnny Nitro band.

Looking to wet your whistle? Ask the cheerful bartenders for their number-one concoction – Stoli Pink Lemonade ($4.50). Most likely they'll join you in a toast, or two, or three ....

PP Two for one draft beer of choice.

85: Hi-Ball Lounge
Lounge/Dance Club

473 Broadway (between Kearny & Montgomery). 415-39-SWING. North Beach. **HOURS:** Tue-Thur, 7p.m.-1a.m.; Fri-Sat, 8:30p.m.-2a.m.; Sun, 8p.m.-1a.m. **ENTRANCE CHARGE:** Tue-Wed, Free, Thur & Sun, $5.00, Fri-Sat, $7.00.

The same Young brothers who brought you the Desert Moon and Blues conspired late last year to open this trendy jazz and swing lounge. According to owner Max Young, the crowd is mostly locals and City people, from 25 to 35. Inside, soft, red candlelight flickers off tigerskin and Barbary Coast brick walls. Red globes of light dangle from ceiling fans. Regulars and early arrivals sit in red velvet booths, while everyone else sits at cabaret tables or jostles for space near the bar. All in all, it's a classy, but not too upscale, scene in an area more known for strip clubs than swing clubs.

The HiBall is very new, and musical programming is still being set, but the central theme is Jazz and Swing-based live bands, with particularly upbeat and danceable music on weekends. Current offerings are: swing lessons on Tuesdays; experimental and Latin Jazz on Wednesdays; mainstream Jazz on Thursdays; and live Swing bands on Fridays and Saturdays. By mid-96, the owners plan to open on Sundays and Mondays as well.

The Young brothers aim for a slightly upscale crowd, and the crowd is willing to dress the part. This is particularly evident on weekends, as the serious Swingsters

break out their Zoot suits and fedoras for the big night out. The bar service seems to echo this retro, upscale feel, with shaker drinks (martinis, Cosmopolitans) the beverages of choice. Max has gone so far as to have an enormous, 25-ounce martini glass custom blown. It's only available for special occasions, and you can expect to pay about $30 for what Max bills as "the world's largest Martini." For the less ostentatious among you, *The HiBall* Happy Hour offers $3.00 call martinis Thursdays and Fridays from 5:00 to 9:00 p.m.

86: Jazz at Pearl's   Jazz House

256 Columbus Ave. (at Broadway). 415-291-8255. North Beach. **HOURS:** Mon-Sat, 7p.m.-2a.m.; Sun, Closed. **ENTRANCE CHARGE:** Fri & Sat, 2 drink minimum per set, per person; Sun-Thur, 2 drink minimum per person.

Pearl's has stayed true to its billing as the home of great Bay Area Jazz, and it is practically a clubhouse for area Jazz musicians. On any given night, for example, you may be treated to the music of Manny Duran, or the beat of Vince Lateano. Although there is a daily scheduled set, most musicians who drop in, sit in and, as the night moves along, many surprise appearances can take the stage.

Throughout, you'll find the owner, Mr. Jazz-man Sunny Buxton, 'rotating' the room, making sure everyone is happy. His presence is that of welcoming house-party host. *Pearl's* 50s-style setup is an acoustic wonder, and you can enjoy a beautiful meal while grooving off the tunes of New York post-bebop. On the weekend, expect a standing-room-only scene. Take our word for it, and check out *Pearl's* Home Cookin' Ribs ($7.50).

87: The Lost & Found Saloon   Neighborhood Blues Saloon

1353 Grant Ave. (between Green & Union). 415-392-9126. North Beach. **HOURS:** Daily, noon-2a.m. **ENTRANCE CHARGE:** Fri & Sat $2.00 for live music. **SPECIALS:** Live Blues, Tue-Sun 9:30p.m.-1:30a.m. **RESTRICTIONS:** Cash only.

Nobody quite knows how the name of this saloon came about, but we suspect that many stray cats – during beer-drenched nights – have lost, found, and again lost themselves along side this bar's mahogany edge.

More than we can say for some of its patrons, *Lost & Found* is holding its own among North Beach's fossilized fraternity of dive bars and saloons. Within its austere walls, time has shown this drinking hole its share of trolloping prostitutes, brawling sailors, pontificating beatniks, and happy hippies – all seeking something lost ... perhaps found. In fact, it was from this place that Janice Joplin and Clearance Clearwater Revival catapulted onto the world's stage.

Much as this delightfully dingy saloon is but a whisper of its more rambunctious days, it remains a favorite among local beer quaffers. The interior is wonderfully worn-in, and a second room provides a tiny stage, dance floor and row-boat bar *(ya just gotta see it!).* With the exception of Mondays, you'll hear strictly live Blues daily, as *Lost & Found* competes for supremacy within the BBB-Zone (that's the Blues-Band-Battle-Zone – defined as the equally measured open air of audible space residing between one bar's live Blues music and another's, which, in this case, is *Grant & Green* – and not so ample).

88: Mario's Bohemian Cigar Store Cafe   Eat!

566 Columbus Ave. (at Union). 415-362-0536. North Beach. **HOURS:** Mon-Sat, 10a.m.-Midnight; Sun, 10a.m.-11p.m. **RESTRICTIONS:** Cash only.

This is *not* a cigar store. The name is a distant remnant from the days when this joint was North Beach's happy distributor of chic sticks. My, how times have changed, and as chic-sticks became better known as 'cancer sticks,' the Italian owners got wise and got into the Cafe business.

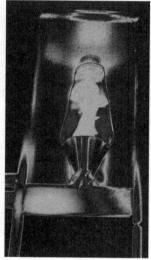

Sitting on the corner of Columbus and Union, across from Washington Square, this cafe offers a quaint jazzy setting for anyone in the mood to just linger. But you'll find much more than that. *Mario's* Focaccia sandwiches are a delightful orchestration of spices likely to leave your taste buds in a state of rapture. Yes, they're that good! Patrons range from the Joe-Shmoe pseudo-intellectuals and tourists to home-grown locals (who happen to know the staff's shift schedule better then the staff does).

Check-out their house Campari, and don't shy away from some of the best espresso drinks around. All in all, *Mario's* is one of the most desired of all chill-locales in San Francisco – not to mention a *Let's Party!* staff favorite (Yes, we actually do take our visiting guests here on hot Saturday afternoons). So sit, eat, drink, and watch the world pass as you gaze on the Church of Sts. Peter and Paul across Washington Square, and contemplate what Catholic Mass sounds like in Chinese.

89: Pier 23 Cafe   Restaurant/Live Music Dance Bar

On the Embarcadero at the end of Lombard St. 415-362-5125. Waterfront. **HOURS:** Tue-Sat, 11:30a.m.-1:30a.m.; Sun, 11a.m.-8p.m. **ENTRANCE CHARGE:** Varies depending on night & performance.

Yes, it's a pier – but it looks more like a tiny white shack. If you don't know anything about Pier numbering, that's okay – we don't really think anyone understands it. What you need to know is that *Pier 23* is on the Bay side of the Embarcadero, between where Front and Battery intersect. If not for the neon sign, you could easily miss it.

Maybe that's what makes this funky little hangout popular among the 20-something crowd and the occasional dock worker. This is a favorite luncheon spot for the droves of ad agency and Levi's workers who populate the old 'waterfront' buildings in this 'artsy' business area in the shadow of Coit Tower. With that in mind, you'd better make reservations.

It's also a cozy spot for dinner followed by a live band session, as the tiny dance floor is crammed with dancers and lookers-on. There's music every night of the week, but we've found that the best times to go are Saturday nights and Sunday afternoons.

Pier 23 has a pretty steady rotating band schedule. Wednesday nights start the week with the *'ritmo'* of Salsa Caliente; Thursday nights are funky Jazz with saxophonist Jules Broussard; Friday evenings have been hosting a *Cajun* band that, if they continue to play Friday evenings, will knock your socks off; Saturday nights are usually devoted to Reggae with Sister I-Live or Rankin' Scroo and Ginger.

With no real 'stage' to speak of, the bands are right there with you – and they're usually a lot of fun! On reggae nights, we go up and do backup with the *Sista*. It gets pretty hot and sweaty, so out back, with the bay as a backdrop, there's a patio area with rusty tables and chairs here and there under heat lamps (the tables are covered with white linen for lunch and dinner). The crowd is usually small, young, jeans-clad , and out for fun! Down a couple of beers and join in the action.

The key to this place, however, is those warm days when the sun is shining (even when there's fog in the West). That is when it seems that just about everyone heads down to *Pier 23* for a little drinking and grooving.

Sunday afternoons are happening. Jules Broussard returns, but turns up the beat a little. The music starts at 4:00 p.m. (but people arrive early, and there's usually a line by 5:00 p.m.). Guests ride bikes, roller-blade, and stroll over to *Pier 23* by the bay. Everyone's out back, grabbing beers from the outdoor bar, meeting people, and hanging out in the sun.

They're all here. You'll find preppies fraternizing with yuppies, and frat boys chatting-up tweekers (who still haven't gone to bed from Saturday night). Berkeley near-grads top off their weekends with Margharitas, as The City's near-elite discuss the sailboat they want so they can be *on* – rather than *by* the bay.

All move together in a mad-mix of social persuasions, downing refreshing cocktails. Inside, the music is pumping ... and the crowd moves indoors and out like the ebb and flow of waves – drinking and scamming and enjoying the scenery.

"Oh, shit, we've got to work tomorrow ... I'll have another ..."

But the fun, *as they say*, must end. You see, *Pier 23* cuts the music around 8:30 p.m. – and don't forget to tip the band. What would we do without *them* on Sundays – something *healthy* or something?!?

The crowd often moves on to Johnny Love's for Sunday night with DJ Maestro or to Blues on Union Street (or for a walk along the bay ... *or whatever your desires call for).*

90: Savoy Tivoli   Bar

1434 Grant Ave. (at Union). 415-662-7023. North Beach. **HOURS:** Tue-Thur, 5p.m.-2a.m.; Fri-Sun, 3p.m.-2a.m. **RESTRICTIONS:** Cash only.

In an authentically "American" way, *Savoy* rivals many of its Parisian counterparts when it comes to eclectic decor. From the tin-snipped palms, antique corner hutches, neon, varied art, and garage sale knick-knacks, it presents patrons enough visual goodies to keep them interested for years – if that's what they came for!

The indoor/outdoor patio is a favorite weekday spot for romantic couples or small gatherings of friends who enjoy the cool San Francisco evenings while sipping a coffee drink or glass of wine (don't worry, there are heaters for those *cold* San Francisco evenings).

Weekends, on the other hand, are another thing altogether. On Friday and Saturday nights, this most popular North Beach retreat transforms into a human party – often of epic proportions. It's here that east meets west ... and north ... and south ... as the local university crowd mixes with tourists and Euro-transplanted natives into a cornucopia of undulating music, bodies, and come-on lines *("say, didn't I meet you in Paris ...?").*

The weekend clientele reeks of T-shirts, chinos, and baseball caps (worn, appropriately, backward), navigating the multi-room duo-bar space, vying for the attention of 'that cute one over there' while never losing track of their turn on one of the pool tables.

Ever wonder where the ceiling lights went that once graced the center of our living rooms? They're above the "back" bar at *Savoy*. The music is recorded and, it seems, has always featured contemporary top 40. The place is well ventilated (although it's not cool to smoke, you know!) and – especially if you belong to the 20-something crowd – you can really have a good time here.

91: Specs' 12 Adler Museum Café   Neighborhood Bar

12 Saroyan Place (off Columbus Ave.). 415-421-4112. North Beach. **HOURS:** Mon-Fri, 4:30p.m.-2a.m.; Sat-Sun, 5:30p.m.-2a.m. **SPECIALS:** Live Irish Folk Music on Tuesdays at 9p.m. **RESTRICTIONS:** Cash only.

Specs' may be the quintessential neighborhood bar. Hidden away in its own little nook off Columbus Avenue, *Specs'* has survived the neon tourist hoopla as one of, if not *the*, last real retreat for North Beach locals. Outside, *Specs'* severely weathered sign serves as a deliberately obtrusive reminder of its status. With a semi-mournful tone, one bar-fly conceded that "times-are-a-changin'," as every day ushers-in new faces.

Specs' first opened its doors in '68, when sailors lorded over the bar and tables. It's mish-mash decor reflects their times and adventures and, from nautical paraphernalia to African masks, *Specs'* is chock-full of items and stories gathered from all corners of the globe. Remember to look for the Oosik – a Walrus penis, which (peculiarly) happens to be an Eskimo's good luck charm ... and not exactly convenient as part of a key ring. In short, Specs' genuinely eclectic interior and rustic charm mirror San Francisco – with an exclamation point ... !

92: Steps of Rome   Italian Cafe/Restaurant

348 Columbus Ave. (at Grant). 415-397-0435. North Beach. **HOURS:** Mon-Thur, 8:30a.m.-2a.m.; Fri-Sat, 8:30p.m.-3a.m. **SPECIALS:** Live Satellite-link of RAI network during Italian Soccer league season, early Sunday afternoons.

When in Rome ... they say! Well, the same goes for North Beach. Without a doubt, the center of this area's outdoor social merrymaking is at the *Steps of Rome*. And so it is, from that ancient city on the Tiberis river to this freewheeling City by the Bay, the Italian brand of linger and mingle found on the famed Italian Steps is present and alive in this North Beach locale. Enzo, the owner, has created a setting that has become arguably the home-away-from-home for ex-pat Italians.

From the musical sounds of Vasco Rossi and Eros to a live RAI Satellite-link of Italian soccer league, this cafe is an Italian original. Enzo can often be found lounging at one of his street-side cafe tables, chatting away with patrons while constantly waving at friends who walk by or stop-in (which, not surprisingly, happens to be the whole neighborhood). You'll also find a festive, flirtatious Italian staff whose charm and happy smiles more then make up for their scanty use of the English language.

While the interior is quite plain, the ambiance is pleasing and perfect for gathering over a Cappuccino, plate of pasta, or one of a delectable assortment of deserts (go for the Tiramisú). While providing that home-like setting where you can comfortably read the newspaper (Italian available), or duel with a friend over a game of chess, the scene here turns to one of community and festivity as the sun descends on North Beach. It's not uncommon to find an improv sing-along, complete with clapping, banging, and dancing.

Outside, *Steps* offers front-row seating for Columbus Avenue's parade of party rangers, and this is one of The City's most fertile settings for meeting new people. Check out their most popular dish – Ravioli – or one of their grilled focaccia sandwiches.

93: The Saloon   Barbary Coast Saloons

1232 Grant Ave. (at Columbus). 415-989-7666. North Beach. **HOURS:** Daily, noon-2a.m. **ENTRANCE CHARGE:** Fri & Sat, $3.00-5.00 for live music. **SPECIALS:** Live R&B: Mon-Fri 9:30p.m.-1:30a.m.; Sat & Sun 4p.m.-8:30p.m.; and 9:30p.m.-1:30a.m.

With the tenacious grip of an old man to his cane, *The Saloon* has held onto its corner of Grant and Fresno – a corner that once was the center of San Francisco's rowdiest section. First opened in 1861, *The Saloon* is the last of the original Barbary Coast saloons to survive the Earthquake and Fire of 1906. More impressive than that, it has survived San Francisco's fickle storm of 'what's hot and what's not' and, with 135 years under its belt, is the grandest-daddy of all North Beach (and perhaps all San Francisco) social haunts.

Although the historic entrance lacks the squeaky swivel door, the front windows are brightened with Art Nouveau stained glass (which happens to be the only bright thing about the place). Not much has changed since its grand opening (and it seems that not much has been cleaned, either). The rickety wood-plank floor, chipped-out bar, pealing plaster, and smoke stained wall murals conjure-up the image of a proud wrinkled face that still welcomes the occasional sailor. Adding new life, 9:00 p.m. brings a youthful, lively crowed in search for live and loud R&B – which may go a long way to explaining the falling plaster.

94: Tosca's   Bar/Cafe Lounge

242 Columbus Ave. (between Broadway & Pacific). 415-986-9651. North Beach. **HOURS:** Daily, 5p.m.-2a.m. **SPECIALS:** Tosca's Cappuccino, $3.50; White Nun $4.00. **RESTRICTIONS:** Cash only.

Open since 1919, this classic North Beach bar resonates with the sort of ambiance and tradition that breathes of post-19th Century Vienna and Paris – an era when the classical arts of a refined society set the tone of the day. Although *Tosca's* is snugly tucked into its own 'time,' the later half of this century has kept its appeal more down to earth. No more must you don your 'attitude' as you check your coat at the door. Both are now totally optional.

Inside, you stand a good chance of seeing a visiting celebrity imbibing beneath nicotine-stained paintings, a la De Timono, while mingling among the scratchy sounds of opera coming from an authentic Wurlitzer juke-box. The long, 25-stool bar is manned by friendly coat-and-tie bartenders who dispense from two dinosaur-sized Espresso machines dating to the 1920s. These, reputed to be responsible for the first cup of espresso in San Francisco, still perform their steamed magic in preparing the bar's staple drink: the Tosca Cappuccino.

It is reputed that Tosca's notorious concoction was created in the 1920s, as a loop-hole around the whole prohibition thing. With a little Ghirardelli Chocolate, steamed milk, and Brandy, this drink is a Cappuccino gone mad – and is *oh-so-good!*

The interior, with its high ceilings, is airy – and pregnant with a goldish-dim luminescence. Oddly, the interior is almost like two worlds juxtaposed against one another as the historic atmosphere is confronted by 50s-style red diner-style booths, chairs, and tables. Ah, but perhaps that all leads to the appeal of this less-than-pretentious milieu.

Wednesdays through Sundays, after 9:00 p.m., dance tunes spin from the neighboring nightclub, faintly penetrating through the walls, and mix with the Wurlitzer selections. The mix of time-lines is surreal.

95: Vesuvio Cafe   Bar/Cafe

255 Columbus Ave. (between Broadway & Pacific). 415-362-3370. North Beach.
HOURS: Daily, 6a.m.-2a.m.

Is it merely a bar – or is it a shrine? If you're just looking to bend your elbow with a couple of cold brews while wrapped by a rustic interior, you can't find a better place than this celebrated North Beach haunt. But, if you're also looking to relive (or perhaps just taste) the notorious revolution of the beat generation, entering the door at *Vesuvio Cafe* is like walking into a time capsule that sits as an immortalized symbol for the disillusioned youth of the 50s.

You see, it was *Vesuvio Cafe,* across from the venerated City Lights bookstore, that offered the celebrated beatniks a round table for the Camelot of their day. And, while tourists find a hodgepodge of beat memorabilia hanging on the walls, today's artists feel the spirit of Jack Kerouac, Allen Ginsberg, Dylan Thomas, and others hanging in the ethereal air.

So set yourself down among the Kerouacs and Ginsbergs of our day, and gesticulate in poetic verse your tomes of change. Who knows – by the time you're through, maybe you'll create something so pertinent to our time that the persecutors of today (often called the Religious Right) will come to break down your door.

At least you'll have their attention!

PORTRERO HILL

96: Bottom of the Hill   Music Bar

1235 17th St. (between Texas & Missouri). 415-621-4455. Portrero Hill **HOURS:** Mon-Fri, 11a.m.-2a.m.; Sat, 8p.m.-2a.m.; Sun, 3p.m.-10p.m. **ENTRANCE CHARGE:** $3.00 to $10.00, depending on event.

A classic San Francisco Victorian on the outside, *Bottom of the Hill* is a classic dive bar on the inside. This mostly neighborhood bar occasionally features bands that bring in folks from all over The Bay Area.

Original live music is the draw, and the bands are generally local, ranging from alternative to out-and-out bizarre. But from time to time they manage to book just-breaking national-level bands, which sell out this small space in no time. Recently, Alanis Morissette played a sold-out show just as her *Jagged Little Pill* CD was starting to get play on alternative stations. Next time she comes, she'll be playing to a crowd of thousands at one of The City's large, impersonal venues (hey, ya gotta stay on top of things!)

The club is smoky and randomly decorated, with a few tables and a lot of 'moshin' room in front of the stage. The back-room billiards area is ringed with red vinyl couches and a fireplace. Out back, a sheltered two-level beer garden is a great place for after-work cocktails. The crowd is often of the early-20s, long-haired ilk, especially when they feature one of their ' Death-Rock' bands.

They serve food here, too. Lunch is from 11:00 a.m. to 3:00 p.m. daily and, at night, you can order burgers, sandwiches and salads until midnight for an average price of $6.00. The $3.00 all-you-can-eat Sunday barbecue and pasta feed is understandably popular, and starts at 4:00 p.m.

RICHMOND DISTRICT

"O ut in 'the territories'" is how we refer to the areas west of the Haight. And those of us who have perfected our San Francisco snobbery rarely even venture to those 'other parts' of The City (other than to visit the park or go to the beach).

What you'll discover if you care to venture *Under the Fog-Belt*, however, is San Francisco's living room – *replete with throw-pillows and home entertainment centers.*

And where there're people, there's stuff to do – so we've pulled a few offerings that merit venturing "out of The City within The City."

97: Ireland's 32   Live Music Irish Bar

3920 Geary Blvd. (at 3rd). 415-386-6173. Richmond District. **HOURS:** Mon-Fri, noon-2a.m.; Sat-Sun, 10a.m.-2a.m.

In case you who don't know, there are 32 counties in Ireland – *including the six that make-up northern Ireland.*

So you probably get the drift that the subliminal influences that pervade this Richmond District pub support Irish nationalism.

There, we warned you!

And, if you're just looking for a good Irish pub, this is one of the best in The City. Located in an area that was once a center for San Francisco's Irish population, *Ireland's 32* holds to the basic tenets of Irish pubs throughout the world – fun; music; darts; *and Guinness!*

The place is large and airy, with ample space to sit or mill around among your fellow *party-ers.* The sparsely placed barrel-pedestal tables dominate a large open room, and a vaulted ceiling rises above the long bar, producing a feeling that's anything *but* claustrophobic.

Of course, when the place gets crowded, it's another thing altogether. But, you can easily retreat up the stairs where a smaller, very personal room has a pool table

and an area reserved for some serious dart play (what other kind is there?). At the far end of the bar, you can expect to find an old-timer, or two, who's presence speaks volumes about this pub's authenticity – and focus.

As with most *good* Irish pubs, you can tell *Ireland's 32* is well set-up for some healthy elbow-bending. There are counters *everywhere* for you to 'set your pint' – on those occasions when you need your hands to embellish a tall tale, or when a hearty Irish jig gets your feet-a-movin'.

The plentiful melodies that come from the raised corner stage and well-stocked jukebox are what you'd expect from a well established American-Irish pub. Traditional Irish music interspersed with Rock & Roll, Blues, Reggae – *"everything – except rap!"* (*Hmmmm* ... 'Irish rap' – what a concept!) there's never a cover for the live music sets between 9:30 p.m. and 1:00 a.m.

Even among the fun, there's no way to escape the posters, paintings, portraits, and propaganda that support the Irish nationalist cause. The *entire bar* is a political statement! Portraits of poets share wall space with political activists, and writers appear shoulder-to-shoulder with martyrs.

A quick look will discover the familiar faces of James Joyce, Oscar Wilde, and Samuel Becket. More in-depth research will show you the likenesses of such 'freedom fighters' as Wolf Tone, Daniel O'Connel, and Sean McBride (author of the McBride Principals – to discourage doing business with Irish companies that discriminate against Irish Catholics). Then there are the posters of the 1981 hunger strikers ....

If you want the whole scoop on 'the Irish thing,' ask the owner, Brendan, who will probably be behind the bar. Otherwise, get yourself a pint of Guinness ($3.50), order up some 'Pub Grub' (e.g., Shepherds Pie or Irish Stew ($5.50)), and get ready for a good time.

Pasport: Two for one beer.

98: Orocco East-West Supper Club   Supper Club

3565 Geary Blvd. (between Arguello & Stanyan). 415-387-8788. Richmond District. **HOURS:** Sun-Thur, 6p.m.-2a.m. (bar food 'til 11 p.m.); Fri-Sat, 6p.m.-2a.m. (bar food 'til Midnight). **ENTRANCE CHARGE:** Reasonable entry on Fri & Sat.

Residing here, smack-dab in the center of The City, without the benefit of a fancy sign, lies San Francisco's classiest club. *Orocco*, an 'east meets west' club, is a recent renovation – and what a renovation it is!

Encumbered by nothing but visual sweeps, the space exudes an air of peaceful chaos (perhaps that's the East - West thing!). Having ripped out a good portion of the upper floor, *Orocco* presents its patrons an open-air space accented with Eastern-style accouterments of elegant simplicity.

If you had wings, from the curved upper balcony (where you can watch the goings on below), you'd fly past large Japanese-style lamps as you swoop down to the comfortable lounge. There, you'd find a welcoming curved, majestically ornate bar, set within a *human* space where you can circulate freely among the other patrons ... or sit comfortably on one of the plush chairs.

Orocco presents "a relaxed, elegant dining experience," and the powers that be want you to "have fun while you eat." (and drink, we suppose!) Your musical evening begins with a piano player, who gives way to a Jazz ensembles around eight. Occupying a unique, elevated stage/dance floor, the live music then gives way to an ethereal mixture of DJ-spun progressive vibe around midnight. Unlike many other clubs or nightly venues, the energy is consistent, as state-of-the-art sound cycles you to move ... or just groove.

Orocco, which features an affordable menu of East-West delights "with a French influence," has alighted upon San Francisco like manna from Heaven. In other words, it's about time The City presented to its residents and guests a world-class dinner-and-dance club akin to those in Barcelona, San Tropez, Tokyo, and New York.

For you drinkers, the Orocco has an impressively full bar with over 250 different varieties of *spirits* (and growing). They're also welcoming you with reasonable pricing for drinks, their selection of 30+ beers, and a wine cellar which will soon offer over 100 types of wines. Check out their Martini glasses, they're very cool.

As far its aesthetic appointments, this is *The Best* club in San Francisco. No, it's not South of Market, nor is it downtown, in the Marina, or on Russian Hill – but maybe that's a blessing! Its location out of San Francisco's established entertainment loops may actually keep the riff-raff away.

All things aside – if you're looking for, well ... everything we described above ... here's our tip: *Orocco* is definitely worth a trip.

Pasport: 20% off dinner (food portion only) Sunday thru Thursday.

99: Pat O'Shea's Mad Hatter   Pub/Sports Bar

3848 Geary Blvd. (at 3rd). 415-752-3148. Richmond District. **HOURS:** Daily (365 days/yr.), Sun-Thur, 11a.m.-2a.m.; Fri-Sat, 9a.m.-2a.m.

Paddy O's is one of the last 'damn-good Irish pubs' in what used to be San Francisco's old Irish neighborhood. The motto on the green awning out front reads, "We cheat tourists and drunks." It's obnoxious, but who cares!?! Back in the olden days, wooden boards covered the windows so passers-by couldn't see the rowdiness inside – and so wives couldn't see the mischief their husbands were getting into. In those days, drunks would turn into mad-hatters, get up on the bar, take off their clothes, and shake their wankers around. Pete, the bartender (and now co-owner), could tell you stories that would make you laugh for days, but "That was before lawyers," he says.

Now they're worried about someone suing someone else. It's still a great pub, though, serving up more than five beers and ciders on tap ... and really good fare too. Nancy Oaks (renowned in the cooking world) founded the kitchen in the mid-80s. Tony, Nancy's right-hand man, delivers good hearty food in big portions. Along with rib-eye and roasted leg-of-lamb, you'll enjoy the traditional corned beef and cabbage on Thursday nights.

On weekends, live bands come out around 9:00 p.m on the tiny stage in back. College kids convene then to drink and smoke, and to talk over the R&B and Funk bands booked by Dave, another bartender. The crowd is really a 'mixed bag,' because the Richmond district is no longer the old Irish neighborhood. Now, it's a concentrated area of blue collar workers, policemen, political celebs, and college students from the University San Francisco. You can join softball teams celebrating a victory, or dart teams one night and pool tournaments the next. The real Pat O'Shea died last year, but the Irish cheer lives on.

Pasport: Two for one on domestic beer, microbrew or well drink cocktails.

100: Tommy's Mexican Restaurant   Mexican Cantina

5929 Geary Blvd. (at 23rd). 415-387-4747. Richmond District. **HOURS:** Sun-Thur, 11a.m.-11p.m.; Fri-Sat, 11a.m.-Midnight. **RESTRICTIONS:** Cash only.

Located in The Avenues, *Tommy's* is a legend among the locals. We first found out about the place from a bartender at a SoMa restaurant. You see, Tommy has been The City's authority on tequila since 1965. And, since that time, he (and now his son Julio) continue to promote the education of tequila to all their customers. Julio, in fact, was interviewed by GQ Magazine in December 94, saying tequila was making a comeback (ya didn't have to tell *us* that!).

Dark and light-blue Mexican tiles adorn the storefront, and all you can see through the windows are big bowls of tortilla chips under an "OPEN" neon sign. Venture in, sit at the bar, and Julio will serve up "the best Margarita in The City." They say this claim is valid because they use only 100 percent agave non-aged tequila (not Cuervo Gold, which only contains a percentage) and fresh lime juice (one of the few places this side of the border to use fresh, hand-squeezed limes). Julio will test-taste each Margarita to make sure it's good and strong. "We don't know 'snow-cone' Margaritas, like they have at Chevy's," he says.

Here's the spiel:

Tequila is Mexico's only origin spirit, and is now produced exclusively in the Mexican state of Jalisco, (It's like, in order to call champagne *champagne*, it must come from the Champagne region in France.) Tequila is distilled from the blue agave plant, a member of the lily family – it's not a cactus as commonly thought. After about 10 years, mature blue-agave 'flowers,' weighing up to 70 kg, are baked, crushed, fermented, and double distilled to produce a fine tequila. This is what gives it that distinctive taste – a taste some of you have vowed never to drink again. But good tequila can be very smooth, and *Tommy's* only serves premium tequilas.

And, for $5.00, you can join *Tommy's* Blue Agave Club. You'll receive a card, and each time you try a new tequila you'll get your card stamped. The goal is to taste all 30 tequilas, and become a certified tequila master – complete with certificate and T-shirt ... promising to educate others about tequila ... and *don't be afraid to eat the worm!*

101: Trad'r Sam's   Cocktail Bar

6150 Geary St. (at 26th). 415-221-0773. Richmond District. **HOURS:** Daily, 10a.m.-2a.m.

This dive bar is across the street from Tommy's, and very popular among local, young hipsters – and two barflies who seem to have been *glued* to the same corner of the bar since it opened in 1939. You'll enter through a half door (like all *good* seedy bars have) into a small bar setting with a tropical theme that died a long time ago. But it' s the dragged out tackiness, which once may have made this place chic, that makes it so *cool* now. It looks kinda how we picture the Costanzas (on *Seinfeld*) designed their living room.

Worn bamboo furniture is divided into little cabanas, each bearing the name of a tropical place (e.g., Maui, Hilo, Tahiti, etc.). Couples like to come in and choose which 'hut' to sit in. Old Christmas lights hang droopily around the room, juxtaposed against a jukebox that bangs out tunes from Van Morrison, Pulp Fiction, and the best of Blondie.

Dorothy's father bought the place in '78, and she bartends almost every night of the week, serving up big fru-fru drinks with enough alcohol to knock you're socks off. We're not lightweights by any means, but we swear that only two Zombies had us pantomiming the *Night of the Living Dead*.

Trad'r Sam's is home of the "Banana Cow" (rum, banana, vodka, and half 'n' half). Dorothy also claims that they were the first introduce the Mai Tai – way before Trad'r Vic's ever thought of it. The original owner, Sam Bailey, who opened the place in '39, still insists that Trad'r Vic's stole his idea for the theme, the drink recipes – *everything* – and then took the credit. So *Trad'r Sam's* remains an obscure *Avenues* haunt reserved for the special few who appreciate it.

Dorothy showed usa picture before we stumbled out. It was signed, "To Trad'r Sam's, Thanks for everything. John Oates."

Let's Party! Favorites
Parks

- Delores Glen
- G G Park Arboratum
- G G Park Dutch Windmill
- G G Park Japanese Tea Garden
- G G Park Rose Garden
- G G Park Polo Fields
- G G Park Rhodedendron Dell
- G G Park Stow Lake
- G G Park Strawberry Hill
- Hippie Hill
- Lincoln Park
- Marina Green
- Ocean Beach
- Presidio
- Sutro Park
- Tank Park
- Washington Square

Let's Party! Favorites
Bike Route

- Golden Gate Park
- Lands Ends
- Marin Headlands
- Marina to Sausalito
- Mount Tamalpais
- Over the Golden Gate Bridge
- Tiberon

Let's Party! Favorites
Hiking Route

- Golden Gate Park (really!)
- Lands End
- Marin Headlands
- Muir Woods
- Up Mount Tamalpais

Let's Party! Favorites
Beach

- Baker's Beach
- China Beach
- Fort Funston
- Lands End
- Sloat Beach
- Stinson Beach

Let's Party! Favorites
Local Bands

- Bill Nayer Show
- Box Set
- Cheeseballs
- Common Sense
- Groovetone
- Fundamentals
- Hot Club of SF
- Jungle Biscuit
- Los Angelitos
- Mother Hips
- Papa's Culture
- Pride & Joy
- Pure Ecstacy
- Undercover SKA
- Slide Five
- The Philbillies
- Ya Ya Littleman

Let's Party! Favorites
Bar Signs

- 330 Ritch
- Blue Light
- Gino & Carlo's
- Hi Ball
- Holy Cow
- Horse Shoe
- Julie's Supper Club
- "open"
- Paragon
- The Red Room
- Savoy Tivoli
- Tommy's
- Vesuvio Cafe

Let's Party! Favorites
Irish Coffee

- Blackthorn Tavern
- Buena Vista
- Little Shamrock

Let's Party! Favorites
Margarita

- Andalé Restaurant
- Baja Cantina
- Balboa Café
- Cadillac Bar & Grill
- Chevy's Mexican Restaurant
- Julie's Supper Club
- Mission
- Tommy's Mexican Restaurant

Let's Party! Favorites
Martini

- Bix
- Blue Light
- Bruno's
- Cafe Le Central
- Eric's (Vodka)
- Garibaldi's
- HiBall
- Icon Cafe
- Occidental Grill
- Orocco
- Persian Zam Zam (if you don't get thrown out before you order)

Let's Party! Favorites
City View Point

- Coit Tower
- Marin Headlands
- Mount Tamalpais
- Portrero Hill
- Tank Park
- Twin Peaks

Let's Party! Favorites
Movie Theater

- Castro
- Century Plaza 8
- Chestnut St.
- Coronet
- Galaxy
- Presidio
- Red Vic
- Union St.

RUSSIAN GULCH

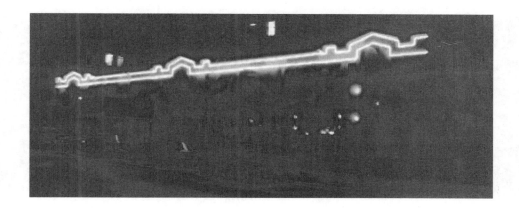

Mimicking Van Ness Avenue – San Francisco's main north/south bisect – Polk Street provides the commercial hub for the neighborhoods of lower Russian Hill and Polk Gulch – *hence our title,* Russian Gulch.

Stretching from the Civic Center in the south to Aquatic Park on The Bay, our hybrid name represents the almost-continuous stretch of shops, restaurants, and bars that line Polk Street and Van Ness Avenue.

Nothing much to speak of – just your typical San Francisco community hub. But, we've culled a few choice delicacies for your enjoyment.

103: Babylon   Bar/Dance Club

2260 Van Ness Ave. (at Vallejo). 415-567-1222. Russian Hill. **HOURS:** Daily, 7p.m.-2a.m. **ENTRANCE CHARGE:** $5.00-$10.00 per person.

Hoping to relive your wild *Let's Party! Europe* experience, but can't quite get all the way to the Continent just yet? No problem. Practice your foreign language pickup lines, and head on down to this trendy Euro-crowd hangout. Inside, broad Roman arches and faux marble walls provide the background for this upscale, yet casual club.

The percentage of international patrons in chic Italian attire is uncanny. Host Tony Kutulas has done a brilliant job of creating the ambiance of Mediterranean nightclub in the middle of San Francisco. Patrons tend to fall into the 21 to 35 year old age group.

High-energy dance tunes are the musical fare on Friday and Saturday nights. DJs spin Top 40 and techno, often playing rare mixes – always with a European edge. Other nights, the music varies, so call for details. Cover ranges from $5.00 to $8.00.

Exhibitionists will enjoy showing off their stuff on the small, upstairs dance floor, from which they can see and be seen by the entire club. Exterior neon accents give

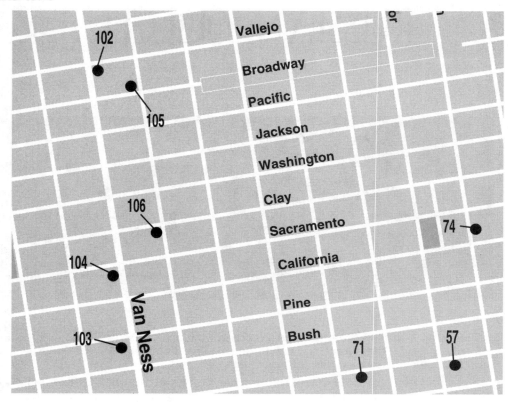

Map showing locations: Vallejo, Broadway, Pacific, Jackson, Washington, Clay, Sacramento, California, Pine, Bush streets crossing Van Ness. Marked points: 102, 105, 106, 104, 103, 74, 71, 57.

a rosy glow to the street scene, which patrons can take in through the huge plate glass windows that make up one side of the club.

Babylon's limited bar menu fits on a four-by-six card, yet is surprisingly broad. Beyond burgers and pizza, they offer chicken satay in peanut sauce ($4.50), fettucine primavera ($6.75), and sautéed chicken marsala ($8.75). Food can be ordered from 7:00 p.m. until closing.

To get a table, it's a very good idea to call for a reservation.

102: Coconut Grove Supper Club   Supper Club/Swing & Jazz Bar

1415 Van Ness Ave. (at Pine). 415-776-1616. Polk Gulch. **HOURS:** Daily, 5 p.m.-2a.m. **ENTRANCE CHARGE:** $12.00-$25.00 depending on performance.

Coconut Grove is a 40s style supper club – the kind of c l a s s y joint you'd see Chili Palmer drive up to in a pink-caddy convertible in decadent Miami. You, too, can step out in style in San Francisco, but be sure to get dolled up. Valet parking at the door. A cabana draped in velvet curtains serves as the lobby. Your host is called a "concierge."

Turning one way, you enter the dining room; the other way, the bar. Inside, the ambiance is soothing, yet dramatic. The dining area is enhanced with theater-quality lighting. The *bronzed* tables are set amidst a sea of alabaster palm trees with lights serving as the coconuts. Front-and-center is an elevated stage showered in colored lights. Picture this: Close your eyes and imagine a huge oyster shell opening up to reveal a sultry singer crooning into one of those huge 40s-era mikes. Your

emcee, Ricky Ricardo (of course). Zoot suits and fancy dresses, powdered noses and classic hairdo's, waiters dressed to the nines in white bow-tied tuxes.

Coconut Grove features such big name artists as Tito Puente, Harry Connick, Jr. – *and even ol' blue eyes himself.* They also book several local favorites, including the Bob Dalpe trio in full Dick Tracy regalia, ready to do bust out the Swing *(schwi-i-in-n-ng!).* Other favorites are Big Bang Beat, and Lavay Smith and the Red Hot Skillet Lickers. There's a $12 show charge when you sit at a table (the cover is higher, and tables more in demand, if a headliner is featured). This is a great *date* place. Oh, by the way, it's *free* to sit at the magnificent, beautiful, copper-topped bar.

You'll definitely have the urge to order a Remy Martin, Manhattan, or other *gentlemanly* drink that'll bring you back 50 years to when it really *was* the good life. The bartender approaches you with a *dee-e-e-p* inviting voice, "How are you doing? ... howsa-bout a Martini? I make an e x c e l l e n t Martini..." (and he does!). It's served very dry, with two gigantic olives. One guest walks in commenting under his breath, *"Isn't it neat?"*

Whether you're in the mood for Motown, Salsa or the Big Band sound, head uptown to the *Coconut Grove* and swing the night away.

Passport: A complimentary show for two. Sunday thru Thursday (National Headliner excluded). Reservations required.

104: Hard Rock Cafe   Restaurant

1699 Van Ness Ave. (at Sacramento). 415-885-1699. Pacific Heights. **HOURS:** Sun-Thur, 11a.m.-11:30p.m.; Fri-Sat, 11a.m.-Midnight.

The original *Hard Rock Cafe* (HRC) was founded on Old Park Lane in London in 1971 by two young Americans who were yearning for good old American cooking. They set out to give London the best down-home American food – at reasonable prices *(shyeah right,* that's what the *brochure* says; we think it's overpriced ... but you do get good-sized portions).

Seasoned with healthy dose of Rock n' Roll. The two young men have parted their ways, but since that first restaurant, Hard Rock Cafes have spread all over the world – including Tel Aviv. By the way, last we heard the Hard Rock on Meinekestraße in Berlin has closed.

Okay, here it is if you're one of those die-harders who 'just-must' get the Hard Rock San Francisco T-shirt (at $15.50 a pop). 'Our' *Hard Rock* is on Van Ness Avenue right off the California cable car line (and easily accessible for tourists). It was built way back in 1984, so it's not as fancy-shmancy as, say, the one in Orlando.

A plastic cow and thousands of a camera-toting tourists mark the entrance to HRC. Upon entering, just overhead is a '67 candy-apple-red Cadillac convertible stuck into the wall – a signature, recalling classic 'decadent Americana,' of all HRC's. Just ahead, in the center of the main room, is a large rectangular bar that's buzzing most every night of the week.

Just to the left, a new addition holds a glass-encased, sequin-studded outfit Madonna wore on her Erotica tour (and a small TV screen that runs a live concert video of Madonna doing her stuff with her dance slaves. HRC boasts the largest collection of rock memorabilia in the world.

When you think of San Francisco's music scene, you think of the late, great, Jerry Garcia (may he *rock* in Heaven). And, look for the "All is one" Haight/Ashbury wall ... including an original poster by Alton Kelly saved from the Fillmore Auditorium fire in 1967. We all have our memories from that era, and the San Francisco HRC is worth a stop-by visit. Every once in a while you may even catch a celeb or two (between your beer, or two).

105: Johnny Love's   Dance Bar/Restaurant

1500 Polk St. (at Broadway). 415-931-6053. Russian Hill. **HOURS:** Daily, 5 p.m.-2a.m.
ENTRANCE CHARGE: Varies depending on night & event.

Ask anyone in The City, and they'll tell you they're friends of Johnny Love (aka Johnny Methany). We don't know if it's *love* you're looking for, but you'll sure find plenty of action (guaranteed-to-get-laid-condoms-sold-in-the-bathroom) – just ask the girls who come to dance on the bar (including one from the *Let's Party!* staff).

If you're a *guy* who wants to dance on the bar, you're out of luck. So pound some shots, grab a girl, and proceed to the dance floor for a little bump and grind. It's a 'happening' every night of the week, featuring live bands six nights, and DJ Maestro on Sundays (which is actually really a great night to go).

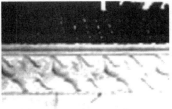

The bands play that funky disco that even white boys can dance to and, on any given night, you're more than likely going to hear the song "she's a Brick ... House." The cover is usually only $3.00 to $5.00, but Johnny really makes his killing on the drinks. He's been a bartender in The City for years, and just recently published his own book on cocktail recipes (the down-and-dirtier the better). He's there just about every night, doing the Tom-Cruise-pouring-and-dancing routine" – and kissing the chicks. Johnny is definitely a *faux-celeb*. Come on down, and prepare to get loaded ... it's inevitable!

February's 'shot of the month' featured Warm Creamy Bush for $3.00, but a round of 'Jaegers' does the trick for us just fine. The friendly bar staff (scammers) will usually do a shooter along with you – which just adds to the drunken fun.

Girls – watch out for the credit-card-clickers (you know the guys ... the kind that slam their credit cards down on the bar when they want to order a drink). Either they really do have money ... *or they're just waiting for the 'prey' of the evening.* Guys – don't just hang around the bar gawking (does the word 'l-o-o-s-e-r' mean anything to you?) ... dance and get busy!

This place is really 'cheesy,' but can be a lot of fun. The clientele 'is' mixed. Tourists from Europe and beyond come to groove with the locals. Pictures of Johnny with all kinds of celebs cover the walls, and on any given night you might just bump into Michael Jordan or Jake and Sydney of Melrose Place. Dress is anything from jeans and a T-shirt to slut-wear and, on weekends, the crowd turns more toward the local-tourist bridge-and-tunnel (imports from the burbs) variety, a little more dressed-to-impress.

Look for us *Let's Party!-ers* whenever the *Cheeseballs* are playing.

106: Julie Ring's Heart and Soul   Supper Club

1695 Polk St. (at Clay). 415-673-7100. Russian Hill. **HOURS:** Daily, 5p.m.-2a.m.
ENTRANCE CHARGE: Mon-Sat, $4.00-$8.00 no cover Sunday.

40s-style supper clubs seem to what San Franciscans are looking for these days. Perhaps we're looking for blast to the past ... elegant decor ... haute cuisine ... classic drinks ... and some Jazz-turned-funky to make us feel comfortable in this ever-changing world.. With the success of Julie's Supper Club on 7th & Folsom, Julie Ring sought new horizons, giving heart and soul when creating her Polk Street dinner club (just below Pacific Heights).

It's obvious that this club aimed at the 30- to 40-something crowd ... people more Julie's age. And it's absolutely gorgeous. Julie has mixed art with restau-rateur-*ing*, and what you have is an elegant, romantic little bevy of nooks that swoon you into another era.

Julie named her new club as a tribute to her grandmother, who died recently, and granny has her place, there, in a black and white photograph by the entrance. Her grandmother was a feisty one, Julie says. She traveled the world, and partied in an age when women just didn't do those things *(... go Grandma!)*. Her strong spirit lives on in *Heart & Soul*.

"Only those who lack imagination cannot find a good reason for drinking champagne," Oscar Wilde once said (and who could disagree). *Heart & Soul* offers 'really good' Perrier French champagne that's a bit pricey at $8.50 a glass. Bring a date, and ask him to get the Perrier Jouet Flower Bottle Rose at $95 a bottle (c'mon, don't be cheap!).

The silver menu card offers an enticing array of drink classics. Think of someone cool and suave like Humphrey Bogart. He walks in, and orders a Polk & Clay Side Car, *superbly sip-able*, Martell cognac, shaken with orange-flavored triple sec and lemon juice, served in a chilled glass with a twist. What would Rita Moreno go for? Probably a Julie's Hot Mary, red-hot, made with Absolut Peppar and Julies Spicy Mary Mix, complete with a spear of fresh cucumber.

What next, Maestro? Some very talented local trios and quartets provide excellent musical ambiance that rounds off the sensual elements. Then, on to supper and a nightcap in a magical surrounding of art deco sconces and sculptures, candlelight, and the man across from you. No party could go wrong with Julie as the host.

Passport: Two for one entry (not valid during special events-call to verify).

SOMA

W hile many of San Francisco's neighborhoods have their own character, none stand apart as much as the South of Market area ... *commonly known as SoMa.*

Slicing diagonally through The City, **Market Street** is San Francisco's main thoroughfare. It's also the demarcation line between SoMa – and *the rest* of San Francisco. In relation to other San Francisco neighborhoods, SoMa, with its flat-industrial-warehouse setting, could be considered an eyesore. But *So What!* More importantly, the mere mention of its name should conjure images of night life (and the long club lines that *come-with*). That's right, SoMa is The City's nocturnal playground. *So much so,* that we took the liberty of changing the acronym from standing for South of Market to meaning *Sweet Mama, this place is happening!* (but we'll get to that shortly).

Unlike most San Francisco neighborhoods, SoMa's infant beginnings were far from humble. In fact, owning an address in SoMa's Rincon Hill or South Park areas was once boasting material. Like most of The City's early neighborhoods, the destructive effects of the 1906 Earthquake and Fire were total. Along with the Financial District, SoMa was devastated. Hammered beyond recognition, it's fling with wealth and affluence ended in a matter of shaky minutes.

During the rebuilding years – making use of the extensive network of Cable Cars – the center of wealth shifted to the higher grounds of Pacific Heights and Nob Hill. But, while their mansions had burned to a crisp, many of SoMa's wealthy landowners added to their treasure chests by turning the land they once lived on into ship-yards, rail yards, warehouses, and factories. In a flash, the area south of Market Street had gone from a posh, residential neighborhood to an industrial park.

SOMA
Intro

L ater in the century – about the time the swinging 70's swung in – San Francisco's industrial base had declined to a handful of small businesses. Property was cheaper then ever (and ripe for the picking!).

Among the first to pick was a steady influx of gay businesses, restaurants, bars, clubs, and bathhouses. At the height of SoMa's gay scene, more than 30 gay social haunts operated. But that did not last. With the 80's, AIDS grabbed the spotlight, and the gay scene mellowed and side stepped over to the Castro district.

SoMa's renaissance continued, however, and the spark lit in the 70's led to a cultural explosion of fashion and style (not to mention an onslaught of marauding youth). Old warehouses were transformed into lofts, art studious, galleries, and shops. Suddenly, SoMa's image went from an ugly industrial neighborhood, to an ugly, *yet fashionable* scene – and here is where the deception lies. By day, between **Folsom and Townsend Streets**, you'll still find rows and rows of large squat build-

ings sheltering printers and auto repair shops, warehouses and clothing outlets. By night, however, a sleeping giant comes to life, as Soma is invaded by an attack-force of night owls and alley cats, who join in a safari hunt for The City's premiere bars and clubs.

R isking mind and body, the *Let's Party!* staff set out on a SoMa safari, hunting down *the best of the best.* On our quest, we discovered a few peculiarities:

- While planet-bohemia can be found in the micro galaxies of the Mission and Lower Haight ... and the yuppie-fied singles set of the Marina share a cocktail of flirtations ... the nocturnal playgrounds of SoMa undulate with The City's premier mix of mad revelers.

- From the see-and-be-seen crowd; the strait to the slanted; fashion gurus to fashion misfits; the lookers and the shakers; the techno-tripper tweekers; the ravers, funksters, fools and flippsters, the whole gang is here.

- We believe, in fact, that if three-eyed purple Martians were to touch down in SoMa, chances are it would go unnoticed. You'll find, actually, that many SoMa residents are of the honest opinion that this happens all the time.

- *Yes-sir-ee-Bob,* you'll find someone or something for everyone and everything in SoMa!

S oMa is where discriminating tastes and uninhibited eccentricity are flip sides of the same coin. From bondage clubs catering to the hand-cuffed and leather-clad; limousine drawn patrons paying an upscale restaurant tab; dive bars with graffiti jammed walls; piano bars with lounge-lizards in the stalls; to everything in-between ...

And then, in a class all its own, there's the club-scene *scene!*

Ahhh, and what *about* that scene? Precocious, restless, and fickle – all characterize SoMa's multi-stimulating temples of dance. San Francisco is world renowned for its 'sound,' and throughout The City (but primarily South of Market) you'll find some of the best House, Acid Jazz, Hip Hop, Techno, Trance, Dub, and some of the most *Wicked* Metabolic Mix you'll find anywhere.

Ranking high when compared to the best clubs of London and New York, San Francisco's club scene offers a wild web of action for you to navigate through – oh, but what web has no spiders? Adding to a setting that can be very confusing to the uninitiated, you'll find weekly theme nights that are alive and blasting one week, and extinct as a dinosaur the next. If there is any rhyme or reason to be found ... *uh ... um ...* on second thought, don't even try!

Due to fierce competition, promoters find SoMa's large selection of dance offerings a battle ground where they wage a leaflet war as they vie for notoriety. Although most promoters have the life cycle of a mosquito, a few have become established ... practically reaching a cult-of-personality status. There are three good ways to reach the nightly 'Know-Zone':

- The first is to visit our site on the World Wide Web. (http://EntertainNET.com), There you will find our take on what's happening.

- Another is to frequent bars and clubs where promoters have people handing out colorful, card-sized leaflets outlining themes, featured DJs, hours, and entrance charges, etc.

- The next-to-last is to call a promoter's hot line – many of which are printed in the back of this book.

- Last – and certainly not least – for the most up-to-date happenings in the SF scenes, head to **Behind the Post Office**, located 1510 Haight (at Ashbury), 415-861-2507. (Tell 'em we sent you.)

A kin to concocting a magic potion, promoters craftily mix their ingredients. They start by finding that perfect venue – usually a warehouse-sized, often-multi-leveled building. They then call onboard a team of spin doctors who 'practice' their unique brand of music and vibe. Thrown into the potion a visual attack of light, a few dancers and, for good measure, a chill room, and you've got the formula for an all-night groove. Some have a VIP, or 'vip' room where, if you gain access, you'll find a second room that can sometimes lead to a third ... or even a forth. Earning your way though this succession of thresholds is based, surprisingly, more on attitude than looks (but having 'the look' doesn't hurt!).

If you're going to pay any type of homage to this neighborhood's formidable selection of cafes, bars, live music venues, clubs, after hours clubs, and after-after hours clubs, you'd better charge your batteries. Because this Magical SoMa Tour begins in the morning, and ends 24 hours later, *only the strong survive!* "If, Jim, you choose to accept this mission ..."

Expect your body to take a flying leap in 10 different directions as it clatters, collapses, and crashes under the morning sun of the day after. But fear not, brave warrior, after you pass the finish line and end up at the **End Up**, you can take comfort in the fact that you're among the few who have survived this area's marauding adventure.

So here's the low-down on where to get-down. Because SoMa hot spots are scattered like freckles on the bosom of an Irish Lass, you'll need to take care of three things:

- Make sure you have comfortable, *yet fashionable* shoes
- Eat a good breakfast
- Make certain you know how to hail a cab.

Okay, the shoe thing is covered, and you're ready for the morning tank-up. Trot on over to South Park – smack, dab in the heart of SoMa's Outlet hub. This hidden little 'nook of a park' is a rare leftover from those prominent days when the area

paraded a landscape of stately abodes. Around the oval-shaped park you'll find a few cafes offering a hearty breakfast and decent coffee ... so what more can you ask?

Ha, but there's more! It may not be Golden Gate Park, but in this city of scarcely found greenery, this smallish park gives you a rare inter-city glimpse of what grass looks like. While not the type of pastoral view that would make a Parisian painter's brush do an Impressionist jig, a mornings repast at the **South Park Cafe** is where you can taste the French flavor of a neighborly bistro amid the smell fresh baked baguettes and croissants.

If your morning appetite demands more then croissants, walk over to **Caffe Centro**. With its stylish decor and gourmet breakfasts, complete with gourmet prices, you can turn your morning pit-stop into an event.

Now, if you're the type who feels 'all play and no work' will weigh too heavily on your conscience – and doing the laundry is no longer avoidable – then get it over with ... *but have a good time while your doing it!* Lug your load to the **Brain Wash,** on **Folsom,** where you can let the cycle spin itself dizzy as you relax in a cafe setting.

And wait for the day to pass ...

As the sun begins its descent, SoMa comes to life with total disregard for the calendar. As you'll discover, there is a full-moon every night here! So, before you enter the happy-happy-joy-joy realm of madness, we recommend another nutritious meal at one of the area's many bar/restaurants or supper clubs.

Starting from the waterfront, on the Embarcadaro and just a hop, skip, and a jump from the **Palomino**, sits **Gorden Biersch.** Renowned for its in-house-brewed beer, upstairs (away from the rollicking crowd), a more sedate setting awaits where you can enjoying the tastes of California cuisine (we kinda like the mushroom pizza, but if you want to torture everyone you encounter the rest of the evening, go for the garlic fries).

Between **First and Second Streets on Natoma,** is the **Caribbean Zone** – with a touch of bizarre irony, because airline food has never been this good! But this is not an airline. It is, however, a DC-3 gooney-bird. Inside the restaurant (and inside the fuselage) you can fill-up on a menu that features ... you guessed it ... Caribbean cuisine. With video monitors in place of windows, *and a busy bar,* this locale falls into our must-see category.

Whenever there's an occasion to enter the Mexican 'Popper-Zone' – especially on May 5th – the **Cadillac Bar** brings Mexican country cooking to SoMa. You shouldn't expect burritos, but it's a mad scene where the Mexican staff keeps you awake with the sounds of shot glasses hitting the table. **Sch-a-mack!** If you're looking for simplicity in food choices, with an ear for music an adventure, to the **Hotel Utah** won't disappoint you. You could say this saloon has seen better times, which is true – it does … several nights a week!

Those looking for Jazz should step into the 'down' of the **Up and Down Club** for a super model-approved feast, accompanied by merriment and melody.

If you're looking to hop on the trendy-train of supper clubs, you can catch it at station **333 Ritch Street**, where after dining on a selection of Tapas goodies, you can take a journey into a wave of moving bodies and rhythmic beats on the dance floor. For a more retro setting, check out a *Let's Party!* favorite, **Julies Super Club**. With its 50's-deco decor, get-down live music, and a catfish dish that's out of this world, you're on the set of the Jetsons meets Doby Gillis in this long standing SoMa Locale.

Moving squarely into the future, sample the fare at the **Icon Byte Bar & Grill** (before you're stuck eating pills that suffice for a meal). And, for a bounty that's out of this world, take a rocket ship ride to **Mars Bar**, where you'll find down-home cookin' – the kind you just can't find here on Earth.

If you want to turn it up a couple notches, enter SoMa's whirlpool of unadulterated wackiness found in, on, and all around **11th and Folsom**. Offering a door-to-door, corner-to-corner roll-call of watering holes, cat-walk clubs, and live music joints, 11th – starting Friday night – takes on the look of a block party that doesn't stop till Sunday morning.

Within all the hubbub, check out **Eleven**, an Italian supper club with live musical jive, simplistic elegance, and beautiful sophistication. It's so 'lofty' we wonder how it manages to keep its feet on the ground and remain casual. And, for that Mexican fast-feast, head across the border to **Wa Ha Ka**, where the Sangria flows freely.

If a watering hole of beer-orgy status is your desire, check out **Twenty Tank** – described by the *Bay Guardian* as the best brewpub this side of Munich (try saying that to a München monk). **Holy Cow** … another watering hole, *oh-my oh-my will our kidneys never rest?* Relying on an override shutdown before a full-systems failure, we pushed on into this veteran haunt to find a come-happy come-lucky crowd, where the mix mingles it up.

Okay, you've baptized your buds at the **Holy Cow**, so just around the corner awaits paradise – the **Paradise Lounge**. Could this be the meaning of life? *Naaa …* too easy! The may not offer salvation, but this multi-level, multi-media venue does feature multi-bands, on multi stages, with multi bars, and pool tables. *Have fun getting lost!*

If you're looking for bigger names – or soon to be 'bigger names' – check out **Slims**, San Francisco's live-music Mecca. Topping out this scene, the **DNA Lounge** is where you can bend more parts of you body (other than your elbow) to the varying sounds of House, Funk, Soul or Reggae.

With no time-out in sight, it's Midnight, and you're halfway there. Whatever it takes, reincarnate yourself if that's what's necessary – *because the night has just begun!* So, don't miss hopping on San Francisco's fast and slippery club train, and get on down the tracks. Theme-night parties prevail over SoMa's club culture, and we've provided a list in the back of the book to help you find them. You'll also find a more detailed descriptions below.

107: 330 Ritch St.   Jazz Supper Club

330 Ritch St. (between Brannan & Townsend). 415-541-9574. SOMA. **HOURS:** Mon-Thur & Sat, 8p.m.-2a.m.; Fri, 5p.m.-2a.m. **ENTRANCE CHARGE:** Varies depending on night & performance. **SPECIALS:** Free Salsa dance lessons on Tuesdays from 8p.m.-9p.m.

Located on historic Ritch Alley, *330 Ritch* is one of San Francisco's new *'hot'* spots – mainly for its versatility and innovativeness.

"Ritch" Street was the first paved street in the south of Market area, and old railroad tracks still run through the building.

The building than is now *300 Ritch* also once functioned as a gay bathhouse. Only the marble slatted door remains. The interior is beautifully restored ... a brick wall lining one side of the club, and low hanging silver/blue lights, stainless steel tables, and red lacquered chairs give the place a modern feel.

A new billiard room located in back has several new tables (hey, for you pool sharks out there, *free pool* before 10:00 p.m.). Bands formerly played in the middle of the dance floor but, since the club became popular, the stage area has been moved to the side wall to make way for Disco, Salsa, or Jazz fusion.

330 Ritch has something new for you every night, but is renowned for Salsa Saturdays. As you may already know, Salsa is making a big comeback, and anyone can learn (lessons included). Just ask our new mayor, Willie (Boss) Brown, who frequents this place.

Mondays you'll want to *jazzid-up* with Mushroom Jazz. Having moved here from its original locale at Cat's Grill, Mushroom at *330 Ritch* is the *only* Mushroom Jazz in existence, and from 9:00 p.m. to 3:00 a.m., it's hybrid grooves for 'huemans.' Mushroom is also popular among the local *gothics. Shroom it up!*

Wednesdays feature live local Jazz duos and trios providing excellent background music for appetizers and a couple of drinks. Try the curried coconut mussels. *Delish.*

Thursdays, DJs spin funk and new soul – this evening is *so* popular, even *330 Ritch* employees hang out on Thursdays. Cover is $5.00.

"Thank god it's": Fridays have a 5:00 p.m. - 8:00 p.m. Happy Hour, when live Jazz is accompanied by $2.00 pints of their 16 beers on tap, 2 for 1 Cosmos and

Kamikazes, and $3.75 Lemon Coolers. Come early – the place gets packed. Then it's *'put on your dancin' shoes,'* 'cause it's Disco Night in The City. Michael Brown (Willie's son) and Kirk 'burn down the house' with '70s and 870s classics.

Saturdays ... *Arriba!* It's Salsa night in *tu pueblo* – it's so hot it'll burn your tongue. Doors open at 8:00 p.m. with DJ Tony "O" pumping out the best Merengue, Salsa, and Latin beats. *What?* You can't Salsa? Garry and Isabel begin lessons at 8:30 p.m., so that by 11:00 p.m. you're sure to be cutting up the rug. It's $5.00 before 9:00 p.m; at 10 p.m. you'll find some of the most happening Latin bands in town at *330 Ritch*. Suddenly in the mood for a Cuban cigar???

Passport: *Two for one entry (not valid during special events-call to verify).*

108: Big Heart City   Dance Club/Venue

836 Mission St. (between 4th and 5th). 415-777-0666. SOMA **HOURS:** Thur-Sat, 10p.m.-4a.m.; Sun-Wed as announced. **ENTRANCE CHARGE:** $10.00 per person. **RESTRICTIONS:** Dress code.

With one of the most advanced sound and visual set-ups in The City, at the time of this writing this upscale spot is home to Thursday night's *Club Plastik* and Friday's *Congo Club.*

The long standing, popular *Plastik* offers a visual feast of fashion and style, where clubbers and lookers become lookers and clubbers as they pass one another in and out of the VIP room. The hardwood dance floor takes a beating from a parade of moves that pop to a variety of House and retro-sample beats.

The *Congo Club* attracts the salsa-shaker set to a DJ mix of salsa rhythms. Saturday nights usually offer a gay event, or the occasional college party. Whichever night blows your whistle, *Big Heart City* pulsates with a class act.

As you enter, to your right sits an opulent Bangkok-style lounge replete with hand-carved antiques from Thailand and a multi-media video gallery. Further in, the ever changing, spacious dance floor is wrapped by a second-floor loft offering a spectator's view of the buzz below. But that gets old quickly so, since you're upstairs, choose between the pool table room, dance floor, or VIP lounge: Rack-it, Shake-it, or Flaunt-it – in other words, use it or loose it, baby!

Passport: *Two for one cocktail.*

109: Bondage a Go Go (Trocadero)   Dance/Leather S&M Venue

520 Fourth St. (at Bryant). 415-995-4600. SOMA. **HOURS:** Wed, 9 p.m.-3a.m. **ENTRANCE CHARGE:** $5.00 per person. **RESTRICTIONS:** 18 and older.

For you *clubsters* who have yet to get your weekend's fill of dance, decadence, and debauchery, fret not. Wednesday night offers an opportunity to catch up on any nocturnal pleasures you may have missed. So, we now present the very-popular and erotic-laced affair – *Bondage-a-Go-Go.* Held in the large-club venue, Trocadero, *Bondage* is San Francisco's house of eye-popping gothic and sexual exhibitionism. Upon entering, you'll immediately encounter a sea of black and leather-clad bodies, many weighed-down with accessories of the handcuff and stud variety (material *and* body piercing, that is!).

Indiana Jones couldn't hold a whip to some of the characters that'll fascinate you here and, if you're looking to stand out, simply wear white.

The large dance floor operates like an open arena; reserved for wild, aggressive gyrations; piloted by industrial and alternative DJ spins. Action on the floor rises to feverish levels inducing the occasional body slam hop-n-bop. Transsexuals, trans-

vestites, *and a few un-identifiables* inhabit a large stage, performing an erotic dance theater of one sort or another.

If you're looking for some eye-popping fun, however, go on up the stairs. Once you get your bearings, coming from the center of what, at first, will appear to be a large crowd huddled together, you'll hear cries and screams that often reach primal heights. So, without delay, feed your curiosity and carefully edge your way through the thick of bodies. As you reach the front, you'll see top-

less, bottomless, and even those with clothes partaking in a sado-masochistic feast of painful fetishes. From butt-spanks to electroshocks, hot melting wax to the torturous feather-to-nipple treatment, there are ample pleasures for all. Most *treatments* are administered by professionals, but if you're into either side of this sort of thing, find yourself a partner and talk to the pit-master. He'll give you some basic rules of engagement, after which you'll be able to let-go your inhibitions – and let that big rubber paddle fly.

Let-'er-*RIP!*

110: The Box   Gay Dance Club

715 Harrison St. (at 3rd). SOMA. 415-647-8258. **HOURS:** Thursday, 9 p.m.-2:30a.m. **ENTRANCE CHARGE:** $6.00 per person.

The Box has been *the* place to dance, party, socialize, and enjoy life on Thursday nights for the past seven years. The club stresses community and diversity, and *The Box* embraces the entire social, economic, ethnic, and sexual spectrum San Francisco has to offer. Although the clientele is basically a 25- to 35-year-old gay crowd, anyone from 21 to 121 is welcome and encouraged to attend the weekly dance fests.

The high-energy dance music is mixed by a long-time San Francisco resident, DJ Page Hodel, whose exhausting schedule also includes a monthly lesbian club called Club Q (held at 177 Townsend on the first Friday of each month), as well as weekly DJ time slots at Club Universe.

111: 111 Minna St. Gallery   Club

111 Minna St. (at 2nd). 415-974-1719. SOMA. **HOURS:** Mon-Sat, noon 'til late. **ENTRANCE CHARGE:** $3.00-$10.00 depending on event. **SPECIALS:** Happy Hour. **RESTRICTIONS:** Positive attitudes only.

Okay, this is absolutely, positively, the last review we're going to write for this book. It's funny, but we started with the idea of doing the best 99 spots in San Francisco, and now that we're finished, we've ended up doing 150 or so. Sure, *there is that much in The City* – in fact there's even more – but we hafta stop somewhere ... we just hafta.

So we're happy to stop with the *111 Minna Street Gallery*. Not only is it a very interesting concept – a gallery that doubles as a club (rather than the other way around), it's also a very *cool* space.

We (that's the *editorial* "I") discovered it when we went to a party hosted by a friend (we so *love* going to parties). When we entered, we were greeted on the wall by the door by x-rays of some guy's head. The fact that it was an art piece didn't matter – we just thought it would be cool to have x-rays of *our* head posted near our front door. That way, anyone who didn't like us after being in our homes would have no excuse ... "Hey, you knew what I was like. You've seen inside my head ..."

What we're sayin' is, *111 Minna* is unlike most bars and clubs you go to regularly. Here, you have no idea whatsoever what your evening of drinking and dancing is going to be surrounded by ... *and that's good!* So, whether it's a view of some guy turned inside out, or a 12-foot-high, two-legged giraffe (or some guy with a spike through his nose sitting next to you), you can be assured of having some interesting visual stimuli.

As for the music (and why not), Eiming (the owner) boasts of playing anything from "classical to good old Rock n Roll," and runs "the gamut of DJ dance ... " The part of their musical proffering we like the best, however, is the *Dance Trance* spun – *as you'll spin* – Thursday and Saturday evenings. Take our word for it, they feature some of the most in-tune DJs in town.

This is a beer-and-wine bar and, most Fridays, hosts an 'event' of some sort. This can range from a 'hosted' party to, well ... *other stuff.* It all fits within *Minna's* unstructured format, which allows for evening presentations of select films and performance art. You'll discover an *event* of some sort four or five evenings a week.

This is a cool space – one that has carried a good *Let's Party!* vibe every time we've managed to stop by. But we gotta warn you of *'the rowdy bunch'* ... this place is pretty low-key, so if you're lookin' for a little 'o dat *slamma-bamma,* look elsewhere.

Passport: Two for one entry, any day.

112: Brain Wash   Cafe/Laundromat

1122 Folsom St. (between 7th & 8th). 415-431-WASH or 415-861-FOOD, Business office: 415-255-4866. SOMA. **HOURS:** Sun-Thur, 7:30a.m.-11p.m. (last wash load 9:30p.m.); Fri-Sat 7:30a.m.-1a.m. (last wash load 11:30a.m.); Kitchen service until Midnight. **SPECIALS:** Live Music, Wed-Fri-Sat 10p.m.-11:30p.m.

Certainly there's much here that the name implies. But that innuendo aside – the *Brain Wash* has managed to turn something people hate doing, into something they love doing. Okay, *love* may be a bit extreme. Perhaps it is societal necessity that is the driving force behind Susan Schindler's creation – a cafe/music bar with a Laundromat (or is it a Laundromat with a bar?). Anyway, since the inception of *'The Wash'* in '89, this 'spot' has been running like a finely tuned Maytag.

Exposed metal beams, polished concrete, clear varnished woods, and wall-sized windows contribute to the feel of this hip neo-industrial locale. The creative environment is a tumble mix that includes a rotating art gallery, live music, an occasional poetry reading, and two thought-provoking omni-sex bathrooms. Yes bathrooms! The 'Readers Room' is covered with eclectic quotes from famous folks. For aspiring philosophers and graffiti-artists, the 'Writers Room' offers a wraparound chalkboard supplied with erasers and chalk. For final touches, Melissa Hutton was set loose to paint the colorful kitschy cafe chairs, covering them with pop-art icons a la Warhol.

The cafe has a short menu with standard cafe fare, and the setting is perfect for a solitary respite or socializing while you await the end of the spin cycle. On many nights, you'll find *Brain Wash* churning with the beat of local bands. Not surprisingly, *The Wash* is also a singles haven, where meeting that significant other is not unusual. To follow through on a particularly happy encounter, this Laundromat has hosted a wedding. During the summer months, this locale caters to many of the young international crowd from the Globe Youth Hostel, located across the street.

Passport: A cup of coffee with breakfast entree. Monday thru Friday only.

113: Cadillac Bar & Grill   Mexican Restaurant/Bar

325 Minna St. (at 4th). 415-543-8226. SOMA. **HOURS:** Mon-Thur, 11a.m.-11p.m.; Fri-Sat, 11a.m.-Midnight; Sun, noon-10p.m.

A fun Mexican bar and restaurant built in an old warehouse, *Cadillac* is not the place for a quiet dinner for two. The loud music, large crowd, and (above all) tequila poppers combine with the warehouse acoustics to make this bar extremely noisy. But *Cadillac* is a great place for group dinner parties of all sorts – birthdays, bachelorette parties, etc.

The restaurant specializes in country-style Mexican cooking, meaning that – when eating here – you are not eating foods invented for Americans. You cannot find a traditional Mission-style burrito on the menu. The seafood platter can feed two or three people, and the fajitas are highly acclaimed.

Patrons arrive in shorts and T-shirts, or walk straight over from nearby Moscone Center in suits and ties. Either way, they're likely to stop for a famous Cadillac Margarita before dining (if you order it blended, you're missing out!). During Happy Hour (3:00 to 7:00 p.m. weekdays) a complimentary buffet of fajitas, tacos, and enchiladas makes a meal in itself. Margaritas and well drinks are also $1 off.

114: Cafe Mars   Bar/Restaurant

798 Brannan (at 7th). 415-621-6277. SOMA. **HOURS:** Tue-Fri, 4p.m.-2a.m.; Sat, 5p.m.-2p.m.

"EAT" – that's the word that radiates, neon ablaze, from behind the earthly kitchen portal. But *we* know better than to believe there are humans back there doing the cooking, because the fare that passes this artificial barrier is simply *out-of-this-world*. Okay, clichés aside *(and this is not a restaurant review in the first place)*, it is rare that we find a bar that has simply great food at reasonable prices – *and* really *rockets* in the social arena.

As you enter this unpretentious venue, you may not feel you've left terra firma, but to spend time in *Mars*, among the local aliens, is to transcend to another time and space.

The amalgamation of what must have been some pretty good fantasies – and garage sales – this uniquely comfortable way station is the alien child of a local bartender/celebrity, now bar owner/extraterrestrial. In fact, John, the owner, has found enough success lately that you're more likely to find him among the patrons than behind the bar.

Popular during the week – but blasting-off like a rocket ship every Friday and Saturday night, this two-room bar-plus-patio takes on the look of the Star Wars Cantina, where a variety of patrons speak in tongues and imbibe intoxicants. Ask for a *Kato Cocktail.*

The music is channeled or DJ driven, with an emphasis on Soul, R&B, and "Space Jazz." When it comes to food, their tapas-style menu has offerings that will please even the most weary space traveler, and your *Let's Party!* sure-hit, from a great bar food menu, is their Rocket Shrimp Tortilla ($7.95).

Stan! Here's your name. How about a free cocktail?

Passport: Free entry, any day.

115: Caribbean Zone   Restaurant/Dance Club

55 Natoma St. (lane at 1st & 2nd, Mission & Howard). 415-541-6416. SOMA. **HOURS:** Mon-Wed & Fri, 11:30a.m.-10p.m.; Thur, 11:30a.m.-1:30a.m.; Sat-Sun, 5p.m.-11p.m. **ENTRANCE CHARGE:** $8.00 per person on Thursday for Salsa.

This bar/restaurant venue is built around an airplane that once belonged to the Doobie Brothers. And, there are a few good reasons to check it out: 1. the spicy island fare; 2. the crazy cocktails, and; 3. the tropical atmosphere. You are now entering the Caribbean Zone … pass a few palm trees, locate the bar.

Drink specials are highlighted on a chalkboard behind the bar. Try a Banana Monkey or a Blue Hawaii, and proceed upstairs to the interior of the airplane – where you can sit. The airplane's windows have been replaced by video screens that simulate take-offs and landings. Remember, this was not your ordinary plane, and the interior accouterments are not what you'd expect. The seating is set up more like a lounge than that 757 you were on last month – you know, the one that had your knees around your chin! "Coffee, tea, or me?" Have your waitress … ahem … *flight attendant,* get you a few more drinks, and you'll *really* be flying. On your way to the privy, check-out the cockpit, which is still intact.

Taste 'Ambient'

Monday nights, the Garden Club stages an 'Ambient' music 'club' here – a total 180 degrees from the tropical scene I just painted for you. 'Ambient' music parties hit big in The City a while back, and have kept their following quite religiously, providing what would be house music to Chicago or Euro-techno is to New York. 'Ambient' music does sets the atmosphere, a "feeling" takes over, and you can dance alone or with your shadow or with a group of people … it doesn't matter! 'Ambient' is trance music with a beat, and its soothing rhythms cycle you to realms of feelings and emotions you may not have experienced before. Whatever your trip, however, you can just sit back on one of the bean bags and let your mind float among the colors and images projected on the walls. When your body spontaneously sets to motion, join the shadowy figures that melt into each other on the 'dance floor.' 'Ambient' music is a mix that doesn't end until it's over. Enjoy! (After all, that's the point, isn't it?)

116: Chalkers Billiard Club   Pool Hall

101 Spear St. (at Mission). 415-512-0450. SOMA. **HOURS:** Mon-Fri, 11:30a.m.-2a.m.; Sat, 2p.m.-2a.m.; Sun, 3p.m.-11p.m.

Historic Rincon Center is home to *Chalker's*, one of The City's best upscale billiards clubs. To get to the club, you pass dozens of murals depicting the early history of Northern California, painted in the 1940s as the largest single project ever commissioned by the Painting and Sculpture Division of FDR's WPA.

Passing through Rincon Center's halls, you'll enter the stunning, five-story Atrium, which is highlighted by a Doug Hollis water sculpture, "Rain Column,"

pouring 3000 gallons of water per hour from the ceiling to the flat, wall-less catch basin in the Atrium's center. *Chalker's* door is just a few steps away, in clear view of the fountain.

Inside, the spacious club is both elegant and comfortable. Concrete ceilings and columns with exposed air ducts give a modern, slightly industrial feel, contrasting with the classic oil paintings in ornate frames dotting the walls. Cherrywood furnishings and sheer-gold gossamer curtains continue the 'modern classic' feel. Interior decorating was completed according to traditional Chinese *feng schwee* principles of harmonious design, resulting in a place with an open, inviting feel.

The white collar crowd ranges from business people, to couples, to locals celebrating special occasions. The hip modern music is a bit loud, and likely to appeal to the younger end of the age spectrum.

A full menu is served Monday through Thursday 11:30 a.m. to 10 p.m., Fridays 11:30 a.m. to midnight, and Saturdays 6:00 p.m. to midnight. The simpler bar menu is available for late-night snacks, from 2:00 to 6:00 p.m. Saturdays, and from 3:00 to 10:00 p.m. Sundays. Patrons can dine in the bar area, or request table-side service. Menu choices range from country pate ($5.00) to Caesar Salad ($7.00) to the grilled Ahi sandwich ($7.00). The delicately flavorful crab cakes ($8.00) are highly recommended.

Table rentals range from $5.00 to $15.00 an hour, depending on number of people playing, and the day and time of play. The *Chalker's* folks are high-tech: their computer table-management system prorates your table time to the minute. There are 29 custom-made billiards tables, and one antique 12-foot snooker table.

A variety of special deals are available: Tuesday is 'Ladies Night,' with half-price table rentals to parties with at least one woman player; Wednesday is College Night, when a valid-looking student ID will get you a half-price deal on tables; Monday through Friday, a 5:00 to 7:00 p.m. Happy Hour features draft beer, wine by the glass, and Skyy Vodka cocktails for $2.50.

117: Club DV8

Venue

538 Howard St., (415-267-5957) / 55 Natoma St. (415-267-5984) (between 1st & 2nd). SOMA. **HOURS:** Vary per night depending on events. Usually 'til dawn. **ENTRANCE CHARGE:** Varies depending on event, usually between $5.00 and $10.00. **RESTRICTIONS:** Also varies, but usually *'cool'* works!.

We'd be remiss if we left out this granddaddy of SoMa clubs. DV8 has been dishing out the late-night club thing so long that it seems *everyone* has *some* opinion about the place. There's been so much drama in and around DV8 that, if a mini-series were made about San Francisco's night scene, DV8 could provide the script.

So why would we consider not reviewing it? After all, DV8 has certainly established itself as a San Francisco SoMa night-life fixture – or 'nightlite,' if you will ... or 'night life,' as in "hey honey, can you turn on the *night life* in the bathroom ..."

But, we digress. The point is that DV8 – and its merry-maker, Dr. Winkie – have seen better times. And, while it would be totally within our *Let's Party!* "you gotta be happenin' to grace our pages" *snob* mentality to leave it out (and only mention the 'clubs'), in this case we would be doing you ... if not The City as a whole ... a disservice.

You see, DV8 is the night-child of Dr. Winkie. As for Dr. Winkie, all we really know is that the Honorable Doctor found some modicum of regional fame when he attached a small mini-battery-powered flashing red light in buttons or on pins or something similar. This little thing was called a 'Winkie' and, as you can imagine, the little gimmick was *all the rage in La La Land*– the land of 'me, me, me." ... and Winkie cleaned up. As for the 'Dr.' part, we don't have a clue where that came from.

The story goes that Dr. Winkie – a true benefactor of modern art – opened this club, and for the longest time it was *'the place'* for night life in San Francisco (but that was before *Release* left). We don't know the workings of San Francisco's club promoters, but when Release went, well, so did DV8's Saturday night fix.

Bored yet? Sorry if this 'review' is sounding sorta like the bland stuff you read in *those other* travel guides. The bottom line is: at the direction of the fine Doctor, DV8 has the coolest, most-artistic interior of any club in The City. It seems Winkie has been into artists like Keith Haring, but *way* before even Keith Haring was into Haring – and he didn't stop collecting cool art after Haring's death.

In fact, jumping out at you from many of DV8's walls are the works of some of today's most-progressive modern artists. Much of the art is on the second floor of this four-floor party Mecca (check out *Lift*, which gets going around Midnight).

On any given night, you'll enjoy all sorts of progressive beats – from Jive/Funk, to House, to Acid, to Fusion, to Metabolic Rave, to Trance, to, to, to ... the list goes on and on. And, although San Francisco's established night life 'elite' have, on many nights, found other places to go, DV8 still maintains some of the best, most groovin' times in The City.

So there ya have it! If you're on the San Francisco night life tour, it would not be complete without a visit (or two) to DV8 – San Francisco's dressed up child of the night.

118: Club Universe Gay Dance Club

177 Townsend St. (at 2nd). 415-985-5241. SOMA. **HOURS:** Saturday, 9:30 p.m.-7a.m. **ENTRANCE CHARGE:** $10.00 per person.

Club Universe is the quintessential San Francisco nightclub. Not only is it the *biggest* club in San Francisco, it's also the best club The City has seen in a long time. Dance and sweat alongside shirtless muscle boys who grind and gyrate until the sun rises the next morning. On any given Saturday night, there'll be at least 2000 20- to 30-something gay, bisexual, and, yes, even a few 'straight' boys and girls passing through the doors and entering a themed fantasy land that changes weekly.

Club Universe has transported patrons through time and space, into the streets of the great capitals of Europe and the Orient, and even into the swamplands of Dinosaur-inhabited, prehistoric planet Earth! If you who don't care about a packed house or elaborate decorations, don't despair – *Club Universe* is home to the best sound system in the city, and the most-talented DJs spin an eloquent blend of cutting-edge, high-energy House music. *Club Universe* is also a space where international music performers do their thing on the club's sizable stage.

119: Covered Wagon Dance Bar

917 Folsom St. (at 5th). 415-974-1585. SOMA. **HOURS:** Mon-Sat, 4:30p.m.-2a.m. **ENTRANCE CHARGE:** Around $4.00 per person.

College kids and early 20's single-suburbanites-on-the-prowl populate this SoMa dance club. The grungy decor involves black walls, black light, and lots of neon, and a tiny Karaoke lounge is hidden in the back.

The 'CW' (as it is known by regulars) features 25 beers on tap, a Jäegermeister shot machine, and a full bar. Fridays, The City's bicycle messengers take the place over for the 4:30 to 9:30 p.m. Happy Hour, made popular by the free flow of $2.00 pints (but where's Puck?).

The crowd varies, depending on the night: Monday is Hip-Hop night; Tuesday is not the night to bring your parents to *CW*; it is time for Playland – a bondage and discipline theme night involving black leather, whips, live shows, and even *loaner* 'pleasure toys'; Wednesday, the alternative trend is continued by Faster Pussycat, the club's lesbian night; Thursdays, the focus is alternative music at the Tainted Love Club, a cool all-80s dance scene brought to you by the people who do New Wave City; Fridays is *CW's* lively 70s Funk and Soul night; and Saturday, the party week peaks with a variety of 70s, 80s, and 90s dance tunes.

Isn't that enough?

120: DNA Lounge Live Music/Dance Club

375 11th St. (at Harrison). 415-626-1409. SOMA. **HOURS:** Tue-Sat, 9p.m.-4p.m. **ENTRANCE CHARGE:** Varies depending on time and event.

The top two reasons to go to *DNA*: 1. it's one the of few regular clubs open 'til 4:00 a.m. (for San Francisco, that's *late*!); 2. Friday nights. Over a year ago, Grooveline – not just a band, a show – made Fridays their stint at *DNA*. So, put on your halter tops, your hip-huggers, your platform shoes, and your disco weave, 'cause everybody's *kung-fu-fight-ing*. This three-man band puts on the full gear, and does every conceivable rendition of the Village People.

The singer, a white guy with a huge Afro, is the real kick of the show. When he takes off his satin shirt to reveal his skinny torso and huge gold medallions, the crowd goes wild. He works up a sweat boogying and oog-y-ing 'til "you just can't boogie no more." He sings pretty good, too, and sounds just Sly. On the night we were there Rob Sneider (you know, the Copy Guy from SNL – also co-owner of the club) was on stage doin' the Y-M-C-A with Grooveline. You know, this disco kick really gets the babe, 'cause when that scrawny singer starts doin' the hustle and invites the girls on stage, there aren't enough bouncers to keep the chicks off him.

Cover is $7.00 before 11:00 p.m., and $10 later – but arrive early to avoid the lines that, by 11:00 p.m., are something to reckon with. The band ends at 1:30 a.m., but a funky DJ spins tunes 'til everyone leaves (which is usually about 4:00 a.m. or so on a good night).

This is a big club with a large dance floor, stage, and a second level for dance floor viewing. The upstairs is decorated with red velvet curtains to match red couches and a smart bar serving up smart drinks. The club seems never-ending, and there are seemingly endless back rooms to host private parties – where only the correct name or a good attitude will get you in. We found one room that had a Twister-game dance floor and psychedelia projected onto the walls.

DNA features different themes every night, so we suggest you call to see what's up on a specific evening. One thing's for sure – the visionaries there offer 'something for everybody.' Disco is back as this is written ... but whatever the next trend, they'll adapt.

121: Eleven Ristorante & Bar   Restaurant/Jazz Bar

374 Eleventh St. (at Harrison). 415-431-3337. SOMA. **HOURS:** Dinner: Mon-Thur 6 p.m.-11 p.m.; Fri & Sat 6 p.m.-Midnight; Club open til 2a.m. **ENTRANCE CHARGE:** $3.00-$5.00, depending on night.

Romantic candlelit tables on two levels offer great vantage points to share dinner, a Martini, and conversation while excellent live jazz filter down from the musical loft. Against a red-lit background, as-if suspended in midair, *Eleven* features such Acid Jazz combos as Jungle Biskit, Eddie Duran and One Nation Underground – some of The City's Acid Jazz pioneers. Their ability to waiver between soft dinner Jazz to a late night funky beat is part of what makes this place hip and trendy.

The loft and bar area provide excellent acoustics for the *chic*-ly garbed trendsetters who flock to this club. The beautiful wooden bar offers 18 beers on tap, including Anchor Liberty ale, Sierra Nevada, and Thomas Kemper Amber Lager. Specialty drinks include the very dry Skytini (shaken, not stirred), Orange Stoli Cosmopolitan, or *Citronade* served in a fluted glass.

Food is in the *Italian American California-cuisine* category, and you can choose from a snack of gourmet pizza or tasty fettucini with scallops, garlic, and anchovies. Or, maybe you just came for dessert and a nightcap – not an uncommon occurrence at *Eleven*. An espresso pleasingly accompanies your tiramisu or decadent flourless chocolate cake.

On Wednesdays, local promoters host a social-weekend kickoff, where you can be pretty assured of running into some of those same people you were hanging with last Saturday at 4:00 a.m.. On occasional Wednesday nights, you may catch a fashion show starring local models and designers. *"I'm too sexy for this place, too sexy ..."*

Other happening nights are Thursday and Friday, when the crowd arrives in black Armani-wear and slicked-back model looks. Saturdays bring a heavy influx of tourists, the *near* variety – like from Walnut Creek, *for example.*

Rob Scheider, who co-owns the DNA Lounge across the street, also has a part interest in *Eleven*. You may catch even the comedian having supper or grooving to One Nation Underground.

After dinner and your fill of Jazz, get your hand stamped as you walk out the door so you can get into the DNA. *Welcome to the planet Soul.*

122: The Endup   Mixed Dance Club

401 6th St. (at Harrison). 415-487-6277. SOMA. **HOURS:** Varies depending on event. **ENTRANCE CHARGE:** Varies depending on event.

So, what do we have here? A San Francisco institution – in every sense of the word! The Endup is San Francisco's ultimate mixed club. As such, we have given you both the straight and gay perspectives. Enjoy!

THE STRAIGHT REVIEW: Its 6:00 a.m. on a Sunday; all the late-night clubs are clearing out – but you're still amped. There're no 'after parties' to be found ... what do you do?.

While the good people of San Francisco are getting ready for church, we, he, she, and they *all* still have some mileage left-over on our sins before its time to repent. Week after week, the Endup is your *Let's Party!* off-the-scale option to church.

Although this locale is open on various other days of the week (remember, we don't give guarantees!), we must admit that only on Sunday mornings have we managed to "end up at the Endup." We must be stockpiling our confessions.

As you near the corner gateway, you'll see 'can't-get-enough' like-minded partyers waiting to get in. So, relieve yourself of material pleasures, and hand over a $5 bill for entry.

Inside, you'll vaguely perceive eyes cloaked behind designer shades as the sun begins to rear its blaring face. Part of San Francisco's club culture is recharging for the next wave of indulgence ... *while another group jigs around the dance floor in a seemingly non-stop dance trance.* It's on the dance floor where you'll encounter shirtless muscle boys struttin' their goods among post-party divas and outa-this-world Shivas – all gyrating under the entrancing spell of house, techno, and ambient music. Bongo and conga players sit on the fringe, chasing down DJ mania-driven spins.

All around, you'll sense a faint air of decadence. Suddenly, within and between the relentless dance floor beats, comes the random whisper of a *sound*. Your ears tell you you're imagining things, but it's there – the sound of trickling water.

You're guided from the belly of the whale outside to a large sun-splash patio, where a waterfall commands a green rich corner of a sanctuary-like setting. Benches blend within concealed nooks, offering chill zones for weekend-warrior-tweekers who all seem to be on one potion or another, and caught in that spunday haze of oblivious ecstasy. They all know its the beginning of a beautiful day, worthy – perhaps – of passing out on the beach.

THE GAY REVIEW: *The Endup* continues to dazzle and amaze even the most-hardened club goer with San Francisco's most endearing, bizarre, and just plain crazy environment. This modest-looking club has been going strong for as long as anybody can remember, and enjoys the elevated status of being referred to as "a San Francisco tradition." And it truly is.

While other clubs come and go, like so many tired drag queens whose make-up has been on just a little too long, *The Endup* carries itself with the style and timelessness of a veritable institution that is definitely here to stay. This is not to say *The Endup* is stately or elegant – it's not! On the contrary – it's one of the dirtiest, trashiest clubs in town. But the beauty of it is, dirt and trash never go out of style in San Francisco's SoMa Club Scene! After all the glitz and glamour has been cleared away from the other clubs, every club boy and girl with any energy left to continue their lost weekend of fun and excitement in San Francisco will end up at *The Endup!*

Get it? The best time to enjoy *The Endup's* unique charm is Sunday morning. They open at 6 a.m. and, by the time 8 o'clock rolls around, the place is packed with party animals who couldn't bare to go to sleep the night before (can you say, "meta-amphetamines"?). From doctors to the semi-homeless … from the just-turned-21-year-old to the just-turned-45-year-old … from the serious club goer to the curious tourist … this is *the place to go* on Sundays.

123: Girl Spot   Mixed Dance Club

278 11th St. (at Folsom). 415-337-4962. SOMA. **HOURS:** Saturday, 8 p.m.-7a.m. **ENTRANCE CHARGE:** $7.00 per person.

Girl Spot, now located at the new, lavishly renovated club space V/sf, is *on fire!* It's an amazing display of gorgeous women, tough leather dykes, SoMa club girls, a few 'straight' couples, and a handful of fags bringing down the house at one of the freshest, most vibrant, totally *alive* clubs in San Francisco.

G-Spot burns brightly with a synergistic mix of positive vibrations, high energy, popular House music, and a powerfully charged, sexual atmosphere. There are few (surprisingly) regularly scheduled lesbian clubs in town, and even fewer that occur weekly, so when Saturday night rears it's beautiful head, the girls know where to go if they want to get down and really party.

The host space, V/sf, recently spent over $500,000 on a custom, neo-industrial architecturally designed interior, a state-of-the-art dance floor (you *must* dance on it to believe it!), a crisp sound system, and a spectacular display of disco lights to dazzle and bewilder the senses. Don't miss it!

124: Gordon Biersch   Brewery Bar/Restaurant

2 Harrison St. (on Embarcadero). 415-243-8246. SOMA. **HOURS:** Mon-Thur, 11a.m.-Midnight, kitchen closes 10p.m.; Fri-Sat ,11a.m.-2a.m., kitchen closes 10:30p.m.

Besides the lively bunch you'll find waiting after work on Fridays to get in, the front of this trendy brew-pub-wine-bar is marked by a tall silo that holds *40,000* pounds of barley. As you enter, you'll easily pick up the telltale aroma of boiling hops coming from the large copper casks that bedeck the left side of the bar's large social arena. That's right, in a building that once churned out Hills Brothers coffee, a German-style beer brewery has supplanted one vice with another. Coffee ... beer ... coffee ... beer ... *hmmmmm ...* we'll go for the beer!

This popular watering hole offers a red-brick interior, second-floor restaurant (where you can watch the groove-moves below), and a connoisseur selection of three quality-brewed beers. Testament to its popularity is a nightly invasion force of politically-correct young professionals, cap-topped all Americans, and brew-conscious suburbanites. And, the *Gordon Biersch* brand is on sale at other bars throughout the Bay Area.

On weekends, in true beer-hall style, the liberalized conversation reaches a deafening buzz with a merry making bunch who like to flex their elbow-bending muscles at the long bar. If you're still looking for that extra *oomph,* try their demi-famous *Märzen* beer. It's one of their original Oktoberfest amber brews and, like that special person you just met, this beer is smooth in flavor and full in body (yea, yea, we couldn't resist!). Drink-up – being intoxicated (or appearing as such) provides a perfect excuse for that "she-said-he-said-I-did *WHAT?*" morning after. *Prost!!!*

125: Hamburger Mary's   Restaurant

1582 Folsom St. (at 12th). 415-626-5767. SOMA. **HOURS:** Mon-Fri, 11:30a.m.-12:15a.m., closed at 1a.m.; Sat-Sun, 10a.m.-1:15a.m., closed at 2a.m.

Note: Two of our writers took a shot at writing up Hamburger Marys, so we thought we'd give you both versions.

1. For ardent party-ers about to undertake a night-long exploration of the SoMa scene, there's no better place to start than *Hamburger Mary's*. Meet friends at this popular bar and burger joint, satisfy your caloric needs, and then walk just one block over to 11th Street to begin your club-hopping adventure. Popular with all age groups and sexual orientations, *Mary's* attracts everybody. Inside, the ambiance is that of a busy diner throwing an ongoing garage sale. The place is half bar, half restaurant, all covered in early 20th-Century signage and photos.

As you may have guessed, *Hamburger Mary's* is known for its burgers, served sandwich style on sliced nine-grain bread, held together by a steak knife plunged dramatically through the midst. These babies are messy. According to my waiter, the optimal method for consuming one is to cut it in half with the steak knife, and then use both hands.

Burgers average $8:00, including either standard fries or spicy home fries dusted with garlic and chili powder. Vegetarians will find an entire page of flesh-free menu options. And *Mary's* blends some of the thickest, chocolate-iest malts imaginable. Their $10.00 dinner specials (prime rib or grilled salmon when I visited) are financial loss leaders for the restaurant, so a great deal for you. On weekends, the wait for a table can be about an hour. Insiders know that you can call an hour ahead to put your name on the wait list (wow, now you're an 'insider.' How's *that* feel?).

A separate bar area, known as *Mary's Backside*, takes up most of the 12th Street side of the establishment. With recorded R&B through Hip-Hop music blaring in the background, *Mary's* is a great place to evade police listening devices. Largely deep-fried appetizers are available in the Backside. During Happy Hour (Monday to Friday 4:00 to 7:00 p.m.) patrons enjoy free bar food and half-off drinks.

2. A finer static visual experience can be found nowhere better than *Hamburger Mary's*. A San Francisco institution, in our opinion, the food here – which is best ordered 'sloppy' – compares to any of it's kind anywhere in the U.S., if not the world (please don't repeat that to any of the other 'burger places' we write about).

Not really a bar scene *scene*, Hamburger Mary's attracts a mixed crowd of straights, gays, and lesbians who all feel comfortable beneath and among absolutely the coolest mixture of *stuff* found anywhere in the city.

This is truly a *Let's Party!* favorite, and if it's not for lunch, you may find us there winding down after a long pre-party day, or lining our stomachs before one of our patented *long San Francisco nights*.

And while sometimes a little curt, the staff is always attentive. But who cares, when the food is this good?

Passport: 10% off bill (food only).

126: Harry Denton's   Brasserie-style Restaurant/Nightclub

161 Steuart St. (at Howard). 415-882-1333. SOMA. **HOURS:** Dinner Sun-Thur, 5:30 p.m.-9 p.m.; Fri & Sat, 5:30 p.m.-10 p.m.; Nightclub: Thur-Sat ,10 p.m.-2a.m. **ENTRANCE CHARGE:** $5.00-$8.00.

Harry is a San Francisco success story.

He began his restaurant career 22 years ago at the former Henry Africa's after moving to San Francisco from his native Kimberly, Idaho (pop. 800). "After six weeks in San Francisco, the light went on in my head, " Denton said. "I knew I had to have my own place."

After the success of Harry's Bar on Fillmore in 1986, Denton moved SoMa, and joined forces with Bill Kimpton to open a popular brasiere-style restaurant and dance club. The result was *Harry Denton's*. It opened in April of 1991 on Steuart Street, attached to the Harbor Court Hotel (which once housed the Embarcadero YMCA). Once a seedy neighborhood, now fancy restaurants and hotels line the street, which is just one block away from The Bay.

The crowd is 30-*somethingish* – sleek, beautiful, and affluent. It's the kind of place you ride up to in a limo, and stop by to party. It's relatively affordable ($5.00 to $10 cover charge) and, who knows, you may meet Mr. Right, who'll sweep you away in his *Beemer*.

Harry is on the premises most nights, greeting customers, and making sure you're having a good time. "We only have one rule here," he says. "No-one dances on the bar without me." Get there before 10:00 p.m. to avoid long lines.

You enter a magnificent saloon painted in three coats of Jaguar-red automobile paint, red velvet-scalloped curtains, mahogany pillars, and art-deco lamps. Palm leaves are painted on the ceiling against a sky-blue background. If you're lucky, you'll get a seat at the bar, a massive Brunswick beauty rescued from a Cleveland train station and widened by 18 inches to facilitate bar-top dancing (with Harry, of course.)

In the center of the back bar is a brass statue of the Bacchante, the high priestess of Bacchus – appropriately, the god of wine and good times. Years back, at his

heaviest, Harry Denton was 306 pounds and *looked* like Bacchus. A real madcap, he was never seen without a glass of wine in his hand, but he went overboard. Now, 120 pounds lighter, he swears to no booze, but still likes to make sure his guests are having a ball.

The nine porcelain beer taps from Milan dispense locally brewed Anchor beers and porters, Holsten, and Abbey of Leffe (a Belgian beer first brewed by the monks in 1152). They also serve a wide variety of wines by the glass. All classic drinks are made according to original recipes, including a Brandy Alexander or Bull Shot.

Hungry? Try the mussels appetizer steamed in Anchor Steam beer, garlic and tomatoes ($7.50). Their excellent food selection entrees range between $10.95 and $18.95 – for their Veal Cutlet.

After 'the dinner hour,' the tables in the back dining and bar area are cleared to make room for a dance floor and stage. Some nights you may find a live band (Pure Ecstasy is a favorite, playing funk and R&B). On other nights you'll find DJs spinning dance tracks mixed specially for dancing. Weekends are popular, so come early and stay late.

When you ask Harry what makes a good saloon-keeper, he says, "It's making sure everyone's taken care of and comfortable, and doing it with some oomph!" Harry just reopened the Starlight Room at the Sir Francis Drake, and continues to liven up San Francisco's club scene.

Passport: Free entry for two persons.

127: Hole in the Wall Saloon   Gay Bar

289 8th St. (at Howard). 415-431-HOWL. SOMA. **HOURS:** Tue-Thur, noon-2a.m.; Fri-Mon, 6a.m.-2a.m. **SPECIALS:** Happy Hour.

Hole in the Wall Saloon has only been around since 1994, but has already established itself as San Francisco's ultimate leather/biker bar. The place is oozing with character and personality. Be prepared for a visual extravaganza with Rock and Roll and hard-core biker memorabilia attacking you from floor to ceiling, and everywhere in between. It's like a cosmic explosion happened inside the place, and nobody bothered to clean up afterwards.

Every time I visit, the place is slightly physically altered. An alien life form slowly mutating and evolving, or merely the handiwork of some very talented and twisted individuals? You decide.

As for the crowd, the 20- to 50-something clientele looks rough, tough, and nasty, and they are – but they're also friendly, unpretentious, and just plain *fun!* This can be a rowdy bar (don't be surprised if a fight breaks out), but if you're adventurous – and not too shy – *Hole in the Wall Saloon* is on of The City's coolest bars.

128: Holy Cow   Dance Bar

1535 Folsom St. (at 12th). 415-621-6087. SOMA. **HOURS:** Tues-Sun, 6p.m.-2a.m.

This little dance 'barn' in the middle of SoMa's hot 11th and Folsom Street area is best found by seeking the large plastic Jersey cow hanging above the entrance. On the night we went, recent rainstorms had blown the cow down the street, but he's back up again.

The cool thing at *Holy Cow* is that there is usually is no cover charge other than the occasional $2.00 on busy Saturday nights. You *must* have an ID to get in (but that's true everywhere in the city – especially SoMa). A large rectangle bar is in the center of what once was probably two distinct rooms *(two ... two ... two ... bars in one!)*.

Beer and mixed drinks are reasonable, but beware ... no matter how big the bar, ordering a drink on Saturday nights is almost impossible. Even waving your money doesn't help (and make sure *not* to *whistle)*. The crowd is a mixed bag of SoMa party-goers, suburbanites, tourists – and that old *Suavé* guy in a patterned silk shirt and gold chains.

The music is fast and fun ... *and eclectic* ... and that's what makes it good! Thursday night is Euro-techno, and attracts European tourists, (especially local Swedish expatriates, Euro-wannabees, and those who *like* Swedes). Weekends, the DJs offer a mix of 70s 870s and 90s tunes – the kind where when you're dancing you say, "Oh yeah, remember that song? I used to love that song." Just to clue you in, the code is: *The Tide is High* on *Dancing Queen* in a *Bizarre Love Triangle* high on *99 Red Luft Balloons ... Come on Eileen!*

It's funny, we always run into people we know at *The Cow* ... or *meet* people we run into later in Chicago, Copenhagen, or someplace else. It's cheap, it's casual, and it's a change from the huge dance scene down the block. Don't forget to bow down and pay homage to the cow on the way out.

Passport: Two for one draft beer or well drink cocktail.

129: Hotel Utah Saloon   Live Music/Bar

500 Fourth St. (at Bryant). 415-421-8308. SOMA. **HOURS:** Mon-Fri, 11:30a.m.-2a.m.; Sat-Sun, 6p.m.-2a.m. **ENTRANCE CHARGE:** On Thursday thru Saturday evenings, varies.

History, you're calling me home!

If you're looking, or interested, in experiencing a real piece of San Francisco's past, check-out the *Hotel Utah Saloon* – "a funky old bar with *great* live music." From its historically restored exterior architecture, to the ornately carved wooden bar imported from Belgium in 1908, *Utah* reeks of a beauty that is age-old.

Once a club for duck hunters before deriving fame in Clint Eastwood's *Dirty Harry* as Al's Transbay Tavern, the atmosphere in *Utah* can seem like a circus (especially when Cirque du Soleil is in town).

Daily, it attracts a mixture of "hard core regulars from all walks of life" mixing it up with weekend socialites, bridge-and-tunnelers, and SoMa locals. "It's *not* the kind-a-joint where you'll find a lotta attitude!"

Featuring some of the best-in-Bay Area live music, the atmosphere – and the music – can best be described as *casual*. That doesn't mean the place doesn't get-a-rockin', because this place can *jam!*

We'd get into describing the entire layout, but that wouldn't do *Utah* justice. Suffice it to say that the dance floor is 'cozy,' made especially appealing by its proximity to the band (and, perhaps, forced proximity to the person partying next to you). Every way you look at it, this is an 'intimate' saloon.

Utah also has a small menu featuring one of the best selections of 'bar food' anywhere in The City. In addition, their full bar and 10 tap beers are served by a bar staff that never seems to change. They'll attentively keep you refreshed all night long – *just hold your horses!*

To tell you something about the clientele and the staff, an innocent statement such as, *"I ought to check that place out"* can be dangerous. Once you cross *Utah's* threshold, you're liable to spend many a night poundin' back a brew, or two, and flirtin' with the bartender while soaking in some great tunes.

So beware, lest you begin to resemble Norm from Cheers. A stop into the *Hotel Utah Saloon* may keep you from getting to Bondage-a-go-go at the Trocadero, on Wednesdays, next door.

Passport: Two for one draft beer.

130: Icon Byte   Bar & Grill

299 9th St. (at Folsom). 415-861-2983. Icon@ByetBar.com. http://www.well.com/user/tcricus/Icon/. SOMA. **HOURS:** Lunch, Mon-Fri, 11a.m.-4p.m.; Dinner, Tue-Sat, 5p.m.-10p.m.; Club menu, Fri & Sat 10p.m.-Midnight. **SPECIALS:** Dinner Theater, Wednesday, Thursday & Saturday starting 8p.m. (Call for update and up and coming events).

"Hook it up and they will come ..." – and they did. *Icon* is not only the first in the world, but (at the time of this review) it is the only bar in San Francisco where you can, with beer in hand, surf the Internet (or wade the World Wide Web). The interior is heavily charged with a circuitry-laden, digitized decor. The visuals are synaptic, from the glory of an electro-lit techno sculpture to an Earth-caveman's pre-interpretation of futuristic high-tech wizardry. Presiding alongside the wide-eyed visionary virtually glued to the ISDN-sped-web, you'll be continually entertained by the latest in RAM-intensive animation.

At the bar, (human or android – you guess) is Vince, known as the mad mixer. He concocts some of the strangest drinks, and proclaims notoriety for the driest Martini this side of Dune. He demonstrated his formula for us, creating it while a bar-back stood outside the bar-backed-window holding a bottle of Vermouth. Take our word for it, it was dry. Whatever you're drinking, grab that special brew and plunge into the Net ... or fall into the Web ... or grab a seat for dinner (or dinner theater). We're not going to say "it's outta this world," but aliens seeking the equipment to 'phone home,' are more likely to find it here than at any other Bay Area way station.

Entrees are classified as American food from around the world ... in other words, it's the American slant on Italian, French, Jamaican, Thai, (etc.) foods. For those of you who fall in the 'my-body-is-my-temple' category, *Icon* boasts a varied selection of vegetarian dishes. A sure bet is the Buddha's Szechuan Feast – ($7.95): veggie stir-fry served w/jasmine rice (spicy or mild). With chicken or shrimp, add $2.00.

131: Infusion   Bar/Restaurant/Live Music

555 Second St. (between Bryant & Brannan). 415-543-2282. SOMA. **HOURS:** Tue-Sun, 11:30a.m.-2a.m. **ENTRANCE CHARGE:** $3.00, Thur; $5.00, Fri & Sat. (without dinner).

This may risky – *reviewing a bar that's not yet open* – but with our World Wide Web site on the Internet (http://EntertainNET.com), you will be able to get the current lowdown on this club – *and more.* Besides, we believe in giving everybody a fair shake, and this is one of those occasions where *it just feels right!* So here goes ...

Located in what was recently one of San Francisco's classier 'rendezvous' spots, where upper income 'suits' came with their *belle du jour,* now lies a cat of a different color. Where dark mood lighting and secluded seating once provided the setting for Jazz and romantic innuendoes, a more welcoming and airy scene now awaits.

With an innovative approach, the new owners of this 'destination' have an enticing mixture of ambiance and philosophy to share with their new patrons. The decor, well , that remains to be seen (at least for us) ... but we're *told* that it will be cool – we'll let you be the judge.

What we *do* know, is that the philosophy behind *Infusion* is one that encompasses a mixture of 'good food' (that's not too expensive), 'good music' (acoustic Rock-n-Roll), and Vodka Infusions (Sky Vodka imbibing the flavorful ingredients of 'mostly fruits').

One thing that excites us, is that their 'something for everyone' *new-American-cuisine* menu has just that – something for everyone. What excites us even more is that their extensive list of starters, salads, pastas, and entrees is priced *amazingly* low for what's offered. If we hadn't spoken with the chef, we'd doubt anything would be any good. When their top-priced *Peppered Filet Mignon flamed in Jameson's* priced out at a meager *$14.50,* however, we have to ask – *what do you have to lose?*

When it comes to music, we voluntarily stand up for (or sit contentedly below) their plan to strictly feature acoustic music. Now, starting every evening at 9:00 p.m., you can stroll in for a pleasing set, or two, of music delicately composed – *in a manner where you can actually understand the words!*

And providing this setting has its advantages! Not only is there a market for this MTV Unplugged-type offering – the owners have expressed substantial interest from many local 'on the verge ...' bands, as well as major name possibilities – especially in performing for their 'Acoustic Brunch,' every Sunday between noon and 4:00 p.m. (brunch is served 11:30 a.m. to 3:00 p.m.).

As for their beverage *'hook,'* well, the name of this bar says it all! It stands for Infusions of Vodka (and any other 'entendre' you can think up!). What you'll see, as you check out your *presence* in the mirror behind the bar, is a line-up of no fewer than seven glass decanters displaying their contents for your perusal. With two reserved for olives and Jalepeños, the remaining vials will hold with such fruits as cherries, blueberries, and oranges. Served in martini-style glasses, they''' let us 'do' little mix-n-match combinations, the way we like our Italian sodas. *Jalepeño infused Vodka!* Can't *wait* for those Bloody Marys!

So it goes like this: If you're lookin' for a place where you can find good food and an 'intimate groove'; a place where you can have fun among an eclectic gathering of people of like mind and tastes; a place where musicians like to come to hear music – and even the employees like to hang out on their day off, it seems the folks at *Infusion* have the formula. We wish them luck.

Passport: Two Infusions for the price of one.

132: Julie's Supper Club   Supper Club

1123 Folsom St. (at 7th). 415-861-0707. SOMA. **HOURS:** Mon-Thur, 5:30p.m.-10:30p.m.; Fri-Sat, 5:30p.m.-11:30p.m.; bar open 'til 2a.m. **ENTRANCE CHARGE:** $5.00 after 10:30 p.m., Thur-Sat. only.

Bam Bam Flintstone becomes an interior designer – but not until memorizing every episode of the Jetsons. This is the sort of notion you can easily gain as you

enter this *Grandmother* of San Francisco dinner clubs. Julie is long gone – having moved across town to wile her wares at Julie Rings Heart and Soul, but her legacy lives on in the kitchen *and on the menu* of this most-established of all SoMa entertainment haunts.

Success is testament to the food and fun formula that placed *Julie's* on The City's supper club map way back in April of 1987 – a time when many of today's club owners were busboys or bartenders. The unique *social* atmosphere and consistently good food, combined with the eclectic musical whims of the bar staff and committed clients, has fueled *Julie's* longevity

Like any established club, *Julie's* popularity ebbs and flows with the fickle fantasies of The Bay Area's 'we're too trendy' fashion phantoms. Be assured, however, that on any given weekend, you'll find a crowd of late-20s to mid-40s groovers bouncin' to the live-band-beat while groovin' to the moovin' of bar-flys-in-heat.

Oops ... sorry ... we've been going to Julie's soooooo long, we thought we could take some artistic liberties. The truth is, Julie's brings to SoMa a stable offering of a solid weekend scene. Operating on a six month (or so) cycle of weekday highs and lows, you can almost judge the mood in The City by whether *Julie's* is jammin' or not on a Thursday.

They easily have one of San Francisco's most-affordable menus, featuring such mainstay appetizers as their famous 'Julies' (cheese-filled wontons ($x.xx), killer quesadillas ($x.xx), and deep-fried catfish that will change your mind about catfish. The entries are ever changing, usually with a pasta, chicken, fish, lamb (to die for), and other offerings that are good enough that we have yet to try Dave's Burger ($x.xx), a menu mainstay.

On the drink side, their full bar presents full-attention bartenders who seem to like their jobs *(they stay so* damn *long),* and who produce – in our humble *Let's Party!* opinion – the best Top-Shelf Margarita on the West Coast.

Oh, for you history buffs. Did you know that Patty Hearst – you know, the chic who was abducted and branwashed by the Symbionese Liberation Army? Well, they did her thing on her in what is now Julie's basement *(Mom, guess who's over for dinner?!?)*. Perhaps that's why the laundromat across the street is called the *Brain Wash!*

A Personal Note From the Publisher: To Julie's, *the first bar I visited upon arriving in San Francisco, oh so many years ago. I want to thank you for the good food, and good times ... and could you* please *put the photo of Natalie Wood back up on the wall?!?* Thank you,
Mark J. Maxam

133: My Place   Gay Bar

1225 Folsom St. (at 8th). 415-863-2329. SOMA. **HOURS:** Daily, noon-2a.m. **SPECIALS:** Happy Hour. **RESTRICTIONS:** Cash only.

My Place runs along the lines of the classic late 70s leather hangout. If that sentence alone is not enough to have you scrambling through those extra-thick, ominous-looking leather curtains into one of the most socially outrageous bars in town (and it should), let me explain. Upon entering *My Place,* you'll be greeted by dim red lights, the occasional black light, and an arousing bluish flicker emanating from a large television perched above (and just to the left of) the entranceway.

After your eyes adjust to the darkness, and you have a beer firmly in hand, take a moment to absorb your surroundings. Notice the chandelier above the bar, resplendent with dildoes and other paraphernalia to fit all persuasions; or the dungeon fantasy wall mural; or the wrist shackles suspended from the ceiling next to the pool table; or the spider's-web-like rope arrangement near the back; or the loud, edgy music electrifying the already supercharged, erotic atmosphere. If this isn't enough, you'll soon discover that manager Shawn, his fast and friendly crew, and the motley group of weekend revelers are some of the friendliest guys in town. This and more (if you desire) awaits you at one of the most outstanding leather bars in town, *My Place.*

134: Paradise Lounge   Live Music Bar

501 Folsom St. (at 11th). 415-861-6906. SOMA. **HOURS:** Daily, 3p.m.-2a.m. **ENTRANCE CHARGE:** $3.00-$7.00 per person. **SPECIALS:** Happy Hour, 3p.m.-7p.m., $.75 off drinks, plus free pool tables.

Paradise is live-band central, and has been around as long as I can remember. The cover is never more than $3.00 to $5.00, and it's an arena for several local bands, bands just put together, bands that have done the circuit for years, bands touring from other cities from venues just like this one (whose guitar player you just might recognize from college).

There's Rock n' Roll, Grunge, Funk, Jazz, Swing, Ska, and just about anything else you can name.

Paradise is cut into several different lounges, with a bar and lounge up front, a jazz room on one side, and a larger space in back for bigger bands and a dance

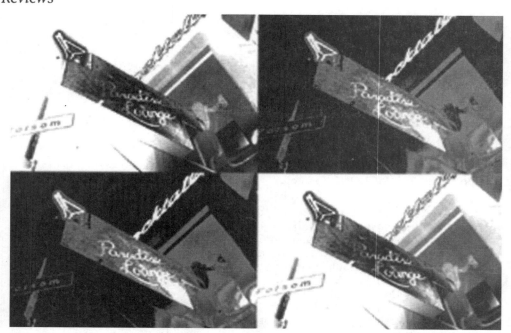

area. The cool thing is, for such a small area, the walls hold the acoustics really well. You simply don't hear the music from the next room so, when you're sick of one type tune, off you venture to the next space for a different groove.

A regular favorite at *Paradise* is the Bud E. Luv show, starring Bud the lounge lizard himself. He does a repertoire of all the tacky tunes you remember from growing up. It's a hilarious show (yeah, who loves ya baby), and he finishes up the set with the theme from Love Boat (but, truthfully, you can only take so much).

Above *Paradise* is a candlelit bar with tables that face the street corner (where you sit as witness to all the craziness going on at SoMa's 11th Street hub). Upstairs are pool tables, and usually a light Jazz combo, acoustic guitar, or – some nights – 'open-mike' and poetry readings.

Paradise has expanded its boundaries to include Transmission Theater next door. The theater houses a larger space for greater versatility – bigger concerts, virtual reality games, avante garde theater, etc. In March 96, *Paradise* and Transmission participated in presenting the Bammies (Bay Area Music Awards), where music legends are made.

Paradise 'has it all' – especially if you aren't into fancy. But *fancy-schmancy* doesn't buy you good vibes, so stop on by.

Somewhere caught between an idea and a beer, Paradise Lounge got reviewed by two of our writers. We won't tell you who is who, but here's another look at this long-blasting SOMA locale:

According to Dante's Inferno, Hell has seven rings. *Paradise*, on the other hand, has only two levels, and three stages to pass through. That's right, if your nocturnal forays call for a nonstop variety of live music, you won't do better than their three daily acts.

Paradise features a spectrum of live acts. On one stage, a musician makes love to his guitar during a Blues ballet; another vibrates to the sounds of Grung-Punk; a third offers the jazzy tunes of a brass ensemble.

The atmosphere is relaxed and roomy- roamer-friendly. Besides live music, Paradise Lounge puts-out entertaining multimedia affairs ranging from provocative readings to a full blown techno circus. If your lounging circuits are on overload, shuffle to the pool room where, at first, you'll probably do nothing more then put your name on the list. You'll discover many come here just to play pool, so it might be a wait – but who cares, you're in paradise!

135: Release   Dance Club

1015 Folsom St. (at 6th). 415-431-1200. SOMA. **HOURS:** Sat, 10 p.m.-7a.m. **ENTRANCE CHARGE:** $10.00 per person. **RESTRICTIONS:** Dress Code.

Oh, how sweet it is – Saturday night has arrived, your juices are flowing to the brim, and you're armed with sparks in your feet. Its time to decompress and release. As we write this, 1015 Folsom is the address for *Release,* The City's premier decompression chamber – *on Saturdays only*. It's a tri-level temple of sight and sound that serves as the royal grounds for the movers and shakers of club culture – as well as who's-who celebrity drop-ins.

Under the watchful wings of Martel and Nabiel, San Francisco's top promoters, you'll experience the spin sermons of some of San Francisco's top DJ's. *Release* has been in the forefront of The City's high powered, competitive club scene for over three years, and has yet to show signs of relinquishing its reign. By relocating from venue to venue before settling into its happy home at 1015 Folsom, *Release* has proven that its not the location that matters. Their San Francisco born and bred formula of energy and vibe has heightened this once-a-week bash into a state of mind.

Its Midnight; the front door is buzzing like a bee hive; fashion funksters emerge from limousines and taxis; a line of club goers wraps around the corner of the building. As you stand waiting to pass the doormen, you feel the outside walls vibrate and expand with every beat. Finally, the wait is over and you enter the 'Gold Room.' Anticipation ultimately unfolds into moments of awareness and presence; bodies under a musical spell dance between the beats, vanishing and reappearing through shafts of light.

As you side-step past the bar and dance floor, you'll encounter a bottle neck of bodies migrating through one large entryway or another leading to the main dance floor. One DJ's universe of sound dissolves into the realm of another's, as the sound from the next room takes over. To the left, a large stage reverberates under platform stomps of exhibitionist groove.

Reminding you of primal lures, you see cage dancers hanging above the dance floor, as manic percussionists keep pace with the powerfully charged House beats. Laser beams cut through the smoke, and bounce off a moving parade of styles. 'Posers,' with lit cigarettes in hand, stand on the sideline of the madness, as Puffs girls rotate through the scene selling candy and smokes, a la 50's-style nightclubs.

You'll see a set of stairs that lead down, and several sets that lead up. Down takes you to another dance floor that sometimes features live music. Up, however, is another subject. Go one way, and you'll wind up in a 'chill room' of the truest kind. The 'time-out terrace' is a music *and roof*-free comfort zone where a grill serves food. It's a perfect setting for relaxing or getting aquatinted with new dance floor run-ins.

The other staircase from the stage leads, literally, nowhere. The sizable bouncer reserves it for exiting the VIP lounges upstairs.

You'll find the stairway to the VIP rooms by backtracking into the hallway between the two main dance floors. Head up this stairway, and you've made it to the club's VIP rooms – *if you have what it takes,* that is!

A dress-code is strictly enforced by the doorman here, so if you're sportin' your torn jeans and "Go 49ers" t-shirt, forget it! It also helps to know someone, but if you look good (and aren't acting like an ass), take our advice: patience pays!

The VIP rooms offer a lounger-laden ambiance where you can pick-up and move to the groove, or set your seat to the beat on one of the plushy cushioned couches. One door further, past another scrutinizing doorman, and you're in the VIP-room-*deluxe*. Carry the right energy (and a little more patience), and you're in!

Now you'll find yourself in a more-intimate space that's pregnant with spirit and wit – at least on most nights. The small dance floor keeps your dancing form intimate, while the surrounding couches mold to forms of another sort. Here is where flirting and networking lead to some of The City's legendary after-parties. If the word doesn't come your way, however, there's always the *Endup*.

136: Slims   Live Music Venue

333 11th St. (at Harrison). 415-522-0333. SOMA. **HOURS:** Fri & Sat doors open 8p.m.; show, 9p.m.-1:30a.m.; Sun-Thur as announced. **ENTRANCE CHARGE:** Range is $5.00-$20.00, depending on performance. **SPECIALS:** VIP seating for dinner reservations. **RESTRICTIONS:** Minimum credit card charge of $10.00 on food.

Since it's grand opening in September of 88, *Slim's* has bulldozed its way to the forefront of San Francisco's live music scene. It's co-owner, Boz Scaggs, envisioned a London-style small music venue where both famous and yet-to-be-famous artists can share their latest compositions. So, thanks to Boz, the SoMa scene is complete for the happy nocturnal prowlers.

Inside, the setting is raw, yet congenial. Flanked with a sprawling bar beneath wrought iron chandeliers, the large, squarish room separates an imposing stage on one side, and a balcony on the other. The balcony offers the best view in the house.

Access to this choicest of spots requires dinner reservations made with a credit card through BASS Ticket Outlets (510-762-2277). The ambiance changes like the colors of a chameleon, depending on the type of music booked. And, when it comes to music, pretty much anything goes at Slim's. From Blues, R&B, Jazz, and Cajun-Zydeco to Alternative Rock, it pays to check the schedule ahead of time. Look in the *Bay Guardian* or *San Francisco Weekly* for a scheduled line-up.

137: Sound Factory   Dance Club

525 Harrison St. (at 1st). 415-543-1300. SOMA. **HOURS:** Fri, 9:30p.m.-7a.m.; Sat, 9:30p.m.-4a.m. **ENTRANCE CHARGE:** $10.00 per person. **RESTRICTIONS:** No sneakers or hooded sweatshirts.

Another of San Francisco's high-drama-dance-club-venues, *Sound Factory* offers a multi-level, multi-media playground for urban and suburban dance junkies alike. *Sound Factory*, with it's vibe-hoisting muscle-man icon, is one of the oldest on-going clubs in The City. Boasting The City's largest dance floor, it's easy to be sucked into the gravitational pull of this house of techno beats (once you get past the ever-present line, that is).

Beneath flying dolphins, you'll witness the beauty and style of some of the Bay Area's eccentric (and just plain weird) inhabitants, flash-dancing to trance-like beats. If you're looking for a change of scenery, *Sound Factory* offers a disorienting maze of corners that lead from one room to the next – each 'tagged' with its own ambiance. From the artfully decked-out bar/lounge, to the competitively charged 'billiard' room, around every corner you transcend from one sound envelope to the next.

Turn another corner, and a set of stairs will lead you up to the VIP-lounge ... and yet another dance floor. Up here, mind-altering substances are not needed – *there are enough interesting people to keep you* well *amused.*

138: South Beach Billiards   Pool Hall

270 Brannan St. (between 1st & 2nd). 415-495-5939. SOMA. **HOURS:** Mon– Fri, noon-2a.m.; Sat-Sun, 2p.m.-2a.m. **ENTRANCE CHARGE:** RATES: Regular, $12.00/hr. (singles 1/2 price); Fri-Sat after 7p.m., $15.00/hr.; Sun, $6.00/hr. (All rates are pro-rated). **SPECIALS:** $10.00 table, all night, Mon nights after 5p.m.; 1/2 price pool with lunch purchase; Mon-Fri, noon-5p.m.; $20.00 "All You Can Play" table rate, Mon– Thur.

You won't run into Steve Mizerack, or any of his contemporary pool wizards here, but that's okay. What you *will* find, is an very-pleasing, oversized pool palace catering to the *"pool is cool"* brigade of casual players and "pool is a good idea for a date" couples.

What *South Beach Billiards* lacks in hustlers, however, it more than makes up for with an environment that encompasses a small bar, a more-than-ample number of high-quality leather-pocket, good-felt tables, and a rotating art gallery – usually showing pieces that are much too big to fit in your apartment. There's also a really cool sign outside pointing you to a very-relaxed atmosphere inside.

Two things – the pool hall is fronted by a large parking lot, which simply makes life easier; and the sign is reproduced on T-shirts, which you can buy at the front counter.

The proximity of South Beach to 'Multi-Media Gulch' and area artsy lofts ensures a constant influx of healthy, well-educated clientele, so you don't have to worry about being on the wrong end of a Scam – unless it's of your own making. The rates are reasonable (by San Francisco standards), and are prorated, so you only pay for the time you play.

And, if you have different tastes, you can try your hand at Snooker (it's that BIG table right inside the front door), or bocce ball.

The food's not going to knock your socks off, but it's good for what it is (mostly 'create your own' sandwiches and snacks), and the selection of tap beers is usually very good. So, grab your buddies or – better yet a date, and strut your stuff. There's *definitely* something to be said for not having to worry about looking bad compared to Minnesota Fats at the next table.

Oh, yeah. Fats died this year ('96), so rack 'em, and break a good one for him. Maybe he'll smile down on you from Heaven – and that 8-ball that seemed to be hanging on the edge of the pocket ... may ... just ... *drop!*

Passport: Half off regular priced pool, any day, plus $2.00 off T-shirt.

139: The Stud   Gay Bar/Dance Club

399 9th St. (at Harrison). 415-252-STUD. SOMA. **HOURS:** Daily, 5 p.m.-2a.m.
ENTRANCE CHARGE: Varies depending on night. **SPECIALS:** Varies depending on night.

The world famous *Stud*, open since 1966, is one of the best-known 'queer' hot
spots in San Francisco, seven days a week, 365 days a year. It's not the biggest –
and by no means the most glamorous – but it *is* the 'queer' standby, where you
know there'll always be something to do. Long-standing theme nights include:

- Funk Night is Monday, with an ethnically mixed 20- to 30-something crowd
  pounding away at the medium-sized dance floor to the beat of funk, soul, and hip
  hop.
- Wednesday's Classic Disco nights have consistently been one of the busiest and
  liveliest crowds *Stud* has ever known. There's always a long waiting line outside of
  'Dancing Queens' ready to pack the sweaty dance floor and sing along to the fab-
  ulous tunes of ABBA, The Village People, and the flawless screaming divas who laid
  foundation for much of today's House music.
- Sunday nights at are no less nostalgic, with their mega-popular '80s-Something'
  theme night where Culture Club, Duran Duran, Soft Cell, and the like are lovingly
  brought back to a nostalgic Generation X crowd by hip DJs Dan and Paul.

Stud is rarely known as a progressive nightspot in The City, but it *is* known as a
casual, relaxed, cruisy, friendly, down-to-earth club where the beer is always cheap,
the cover charge even cheaper, and the fun ... well, you get the picture. Go to *Stud*,
let your hair down, and enjoy San Francisco!

140: Twenty Tank Brewery   Microbrewery Bar/Restaurant

316 Eleventh St. (between Folsom &
Harrison). 415-255-9455. SOMA.
HOURS: Daily, 11:30a.m.-2a.m.

This pub and micro-brewery
opened in September, 1990, when
San Francisco was first discovering
microbrews. Located at 11th and
Folsom, next to Eleven and across the
street from Slim's, puts it in the heart
of the SoMa crawl. *Twenty Tank* provides a good dress-down alternative
to many of the jazzy, *chic*-ey DJ
dance scenes. You'll likely spot frat
guys in jeans and Ivy League sweatshirts hanging out and drinkin' lots of beer
(while looking for a chance to approach small circles of girls clad in miniskirts and
oxford shoes). Wait a minute ... is this really *San Francisco?*

But, then, microbrews always attract the college crowd! The beer is hearty, and
Twenty Tank is proud of producing the award-winning Kinnikinick Brand Ale and
Stout (say that 10 times quickly). You can find as many as 10 brews on tap and,
when the upstairs bar is open on Friday and Saturday nights, there may be even
more to choose from. When the beer is ready to serve, it comes directly from the
serving tanks in the brewery to the bar taps in the adjoining pub.

Twenty Tank also features live Jazz on Tuesday through Thursday nights, and ...
there's no cover charge! That in itself may be just the clincher that'll make you stay
and say "forget the clubs."

Are you hungry (funny how drinking always does that to you)? You'll appreciate the kitchen, which serves pizzas, hearty pub sandwiches, chili, and finger-foods 'til late. Or, you can just drink 'a coupla pints' of stout – a veritable meal-in-a-mug!

In addition to the usual frat crowd, you'll drink with hangers-on from the club-ber-scene, or possibly band members who just finished a set at Slim's across the way. Rambo, one of the bartenders, told us Mike Myers came in when he was filming in San Francisco. They also shot a Don Johnson pilot here ... and that band, The Breeders, came in and raved about the stout.

Twenty Tank is also a big participant in the city's biannual Eleventh Street block parties. They usually feature big name local bands, and set up a beer tent or patio along the closed-off Eleventh Street.

Passport: A beer snack with purchase of any pint of house brewed beer.

141: Up 'n Down Club   Dance Bar/Supper Club

1151 Folsom St. (between 7th & 8th) 415-626-2388. SOMA. **HOURS:** Mon-Tue, 9 p.m.-2a.m. (no dinner); Wed-Thur, 8 p.m.-2a.m.; Fri-Sat, 8:30 p.m.-2a.m. **ENTRANCE CHARGE:** Varies depending on day and event.

Christy Turlington's *UP & down Club* is a hip, one-stop shop for great food, fine cocktails, and cool Jazz. Co-owned by booking guru J.J. Morgan, the club is at the forefront of San Francisco's new Jazz

scene. In fact, *Up & Down* is continually helping to *redefine* "Jazz."

Since 1992, the 100-capacity 'Down' venue has been a steadfast, six-night-a-week outlet for a new school of young players – all of whom combine Jazz with other musical genres. Integrating Hip-Hop to Funk, Rock to Latin, they continue to create distinctive Bay Area styles.

This Jazz-fusion explosion has exposed some huge Bay Areas talents. *UP & down Club* has released two *Bammie*-nominated (Bay Area music awards) CDs that include the likes of the Charlie Hunter trio, the Will Bernard trio, Josh Jones Latin Jazz Ensemble, and Alphabet Soup (whose lead singer appeared as one of the roomies on MTV's Real World, San Francisco).

Bands perform in the back of the room in a softly lit, jazzy-styled room with earth-tone, fabric-lined walls. Jazz flows along the melding curves that canopy the winding bar and cafe tables. Have a couple of glasses of wine with some sautéed prawns and calamari, and you're all set.

After a set or two, venture on upstairs. The '*Up*' in this club is designed like a Harlem speak-easy, where DJ spins permeate the booths, tables, and intimate dance floor. Monday nights are very crowded with locals grooving to the Hip-Hop of DJ *Racer X* – and 2-for-1 drinks. Alphabet Soup also plays downstairs on Monday nights. Wednesday nights are for jive Samba; Thursdays spin classic Funk & Soul; and weekends feature DJ *Roman*, San Francisco's groove king. This is when the whole place *really* gets movin'.

The cover charge averages $5.00, which is a steal for witnessing the birth of a whole new music scene.

Passport: Free entry, any day.

UPPER MARKET

142: Bahia Cabana Brazilian Restaurant & Dance Club

1600 Market St. (at Page & 12th). 415-861-4202. Upper Market. **HOURS:** Mon-Sat, Dinner, 5p.m.-10p.m.; Dance Club 'til 2a.m. **ENTRANCE CHARGE:** Varies depending on night and performance. **SPECIALS:** Happy Hour, Thur, 5:30p.m.-7:30p.m., free Tapas; Fri-Sat, 7p.m.-9p.m., 30-50% off beers.

While the tropical bamboo bungalow bars and Brazilian fantasy murals may not be totally convincing, on the right night (which is very important here), you can certainly get *Carnival Fever*. We visited *Bahia* in Carnival season, so the place was at manic heights. Still, *Bahia's* reputation for evenings of relentless dance crazed mania is increasing daily.

The musical offerings vary, but Thursday and Sunday currently are salsa nights, Friday focuses on house and techno, and Saturdays are appropriately Brazilian. Cover charges range from $5.00 to $10.00, and are half price for restaurant patrons.

The restaurant serves a simple Brazilian menu from 5:00 to 11:00 p.m.. Entrees average $12, while salads and tapas range from $3.00 to $8.00. Thursday nights, the club offers free tapas, $1.50 draft beer, and flamenco guitar performances from 5:30 to 7:30 p.m. Friday and Saturdays from 7:00 to 9:00 p.m. the Happy Hour serves beers for 30 to 50 percent off. We recommend you stick with the imported Brazilian beers

Passport: 30% off the cover charge (get out your calculator!).

143: Cafe Du Nord — Dance Club/Restaurant/Bar

2170 Market St. (at Noe). 415-861-5016. cafedunord@aol.com. Upper Market. **HOURS:** Daily, 4 p.m.-2a.m. **ENTRANCE CHARGE:** $3.00, depending on time and night.

A notorious illicit saloon during the 1920s, Cafe du Nord retains the look and feel of a Prohibition-era speakeasy. The classic oak bar and bordello-red interior, with light emanating softly from period fixtures, further the illusion of a bar that has been transported back in time. When rising star jazz and blues singer Lavay Smith and the Red Hot Skillet Lickers take the stage and belt out their mellifluous melodies, the transformation is complete. Welcome to Prohibition!

The hip, unpretentious mood is enhanced by the dressed, artsy young crowd. Those truly in the know drop by for free swing lessons on Sundays at 8:00 p.m., or for free salsa lessons on Tuesdays at 9:00 p.m. Dozens of singles and couples attend the lessons each evening, and those arriving solo quickly find many willing partners in this eager-to-learn crowd. After an hour of basic lessons, the curtain goes up and a live band hits the stage.

Live music is featured seven nights a week, and runs the gamut from Jazz to Blues, from Salsa to Swing, from Trance Hop to experimental. Blues and Jazz dominate the weekend lineup.

Fridays and Saturdays, free dinner shows run from 7:00 to 9:00 p.m., followed by a second show . Cover runs from $2.00 to $7.00, and can often be avoided if you arrive before 9:00 p.m.. Dinner is served Wednesday through Saturday from 6:30 to 11:00 p.m.

Passport: One free entrance.

144: Orbit Room Cafe — Cafe

1900 Market St. (at Laguna). 415-252-9515. Upper Market. **HOURS:** Daily, 7a.m.-2a.m.

Lordly poised on the busy corner of Market and Laguna, *Orbit's* elegant, yet simple and spacious interior is tattooed from head to toe with a pseudo avant-garde disposition. (Harrumph!!!) From its Art-Deco aluminum tiled ceiling, to the gold and silver wall tones; from the 1944 Wurlitzer Jukebox, to the cone-shaped marble tables; from the windows the size of a movie house viewing screen, to the outdoor cafe tables, your senses can easily be catapulted to the parallel world of Vienna or Paris.

During the day, an international mix of exchange students from the neighboring University share their notes for an upcoming exam, while munching-down on Focaccia sandwiches. As day wanes, however, *Orbit* – with the student's life of academia – transforms into the high-life of San Francisco fashion-gurus and jet-setters. Frank Sinatra, Tony Bennett, Ella Fitzgerald and Miles Davis jump out of the Wurlitzer, joining with the circles of laughter and conversation.

Belonging to the category of 'back to the future' dinner clubs (e.g., Bruno's and the Red Room) sprouting up throughout The City, *Orbit* takes its place – balancing precariously between the 20th and 21st century.

LISTS OF STUFF

S o, you're in San Francisco, you've checked out everything in the front of the book, and you're still looking ... *or,* you want something to do during the day (other than a park) ... *or* you want to see what we added so we're not just a book about places to drink.

Well, in this chapter we have prepared for you our *Lists of Stuff,* an addendum to our compendium.

For you *club-types,* we've compiled a comprehensive *Club Calendar.* Following it, you will find info on *Salsa Clubs* and *Swing clubs*-so you can (finally learn to) dance that stuff. We also have listings for City *Events* (because you just gotta hit those block parties), *Tours* (for that *something different),* and a list of *Radio Stations* (so you can stay *in-tune).*

Last, and the proverbial *'certainly not least,'* we have our listing of *Late Night Food.* Because we know as you do, when the hunger hits ....

We hope this rounds out your need for us, because we're tired and we're going home. You're welcome, and ... *the rest, is up, to you!*

Just remember, behind these pages we have given you a ••• BONUS •••. Coupons worth a couple hundred dollars of *Two-fers* and *discounts* at San Francisco establishments. Tell 'em we sent ya.

Okay, is *that* enough?

We'll see ya later ....

Club Calendar
Monday

• *Club Dread* at the Endup, 401 Harrison Street, 415-284-6331, 9p.m.+. *Reggae.*

• *Death Guild* at Trocadero Transfer, 520 4th Street, 415-974-4396, 9p.m.-3a.m. *Gothic*

• *Grateful Dead Jam* at Nicky's BBQ, 460 Haight Street, 415-621-6508, 9p.m.-2a.m. *Rock 'n roll.*

• *Mushroom Jazz* at 330 Ritch Street at 330 Ritch Street, 415-541-9574, 9p.m.-2a.m. *Jazz Fusion.*

(Sort of a tradition now, to relax after a rough weekend ... or maybe to continue the weekend (depending on your perspective).)

Tuesday

- *505* at 9th & Howard
- *Asia, Africa and Arabia* at Nicky's BBQ, 460 Haight Street, 415-621-6508, 9p.m.-2a.m.
- *Breathe Deep* at 1015 Folsom, 415-998-9515, 10p.m.-4a.m. *House music.*
- *Butterfly* at Casanova Cocktail Longe, 527 Valencia at 16th, 415-863-9328
- *Spaceport* at 1840 Hayes Street

Wednesday

- **a little more** at Ristorante Eleven, 374 11th Street, 415-431-3337, 9p.m.-2a.m. *Acid fusion.*
- *Black Diamond* at 1015 Folsom, 1015 Folsom Street, 415-998-9515. *House music.*
- *Bondage a GoGo* at The Trocadero 520 4th Street, 415-995-4600. *Gothic Industrial.*
- *Country Western Wednesday* at V/sf, 278 11th Street, 415-621-1530. *Country.*
- *Energy* at Bahia Cabana, 1600 Market Street, 415-861-8657.
- *Funk and Soul* at DNA Lounge, 375 11th Street, 415-626-1409, 9p.m.-2a.m.
- *Hip Hop* at Nickie's BBQ, 460 Haight Street, 415-621-6508, 9p.m.-2a.m.
- *Simply Done* at DV8

Thursday

- *Bedlam* at The Endup, 401 Harrison Street, 415-284-6331. *Gothic & Industrial*
- *The Box* at 715 Harrison Street (at 3rd St.),415-647-8258, 9p.m.-2a.m. *Gay, lesbian and straight.*
- *Booty Shake* at Club 181, 181 Eddy Street, 415-673-8181
- *Full House* at Miss Pearls Jam House, 601 Eddy Street, 415-775-4992
- *Groove Jazz* at Nickie's BBQ, 460 Haight Street, 415-621-6508, 9p.m.-2a.m.
- *Lift* at 55 Natoma Street, 415-267-5984, 11p.m.-5a.m. *Deep House.*
- *Pack a Bowl* at Park Bowl, 1855 Haight Street
- *Plastik* at Big Heart City, 836 Mission Street, 415-979-3031, 10p.m.-3a.m. *Acid Jazz, Ambient, and Int'l House.*
- *Rockabilly* at DNA Lounge, 375 11th Street. *Rock 'n roll, Swing.*
- *Soulvation* at Elbo Room, 647 Valencia Street, 415-252-7788. *R&B.*
- *Swing Mode* at Bahia Cabana, 1600 Market Street, 415-861-4202
- *Top* at The Top, 424 Haight Street, 415-864-7386
- *White Trash* at The Stud, 399 Harrison Street, 415-252-7883, 5p.m.-2a.m. *Rock 'n Roll queer bar.*
- *Zanzibar* at 330 Ritch Street, 330 Ritch Street, 415-541-9574
- *Zion* at Deco Reggae Dancehall

Friday

- *Bulletproof* at (Find it!)
- *Cabana* at 1015 Folsom, 1015 Folsom Street, 415-998-9515, 11p.m.-4a.m.
- *Club 107* at DV8, 540 Howard Street, 415-957-1730, 10p.m.-5a.m.
- *Club X* at 715 Harrison Street, 415-979-8686, 9:30p.m.-2:30a.m. *An 18+ club.*
- *Luxor* at Sol Y Luna, 475 Sacramento Street, 415-860-6985, 10:30p.m.-2a.m. *Int'l House.*
- *Sophie's* at the Beer Cellar, 685 Sutter Street, 415-995-2387, 9p.m.+
- *Terminator* at Trocadero Transfer, 520 4th Street, 415-995-4600, 9p.m.-3a.m.
- *Viva* at V/sf, 278 11th Street, 415-267-3936, 9:30p.m.-4a.m. Gay club. *House.*

Saturday

- *Cream of Beat* at tbd, call 415-469-2081. *A once a month club hosted by the San Francisco mayor, 'Boss' Brown's son. Typically on Saturday. Old school and hip-hop.*
- *City Nights* at 715 Harrison Street, 415-979-8686, 9:30p.m.-2:30a.m. *An 18+ club.*
- *Club Universe* at Club Townsend, 177 Townsend Street, 415-985-5241, 9:30p.m.-7a.m. *House.*
- *'80's Dance Hall* at DNA Lounge, 375 11th Street, 415-626-1409, 9p.m.-4a.m.

LET'S PARTY!
Club Calendar

- **Eden** at Club DV8, 538 Howard Street, 415-267-5957, 10p.m.-7a.m. *R&B, Hip-Hop and 70's.*
- **G-Spot** at V/sf, 278 11th Street, 415-621-1530, 8p.m.- 4a.m. *Lesbian club.*
- **New Wave City** at Trocadero Transfer, 520 4th Street, 415-995-4600, 9p.m.-3a.m. *One Saturday a month.*
- **Release** at 1015 Folsom Street, 415-985-7131, 10p.m.-7a.m. *Multi-room club with 70's disco, funk, and house.*
- **Vegas Lounge** at DNA Lounge, 375 11th Street, 415-979-3031, 10p.m.-3a.m. *70's Remixes and Ambient.*
- **Wicked**-call 415-512-5173. *First Saturday every month-It's 'Wicked!'*

Sunday

- **Leopard Lounge** at Blues, 2125 Lombard Street, 415-771-2583, 9:30p.m.-2a.m. *Acid Jazz.*
- **Pandulce** at V/sf, 278 11th Street, 415-621-1530, 10p.m.-2a.m. *A gay and lesbian latin dance party.*
- **Spundae** at DV8, 55 Natoma Street, 415-974-9389, 8p.m.-'til dawn. *Deep House.*
- **Sunday Tea Dance** at the Endup, 401 Harrison Street, 415-487-6277, 6a.m.-2a.m. *House and Funk.*

Salsa Clubs

Some of the following are dedicated Salsa clubs, and some *Salsa* on certain nights only. Most Salsa clubs offer some form of dance lessons if you get there early. If you don't know how to Salsa, or are rusty, we highly recomend this route. Usually the lessons are free with the cover charge anyway.

- **Sol y Luna**, 475 Sacramento Street, 415-296-8696; Wed-Sat; $10.00 per person. Dress code.
- **Cesar's Latin Palace**, 3140 Mission Street, 415-648-6611; Fri-Sat 'till 5a.m.; $8.00 per person.
- **Coconut Grove**, 1415 Van Ness Avenue, 415-776-1616; Sun, 10p.m.-1:30a.m.; No cover.
- **330 Ritch Street**, 330 Ritch Street, 415-415-541-9574; Sat; $5.00 per person before 9p.m., $10.00 per person after 9p.m. Dance lessons at 8:30p.m.
- **Bruno's Cork Club**, 2389 Mission Street, 415-550-7455; Thur, 11p.m.-2a.m.; $2.00 per person.
- **Kimball's SF**, 300 Grove Street; 415-861-5555; Fri-Sat, 10p.m.-2a.m.; $10.00 per person. Dance lessons at 9p.m.
- **El Rio**, 3158 Mission Street, 415-282-3325; Sun, 4p.m.-8p.m.; $7.00 per person.
- **Cafe Du Nord**, 2170 Mission Street,415-979-6545; Tue, 10p.m.-2a.m.; $3.00 per person. Lessons at 9p.m. This club is *hot* , so dress light.
- **Futura**, 174 King Street, 415-665-6715; second & fourth Saturday of the month, 10p.m.-3a.m., $10.00 per person. Gay club.
- **Alex DaSilva** teaches Wednesday night @ 970 Harrison. Beginner classes at 7p.m., intermediates at 8p.m. The cost is $10.00. Alex is a great Salsa instructorand, and has a relationship with Sol Y luna on Wednesday nights. Start at 970 Harrison at 7p.m., practice for 2 hours, then go to Sol y Luna to dance all night long. 415-546-0321 or 546-1269.

Swing Clubs

- **Friday & Saturday** at Hi-Ball Lounge, 473 Broadway
- **Friday & Sunday** at **Cafe Du Nord**, 2170 Market Street; Sunday with lessons at 8pm
- **Friday** at **The Palace Hotel**, 2 New Montgomery Street
- **Saturday** at **Metronome Ballroom** at 1830 17th Street, Lessons at 7:30p.m.
- **Saturday & Monday** at Coconut Grove at 1415 Van Ness Avenue
- **Thurdsday** at Rockabilly, DNA Lounge, 375 11th Street. Let your sideburns grow for this one.

The Galleries

San Francisco has always been one of the coolest places to enjoy art. Maybe it's the atmosphere, the mix, or perhaps the wide variety of perspectives. Here in *'Baghdad by the Bay,'* there's a climate of tolerance that enables a creativity you'll not find elsewhere in the world. Whether strolling among the many downtown galleries, or cruising SoMa, there's something to capture your particular fancy – *or just blows your mind.*

As a respected New York art dealer once explained, "Art is the least expensive form of entertainment in any city. Usually there is no admission charged, the galleries and museums are well-lit, comfortable places to go, and often you will get a free drink or two to go with it." San Francisco is no exception. The operative word here is *free!*

If you want to visit the better known, *more commercial* galleries in the city, pick up the *Art Now Gallery Guide* at all major galleries – look for the openings listed in the back, and do your thing. But there are other, alternative ways to look at art – *San Francisco style.*

Grab a copy of the *Bay Guardian* (it comes out every Wednesday, is free, and available everywhere) and flip through to the art listings. There you will find probably the best list of openings in The City. On any given Thursday through Saturday night, you can visit several different galleries, sample their art (and of course the refreshments), and be primed to sample San Francisco's famous 'eats.' Another excellent publication is *Art West*, a newspaper sold for $2.50. The *only* Bay Area art monthly, it's available at many galleries.

A favorite local event is known as 'First Thursdays.' On the first Thursday of each month, most galleries across The City throws open their doors to throngs of people. From the well-heeled upper crust to the pierced, tattooed crowd, you'll see more than you could ever want in a single night. There's also a free day at most museums in town (there's a partial listing at the end of this section). Some of *Our Favorite* alternative art spaces (in alphabetical order):

Catherine Clark Gallery

49 Geary Street (at Kearny), 2nd floor. HOURS: Tue-Fri, 10:30a.m.-5:30p.m., Sat, 11a.m.-5:30p.m., first Thur of month until 7:30 p.m. Director: Catherine Clark.

Formerly known as the Morphos Gallery, this plush, high-rise, downtown space has all the trappings of a traditional gallery – but the similarities end there!

Since her beginnings in Hayes Valley in early 1991, Catherine has developed a group of artists who show work that is by no means traditional. For example, in a recent show, an artist tied fishing wire back and forth, up and down, and all around the space, creating a maze that forced people to go over, under, and around to get inside, where all the action was. Hung from the lines were weird [?]paper mache heads and bodies at all sorts of odd angles. This gallery is always packed.

Collision Gallery

417 14th St. (near Valencia). 415-431-4074. HOURS: Thursday 5p.m.-8p.m., Fri, 1:00p.m.-5p.m., and Sat, 1p.m.-6:00p.m.

Collision Gallery is the collective vision of 10 artists (who live upstairs of this small storefront in a 'seedier' section of the Mission). It always has a large crowd of (mostly) younger artists and eclectic personalities, and features gritty, politically satirical, hard-edged work.

Their community-oriented views have produced a program that permits younger kids to use the gallery's darkroom – and to show their work in the space. Yet another program seeks to help homeless teenagers develop their creative voices.

The work here is always good. It will make you think, perhaps make you uncomfortable, or even rub you the wrong way. *So is the price of free speech* (mind opening can be so painful, sometimes). But, after all, that's what art is about ... or is it what *life's* about ... or what *the art of life* is about!?! You get it!

Take a side trip to the *Collision Gallery* - you won't be disappointed.

Four Walls

3160-A Sixteenth Street at Valencia. 415-626-8515. HOURS: Wed thru Sat, Noon-6p.m. Director: Julie Deamer.

Four Walls is located in the heart of the Mission – just a few doors away from some of the best bars in town. Started in early 1995, it has flourished ever since. They exhibit unusual painting and sculpture, films and videos, to be sure – but there's always something *really* different.

One of their best openings was for artist Brian Stortz. On half of the gallery floor, he constructed a mini-community –´complete with trains and track, dirt, plants, dolls, *army men*, buildings, and lights. Several electric and wind-up toy animals crashed through it all, getting trapped, reversing, and crashing into something else. People stood around and watched, mouths agape, and occasionally helped to create the havoc. His paintings and collages were hung throughout the rest of the gallery, which included a huge birthday cake for *The Director*, a killer jazz band. There was a huge spread of food and drink.

Definitely visit this place – maybe you'll find something as fantastic.

Galeria de la Raza/Studio 24

2875 24th Street (at Bryant). HOURS: Tue thru Sat, Noon-6p.m. Director: Gloria Jaramillo.

This is a real find. Founded in 1970 by local artists active in the Chicano civil rights movement (el Movimiento), *Galeria de la Raza* was the first to introduce Frida Khlo to the Bay Area. It also initiated the city's first community mural program in the early '70s.

One of the oldest, most well-respected Latino arts organizations in the country, they are dedicated to promoting public awareness and appreciation of Chicano and Latino artists and their cultures.

A visit to this studio is an experience you'll not soon forget. The work will make an impression on you, and you may come away thinking quite differently about San Francisco – for the better.

Timothy Higbee Gallery

30 Rose St. (near Market), 2nd floor. 415-621-4923. HOURS: Thur thru Sat, 3p.m.-8p.m. Director: Timothy Higbee.

Although this space sits across the street from Zuni Cafe (an upscale bar and restaurant), it caters to an alternative crowd. On the second floor of an old building, this T-shaped gallery is traditional white-washed walls over brick left exposed to show smaller work.

They recently held an opening for an artist named, simply, *Nelson*. He creates portraits in oils on unprimed wood panels – using only a palette knife. Often the portraits are not recognizable as individuals ... but their *personalities* are. It turned out to be successful for both the artist and the gallery.

One of the few galleries in this part of town, the Higbee gallery is worth the extra effort.

A Gallery Underview

Throughout San Francisco, a multitude of cafes, coffee shops, and bars maintain rotating galleries featuring art of all types. Those we like most are featured in our reviews.

If you haven't already been *jolted* into the San Francisco art reality, you can stop in at one of the 30 or so coffee houses that (for a small fee) permit access to the Internet. You can find so much information about art around the world it'll make your head spin (of course, you can also do this from the comfort of your own home or office – but what's the fun in that?).

One Web Site you'll want to visit is the Pacific Rim Art Exchange, at www.prae.com (for more info, call 415-566-7272). This new global collaboration effort is masterminded by Pierre Reynolds, and features everything from paintings to music clips, to animation, computer art, and electronic art. Within a year, they'll be able to show complete videotapes over the Internet.

One of their offerings will probably be *art/world,* a documentary cable TV series started in 1990, featuring world-famous, long-dead art heroes, as well as lesser-known artists. *art/world* has a large collection of Bay Area artists in it's library, and is well worth watching. For further information, call 415-837-0432.

Finally, if you're near the waterfront by the Bay Bridge, go the park at the end of Townsend St. and spend some time looking at the huge sculpture by renowned artist Mark di Suvero. It's called *Gateway,* and there's an interesting aside about the sculpture. It seems that Mark's father was living in China just prior to World War II. Fleeing aggressiveness, Mark's father packed the family up and sailed to America. As the story goes, the di Suvero family's ship landed at the exact point where the sculpture now stands. Coincidence? You'll know it when you see it. And *really* watch it – you'll see it move.

The bottom line on the San Francisco art world is this: see as much variety as you can handle, and don't be surprised if you fall in love with at least one artist (or their work) on your travels. Remember – to support art is to support life ... or does life support art ... or does life imitate art ... or visa versa ...? Perhaps it's *all of the above!*

Gallery Free Days

San Francisco Museum of Modern Art (SFMOMA)
151 Third St. at Howard. HOURS: Tue thru Sun, 11a.m.-6p.m., Thur, 11a.m.-9:00p.m. Free first Tuesday of each month. Half price every Thur, 6p.m.-9:00p.m.

This venerable institution recently moved into new digs – an awesome, modern, brick building that is a sculpture in and of itself. Great art, great light, and an excellent cafe with tables right out front.

Oh, don't forget to take a 'time-out' at Yerba Buena Garden (park) across the street. Notice the church next to the temple – the temple of affluence.

Mexican Museum
Fort Mason Center, Building D (at Laguna and Marina) HOURS: Wed thru Sun, Noon-5p.m. Free first Wednesday of each month.

Featuring an excellent selection of Latin artists, by the time you read this they may be in a new building across the street and down the block from SFMOMA. Call to find out (415-441-0404)

M.H. de Young Museum
Golden Gate Park. HOURS: Wed thru Sun, 10a.m.-4:45p.m. Free first Wednesday of each month.

Now that the wait for the earthquake retrofitting is over, you can visit one of the oldest – and still one of the best museums in the country – in the best park in the country (and the roof won't fall on your head ... *Chicken Little!).* What more could you ask?

Craft and Folk Art Museum
Fort Mason Center, Building A (at Laguna and Marina). HOURS: Tue thru Sat, 11a.m.-5p.m. Free first Wednesday of each month, and every Sat 10a.m.-Noon.

A great location to visit, and really interesting stuff here, with an unusual selection.

Center for the Arts
701 Mission HOURS: Tue thru Sun, 11a.m.-6:00p.m. Free first Thursday of each month, and 6p.m.-8p.m. every Thursday.

(Juri Koll is a freelance everyman, who can be contacted for ... well ... just about everything, through Vagabond Publishing.)

Events   *1996*

American Conservatory Theater Season   Through June 9
Geary Theater and Stage Door Theatre. 415-749-2ACT

Union Street Easter Parade and Celebration   April 7
Union Street. 415-673-0555

San Francisco Giants' Baseball Season   April 12-September 22
Candlestick Park. 415-800-SF-GIANT

Spike and Mike's Festival of Animation   April 12-May 12
Palace of Fine Arts Theater. 415-957-1205

Cherry Blossom Festival   April 13 -14, 20-21 (Parade April 21 @ 1 p.m.)
  Japantown and Japan Center. 415-563-2313

San Francisco International Film Festival   April 18-May 5
  Various locations. 415-929-5000

Whole Life Expo (New Age and Holistic Healing Expo)   April 26-28
  The Fashion Center San Francisco. 415-721-2484, 510-762-BASS

Mural Awareness Month   May 1-31
  Various locations. 415-285-2287

Olympic Torch Run   May 3-4
  Downtown and Golden Gate Bridge. 1-800-496-COKE

Cinco de Mayo Celebration (Parade at 11a.m.)   May 5
  Mission District. 415-826-1401

San Francisco Youth Arts Festival   May 8-12
  Golden Gate Park. 415-759-2916

KFOG Sky Concert (with fireworks)   May 11
  Justin Herman Plaza. 1-800-733-6318

Bay to Breakers Weekend   May 17-19
  Justin Herman Plaza. 1-800-733-6318

San Francisco Examiner Bay to Breakers Footrace   May 19
  The Embarcadero to The Great Highway. 415-777-7770

Pacific Fine Art Festival   May 24-27
  Maiden Lane. 209-296-1195

Carnaval '96 (Parade on May26 at 10a.m.)   May 25-26
  Mission District. 415-824-8999

Art Deco 50's Sale   June 1-2
  Concourse Exhibition Center. 415-599-3326

Union Street Spring Festival of Arts and Crafts   June 1-2
  Union Street. 415-346-9162

Great San Francisco Bike Adventure   June 9
  Moscone Field. 415-668-2243

Pacific Fine Art Festival   June 12-14
  Golden Gateway. 209-296-1195

An American Festival 1996   June 14-29
  Davies Symphony Hall. 415-864-6000

Make*A*Circus   Mid-June through late-September
  Various locations. 415-776-8470

North Beach Festival (42nd Annual)   June 15-16
  North Beach District (Grant Avenue - Washington Square - Green Street). 415-403-0666

San Francisco Dragon Cup (Chinese dragon boat race)   June 15
  Port of San Francisco promenade. 206-583-0393

Stern Grove Midsummer Music Festival   June 16-August 18
  Stern Grove. 415-252-6252

Making Waves 1996 (5th Annual Summer Soltice's International Music Day Festival)   June 21
  Along Downtown Market Street – Justice Herman Plaza – Ferry Plaza. 415-431-9962

San Francisco International Lesbian and Gay Film Festival   June 21-30
  Castro Theater and other venues. 415-703-8650

San Francisco Soccer Cup and International Youth Festival   June 21-23
  Golden Gate Park. 415-751-8801

Lesbian/Gay Freedom Day Parade and Celebration   June 30
  Castro District (from Civic Center to Embarcadero). 415-864-FREE

San Francisco Chronicle Fourth of July Waterfront Festival (with fireworks)   July 4
    Fisherman's Wharf. 415-777-8498

Jazz and All That Art on Fillmore   July 6-7
    Fillmore Street. 415-346-4561

The Arts Commission/San Francisco POPS   July 12-August 3
    Davies Symphony Hall. 415-431-5400

San Francisco Marathon & 5K Run   July 14
    Golden Gate Bridge to Golden Gate Park. 415-296-7111

Cable Car Bell-Ringing Championship   July 18
    Union Square. 415-923-6202

Blues and Art on Polk   July 20-21
    Polk Street. 415-346-4561

Jazz & Wine Festival   July 26-28
    Embarcadero Center. 800-733-6318

San Francisco 49ers' Football Season   August-December
    Candlestick Park. 408-562-4949

ACC Craft Fair   August 2-4
    Fort Mason. 415-896-5060

Nihonmachi Street Fair   August 3-4
    Japantown and Japan Center. 415-771-9861

Filipino American Arts Exposition   August 24-25
    Center for the Arts at Yerba Buena Gardens. 415-436-9711

Renaissance Pleasure Faire   August 24-September 29
    Black Point Forest (east of Novato in Marin) off Hwy 37 – 1 mile east of Hwy 101. 1-800-52FAIRE

Ringling Brothers and Barnum & Bailey Circus   August 29-September 2
    Cow Palace. 415-469-6065

Absolut a la Carte, a la Park (food & wine festival)   August 31-September 2
    Golden Gate Park. 415-383-9378

Free Shakespeare in the Park   August 31-September 29
    Golden Gate Park. 415-666-2221

San Francisco Fair   August 31-September 2
    Civic Center. 415-703-2729

Sausalito Art Festival   August 31-September 2
    Sausalito. 415-332-3555

San Francisco Symphony 85th Season   September 1 through June 1997
    Davies Symphony Hall. 415-864-6000

Pacific Fine Art Festival   September 6-8
    Maiden Lane. 209-296-1195

San Francisco Fringe Festival   September 6 -15
    Downtown. 415-931-1094

San Francisco Opera's 74th Season   September 6, 1996-February 23, 1997
    Bill Graham Civic Auditorium and Orpheum Theater. 415-565-3227

Opera in the Park   September 8
    Golden Gate Park. 415-864-3330

Viva Mexico! Celebration   September 13-15
    PIER 39. 415-705-5500

Festival of the Sea   September 14-15
    Hyde Street Pier. 415-929-0202

Italian Street Painting Festival   September 14-15
    The Anchorage Shopping Center. 415-775-6000

LET'S PARTY!
Events 1996

Festival De Las Americas — September 15
Mission District. 415-826-1401

Chinatown Autumn Moon Festival — September 21-22
Grant Avenue. 415-982-6306

West Portal Fine Arts Festival — September 21-22
West Portal Avenue. 415-751-0211

San Francisco Hillstride — (tentative) September 22
Seven Mile Walk. Marina Green. 415-668-2243

San Francisco Blues Festival — September 27-29
Justin Herman Plaza and Fort Mason. 415-979-5588

Sukkot -- The Festival of the Booths — September 29
Arts, crafts, music, food & wine. Sacramento and Lake Streets. 415-346-9162

American Conservatory Theater Season — October 1996-June 1997
Geary Theater and Stage Door Theatre. 415-749-2ACT

San Francisco Spiders Hockey Season — October 1996-April 1997
Cow Palace. 510-762-BASS

Citibank Fall Cup '96 Regatta — October 5-6
Sloops carrying former Olympians & Olympic hopefuls. PIER 39. 415-705-5500

World Pumpkin Weigh-Off — October 5
location TBD. 415-346-4561

Bridge to Bridge Run — October 6
Golden Gate Bridge to Bay Bridge. 415-974-6800

Castro Street Fair — October 7
Castro District. 415-467-3354

Fleet Week Celebration (Salute to U.S.Navy with Blue Angels air shows) — October 11-13
PIER 39. 415-705-5500

San Francisco Jazz Festival — October 11-27
Various locations. 415-864-5449

Reggae in the Park — October 12-13
Sharon Meadow in Golden Gate Park. 415-383-9378

Italian Heritage Day Parade (Parade at 1p.m. from Fisherman's Wharf to North Beach) — October 13
North Beach. 415-434-1492, 415-403-0660

Great Halloween and Pumpkin Festival — October 19-20
Polk Street. 415-346-4561

San Francisco International Accordian Festival — October 19-20
The Anchorage Shopping Center. 415-775-6000

Grand National Rodeo, Horse and Stock Show — October 25-November 3
Cow Palace. 415-469-6065

Exotic Erotic Ball — October 26
Concourse Exhibition Center. 415-567-BALL

Film Arts Festival — October 30-November 3
Roxie Cinema. 415-552-FILM

San Francisco Bay Area Book Festival (Meet the producers of the Let's Party Guides) — November 2-3
Concourse Exhibition Center. 415-861-2665

Harvest Festival and Christmas Crafts Market — November 8-10, 15-17
Concourse Exhibition Center. 707-778-6300

Holiday Ice Skating at Embarcadero Center — November 8, 1996-January 1997
Dorothy Hamill Ice Skating Center. 800-733-6318

The Great San Francisco Snow Party — November 9-11

PIER 39. 415-705-5500

ACCA Holiday Clay and Glass Festival	November 23-24
Golden Gate Park. 510-865-0541	
San Francisco International Auto Show	November 24-December 1
Moscone Center. 415-673-2016	
San Francisco Ballet Family Holiday Festival	November 29-December 8
Palace of Fine Arts Theater. 415-865-2000	
Run to the Far Side (10K & 15K Footraces)	December 1
Golden Gate Park. 415-564-0532	
Celebration of Craftswomen	December 7-8, 14-15
Fort Mason. 415-821-6480	
Christmas at Sea	December 8, 14
Hyde Street Pier. 415-929-0202	
First Run (Two-mile walk & run)	December 31
Chrissy Field. 415-668-2243	

Events *1997*

Holiday Ice Skating at Embarcadero Center	Through January
Dorothy Hamill Ice Skating Center. 800-733-6318	
San Francisco Opera's 74th Season	Through February 23
Bill Graham Civic Auditorium and Orpheum Theater. 415-565-3227	
San Francisco Spiders Hockey Season	Through April
Cow Palace. 510-762-BASS	
American Conservatory Theater Season	Through June
Geary Theater and Stage Door Theatre. 415-749-2ACT	
San Francisco Symphony 84th Season	Through June
Davies Symphony Hall. 415-864-6000	
San Francisco Symphony 85th Season	Through June
Davies Symphony Hall. 415-864-6000	
San Francisco Symphony 85th Season	Through June
Davies Symphony Hall. 415-864-6000	
MacWorld Expo	January 7-10
Moscone Center. 415-974-4000	
San Francisco Sports and Boat Show	January 10-19
Cow Palace. 415-469-6065	
Martin Luther King, Jr's Birthday Celebration	January 15
Location to be decided. 415-771-6300	
Chinese New Year Celebration (Year of the Ox, 4695 on the lunar calendar)	February 7-22
Parade February 22, 5:30p.m. From Market and Second to Columbus Avenue. 415-982-3000	
Russian Festival	February 7-9
The Russian Center of San Francisco. 415-921-7531	
USArt Show	February 7-9
Fort Mason . 310-455-2886	
Walt Disney's World on Ice	February 13-17
Cow Palace. 415-469-6065	
San Francisco Tribal, Folk and Textile Art Show	February 14-16
Fort Mason. 310-455-2886	
St. Patrick's Day Parade	March 16
From Civic Center to Spear Street (at 12:30p.m.). 415-661-2700	

San Francisco Tours

Blue & Gold Fleet
Bay Cruise

Pier 39, Box Z-2, San Francisco, CA 94133. 415-705-5555. FREQUENCY & PRICES: Daily. Prices range $8.00-$99.00

1-1/4 hour narrated cruise. Adults $16.00, Children & Seniors $8.00. Seasonal 3-hour Dinner/Dance cruise on Friday and Saturday evenings. $40.00 per person, group rates available.

Marine World Africa USA. Package includes a round-trip ferry and bus shuttle to park. Adults $39.00, Juniors (13-18 and 62+) $32.00, Children $23.50.

Daily Napa Valley Wine Tour. Package includes round-trip ferry and shuttle coach. Enjoy tastings at each of the 2-3 wineries with a personally guided tour. $45.00 per person, groups of 15 or more $40.00 per person.

Napa Valley Wine Train. Package includes round-trip ferry and deluxe bus coach and admission onto the Napa Valley Wine Train. You will enjoy a 4 course gourmet luncheon onboard a 1917 Pullman Dining Car during a 3-hour scenic tour. $99 per person.

CYCLEPATH Mountain Bike Adventure Tours
Bicycle Tours

P.O. Box 191854, San Francisco, CA, 94119. 415-956-6171. FREQUENCY & PRICES: Call for schedule. Prices start at $30.00 per person.

CYCLEPATH offers guided mountain bike tours of San Francisco and surrounding state parks. Imagine, cycling across the Golden Gate Bridge, zooming through the colossal Redwoods of Muir Woods and stopping the fun only to have lunch on the beach. All tours are designed for maximun excitement! Groups will consist of 2-14 people.

Tour will include light weight, high performance mountain bike, helmet and lunch on full day rides.

San Francisco Bicycle Tours
Bicycle Tours

758 11th Avenue, San Francisco, CA 94118. 415-351-BIKE (2453), FAX-346-5786. FREQUENCY & PRICES: Daily, lasting approximately 2-1/2 hours. $30.00 per person includes bicycle rental, helmet, water & energy snack

This tour offers an alternative, healthier way of seeing San Francisco. There are a variety of tours and they can be designed to meet anyone's needs, from the expert cyclist to the novice. Call ahead to reserve since there is a maximum of seven people per guide, guaranteeing individual attention.

3 Babes and A Bus
Bus Tours

54 Oakwood Street, San Francisco, CA 94110. 415-552-2582. FREQUENCY & PRICES: Call for schedule. $30.00 per person

A traveling nightclub tour company, where they (the Babes) and their luxury bus take groups to party in the San Francisco's hottest dance clubs. This is a great way to avoid the usual hassles associated with night time outings. There are no parking or taxi fares, drinking and driving worries, or having to pay cover charges. With priority entry you can experience top 40, live Brazilian music, 70's disco, modern dance, the blues and more.

Private tours can be arranged on any given night.

Cable Car Charters
Bus Tours

2830 Geary Blvd., San Francisco, CA 94118. 415-922-2425 or 800-562-7383, FAX-922-1336. FREQUENCY & PRICES: Call for schedule. Prices depend on tour or type of charter.

See San Francisco from a new vantage point on board motorized cable cars. With four open ends, views are unobstructed, photo opportunities are prime, and it offers quick and efficient loading and unloading ability. A cable car tour is interactive. You can smell the coffee in North Beach and the crab in Fisherman's Wharf as well meet the people of the city.

Cable Car Charters offers over a dozen specialty tours. They also offer customized charter of the cable cars for bar hops, private parties, weddings, and film production.

California Parlor Car Tours
Bus Tours

1101 Van Ness Avenue, San Francisco, CA 94109. 415-474-7500 or U.S. and Canada 800-227-4250. FREQUENCY & PRICES: Call for schedule. Starting at $208.00 per person.

The California Parlor Car Tours offer a variety of scenic tours ranging in length anywhere from two days to nine days. You are introduced to California riding in comforatable coaches and staying in nice hotels. Most tours include some meals.

Gray Line   Bus Tours
415-558-9400 or 1-800-826-0202. FREQUENCY & PRICES: For all other tours call for schedule. Starting at $28.00.

Gray Line offers a large selection of guided tours of San Francisco and the Bay Area including Muir Woods, Sausalito, Sonoma, Napa, Monterey, Carmel, Yosemite National Park and Santa Cruz.

The Deluxe City Tour is offered in the following foreign languages:

French, German, Italian, Japanese, Korean and Spanish. Given daily, 10a.m.- 2:30p.m. Adult $28.00. Child $14.00.

Green Tortoise   Bus Tours/Trips
415-956-7500 or 1-800-Tortoise (867-8647). FREQUENCY & PRICES: Call for schedules. Prices range $120.00-$1,750.00.

Yes, *we know* the Bay Area is blessed with majestic scenery and all that other good stuff. But, when its time for a change-a change of scenery that is-you won't do better then hopping aboard a Green Tortoise bus. There's nothing like it-staying close to beautiful country, Tortoise buses reach high and low in quest for the most awe-inspiring settings-from the glaciers of Alaska to the exotic land of Guatemala.

This San Francisco grass-roots outfit was founded in the wake of the flower-power days, but don't expect to find the drivers and staff clad in dandelions and tie-dyed shirts. And, due to the Tortoises' drop-dead fares and package deals, you should do away with fantasies of a luxury coach trip. Besides, those *other* tours usually turn out to be drab, 'hurry-no-time-to-waste-fixed-in-stone-itinerary' kinda experiences.

Embracing a few ideals made popular during the 60s, however, Green Tortoise Tours focus on the principals of communal travel and respect for nature. Most meals are cookout-style, and feature delicious vegetarian dishes. And, although the food fund covers all cookout meals, everyone is expected to help prepare and clean-up.

Each bus carries 30-plus passengers, who are all treated to the (so called) 'miracle'-a comfortable mattress to sleep on. By personal accounts, it *is* truly a miracle ... you'll just have to find out for yourself.

Happy trekers who hop aboard the Tortoise are an international hodgepodge holding passports from Ireland, Scotland, Britain, Australia, New Zealand, Canada, South Africa, Germany, Japan, and even the United States. All seem to carry in their back-pack the traveler's golden tenet, so well spoken by Robert Louis Stevenson, *"For my part, I travel not to go anywhere, but to go. I travel for travel's sake. The great affair is to move."*

Forget "On the Road" by Kerouac, a Green Tortoise experience can provide your hungry journal enough prime-cut meat to start your own literary piece on adventure travel. Along with every traveled mile, every campfire, every meal preparation, and every hike, a new reality is discovered and new friends are made.

The Green Tortoise is about traveling in the *lapse* of luxury, so don't expect anyone to carry your bags, guaranteed arrival times, make you take showers, or even offer much privacy. But then, a wise man once told us that money and luxury can insulate a traveler from experiencing the kernel of life, so embrace the uncertainty that awaits around every corner-it'll make for one *hell* of an exciting trip.

Some of the trips offered by Green Tortoise (all trips include food) are:
- Alaska Expedition-30 days, $1750.00
- Central American Expedition-21 days, $730.00
- The Maya Trail-18 days, $630.00
- National Parks Loop-16 days, $620.00
- Golden Coast/Baja Loop-16 days, $600.00
- Costa Rica Loop-14 days, $400.00 (does not include return airfare)
- Grand Canyon-9 days, $400.00

LET'S PARTY!
Tours

- Coast to Coast (San Francisco to New York & Boston)-10 days, $370.00
- Desert Loop of the Southwest-9 days, $310.00
- Northern California Redwoods & Parks Loop-8 days, $250.00
- Yosemite-3 days, $120.00

The Mexican Bus (see Map: SoMa – E)   **Dance Club Tours**

At Chevy's Restaurant (4th Street & Mission). 415-546-3747. SOMA. HOURS: Fri & Sat pickup at 9:15 p.m. ENTRANCE CHARGE: $25.00 per person. SPECIALS: Also can be booked for private parties (holds 44). RESTRICTIONS: Cash only. *Passport: $5.00 off full price ticket.*

Board the "mambo cabaret on wheels," and club-hop to 'bop' at local Latin and Caribbean clubs. The party bus makes its rounds every Friday and Saturday night, and is a great opportunity to meet people and experience several clubs without having to drive around and worry about the cover charges. Go with a group of friends and party-on! The bus driver and escort are your party guides for the evening, and ensure that you'll have a blast.

This concept is similar to the booze-cruise idea that they have in Waikiki or Mazatlan. Reservations are required.

You'll meet in front of Chevy's at Howard and Fourth Streets at 9:15 p.m.. The mode of transport is an old school bus repainted in bright funky colors, so you're sure to be seen as you set-out on your party adventure. Down a shot of tequila as you board and take your seat, as a slightly buzzed from the pre-party Margaritas at Chevy's and the shot of tequila take hold.

Take a look around at the crazy Christmas lights that line the interior; the artsy Mexican altar just above the driver; and your party pals for the evening. First stop ... Miss Pearl's Jam House. At this Caribbean bar and restaurant, you may be lucky enough to find a Reggae band jommin-on da tunes, mon – flash the guys at the door your button, and you're in! Take off your button once you're inside so you don't look like a dork – but don't get stupid and lose it! Do the irie for about an hour and a half, and you're back on the bus and headed for 330 Ritch for a live Salsa band. By now, you're havin' a really good time.

On our tour, our bus driver did his best to teach us how to Salsa. We appreciated the lesson, but it was no use (maybe you just have to be born to move like that). For some strange reason, the escort had harder time getting us on the bus this time. Some of our friends opted to stay (they had already 'met' somebody). We, on the other hand, ventured on to Sol y Luna, a Latin Supper and Dance Club. Flashing our buttons, we bypassed the line forming late that Saturday night and Rumba'd, Salsa'd and Boogie'd our way 'til 2:00 a.m., arriving back at Chevy's a little later. It wasn't Mr. Toad's Wild Ride, but it was thoroughly worth it.

Super Sightseeing Tours   **Bus Tours**

Pier 9, Suite 1, San Francisco, CA 94111. 415-777-2288. FREQUENCY & PRICES: Call for schedule. Prices range $12.00-$90.00

They offer 10 different tours of various Northern California scenic attractions:

Tour #1-San Francisco Deluxe City Tour-Approx. 3-1/2 hours, from 10 a.m.-2:15 p.m. The tour features the major attractions of the city, with an extended stop at the Japanese Tea Garden in Golden Gate Park, concluding at Fisherman's Wharf. **Tour #2**-Deluxe City Tour & Bay Cruise. **Tour #3**-Deluxe City Tour & Alcatraz. **Tour #4**-Muir Woods / Giant Redwood & Sausalito. **Tour #5**-Muir Woods / Giant Redwood & Sausalito & Bay Cruise. **Tour #6**-Muir Woods / Giant Redwood & Sausalito & Alcatraz. **Tour #7**-The Super Tour. **Tour #8**-Wine Country Tour. **Tour #9**-Monterey / Carmel and 17-Mile Drive. **Tour #10**-Yosemite National Park.

Tower Tours   **Bus Tours**

77 Jefferson Street, San Francisco, CA . 415-434-8687. FREQUENCY & PRICES: Call for schedule. Prices range $25.00-$95.00.

Deluxe City Tour offered daily. Other tours include: Muir Woods / Sausalito; Alcatraz with Deluxe City Tour or Muir Woods / Sausalito; Bay Cruise with Deluxe City Tour or Muir Woods / Sausalito; the Combo-Deluxe City Tour & Muir Woods / Sausalito; Yosemite in a Day; Monterey / Carmel & 17-Mile Drive.

Incredible Adventures   **Camping**

1517 Clement Street, San Francisco, CA 94118. 1-800-777-8464 or 415-668-9729. FREQUENCY & PRICES: Call for schedule. Prices start at $139.00 per person.

California's most magnificent sights unfold during fun-filled three to five day camping adventures. Discover Yosemite, Lake Tahoe, Napa Valley, Big Sur, Pacific Coast Highway 1 and Los Angeles.

The tour includes the camping equipment (except sleeping bag, which is available for a $5 rental fee), food, transportation and park entrance fees.

European Limousine Tours
Limousine Tours

860 24th Avenue, San Francisco, CA 94121. 415-221-9999, FAX-221-3424. FREQUENCY & PRICES: Half-day and full-day rates. Call for quote.

Elegant transportation and private sightseeing service for European non-English speaking visitors. They offer tailor made city tours which can include walking tours of a certain neighborhood, emphasizing our architectural heritage, or the nature aspect of San Francisco and surroundings. Other choices are excursions to Napa, Mendocino, Eureka, Oregon, Washington, or South along the 17-mile drive, Big Sur, Santa Barbara to Los Angeles.

Another service European Limousine offers is assisting Europeans in their native language with planning their own tour in rental cars and providing foreign speaking tour guides.

Hunting Bargains
Shopping

1760 Indian Valley Road, Novato, CA 94947. 415-892-1088. FREQUENCY & PRICES: Mon-Sat, 9:45a.m. from Fisherman's Wharf, 10a.m. from Union Square. $30.00 per person

Hunting Bargains provides a guided shopping tour of San Francisco's original garment district. Visitors are guided to various warehouses, outlets and designer showrooms where name brand merchandise is discounted 20-70%. Each tour will stop for lunch by the Bay at a location selected for quality food. Lunch is not included. Call ahead for reservations.

Roger's Custom Tours
Tours

2640 Ridgeway Avenue, San Bruno, CA 94066. 415-742-9611, FAX-742-9514. FREQUENCY & PRICES: Tour 1- San Francisco High Points (Approx. 3-1/2 hours). Available daily departing at 9:30a.m. Adult $39.95. Child (under 12) $25.00. Tour 2- Golden Gate Bridge (1-1/2 hours). Adult $25.00. Child $10.00. Tour 3- Exotic Chinatown (1-1/2 hours). Adult $25.00. Child $10.00. Call for schedule.

Roger's Custom walk or bicycle or auto or motorized Cable Car or bus Tours will arrange, organize, and guide tours for you or your group in your native language so you get the most out of your San Francisco visit. Possible tours to select:

A Day In Nature
Walking Tours

1490 Sacramento Street, Suite 4D, San Francisco, CA 94109. 415-673-0548. FREQUENCY & PRICES: Twice daily, starting at 9a.m. and at 2p.m.. $40.00 per person

Naturalist, Colin Sloan, has operated A Day in Nature for 10 years, which has rendered him with the knowledge and wisdom to provide an informative four hour tour of either the spectacular Marin Headlands, the beautiful Muir Woods or other gorgeous scenic spots such as Seacliff. You can choose from a beach tour, a rainy day, a Sunday Brunch, an Executive Afternoon or simply create your own while learning the natural history of Northern California. A light meal and refreshments are included as well as door-to-door service from downtown San Francisco. Advance reservations are required.

All About Chinatown
Walking Tours

812 Clay Street , San Francisco, CA 94108. 415-982-8839, FAX-397-2120. FREQUENCY & PRICES: Daily, departing at 10a.m. (lasting approx. 2 hours). Adult $25.00, Children $10.00

A tour of Chinatown, a city within a city, discover: Architecture and Art, Herbal Pharmacy, a Fortune Cookie Factory and Tea Shop, authentic Chinese Temple, Portsmouth Square, more.

Articulate Art: SF 1930's
Walking Tours

5214-F Diamond Heights Blvd., San Francisco, CA 94131. 415-285-0495. FREQUENCY & PRICES: Call for schedule.

Tours of Coit Tower, concentrating on the murals painted by 25 different artists and their assistants, are given every Tuesday and Thursday at the Tower from 10:15a.m. to 11a.m. for $5.00 per person ($3.00 per child under 12). Call the Tower to confirm: 415-362-0808.

Three mural tours are offered by arrangement, with the basic rate of $50.00 per hour, a group together can divide the cost. Arrangements can be made for individuals as well. The tours are specifically on Mexican muralist Diego Rivera, through buildings of architectural significance. Those being:

- Coit Tower and the Rincon Annex (former Post Office)
- Diego Rivera in SF: Art Institute, City Club, CCSF
- Lucien Labaudt at the Beach Chalet; Bernard Zakheim at UCSF

Chinatown Cultural Tours   Walking Tours
200 Estates Drive, San Francisco, CA 94066. 415-873-6688. FREQUENCY & PRICES: Daily, 9:30a.m.-12:30p.m. Lunch, 12:30p.m.-1:15p.m.. Adult $35:00 with lunch. $25:00 without lunch. (Call for Senior & Child Rates)

Larry Lowe Mak's bi-cultural experience uniquely enables him to share with you some valuable insights to one of the oldest cultures in the world. He will enlighten the group to various points of interest such as Portsmouth Square, a Tea Shop, a Tea Ceremony, an Herb Shop, Feng Shui, a Fortune Cookie Factory, a Jade Shop and much more, including a Dim Sum luncheon.

Cruisin' The Castro from an Historical Perspective   Walking Tours
375 Lexington Street, San Francisco, CA 94110. 415-550-8110. FREQUENCY & PRICES: Tue-Sat, 10a.m.-1:30p.m.. $30.00 per person

This walking tour enables travelers to learn Gay history in a concise and colorful format and why San Francisco got to be literally the Gay Mecca of the world. Available year round, reservations are required as tour has a four person minimum and 16 person maximum. Includes brunch.

Glorious Food Culinary Walktours   Walking Tours
1717 Jones Street, San Francisco, CA 94109. 415-441-5637. FREQUENCY & PRICES: Daily, start and duration depending on tour. Starting at $30.00 per person.

Highlight your visit to the City with an intimate and enlightening culinary, historical and cultural view of Chinatown and Italian North Beach, two unique cultures co-existing in adjacent neighborhoods. Glorious Food offers at least six tours to choose from such as the combined Little Italy and Chinatown tour at $55.00 per person including morning cappuccino and 'dim sum' lunch, to individual neighborhood tours starting at $30.00 per person, to evening walk tours including dinner with price determined by the restaurant chosen.

Javawalk   Walking Tours
1899 California #9, San Francisco, CA 94109. 415-673-WALK (9255). FREQUENCY & PRICES: Twice Tue-Sat, starting at 10a.m. and at noon, lasts approx. 2 hours. Adult $15.00, child (under 12) $7.50

The Javawalk tour starts at Union Square and winds through Chinatown, Jackson Square and North Beach. You will be shown the City's coffee roots (much more significant than Seattle's!) and coffeehouse culture (think beatnik). Some time is spent covering San Francisco's history and interesting trivia. A couple of stops at North Beach cafes for a quick java jolt is a must.

San Francisco City Guides   Walking Tours
Main Library, Civic Center, San Francisco, CA 94102. 415-557-4266 (press "*" leave a message). FREQUENCY & PRICES: Daily, lasting approx. 1-1/2 to 2 hours. FREE

Everyday rain or shine (except Thanksgiving, Christmas Day and New Year's Day) the City Guides conduct a variety of tours throughout the famous and infamous neighborhoods of San Francisco. If the weather threatens, but walkers nonetheless have a need to get out and about, City Guides offers four indoor tours.

Printed schedules with description of each tour, with instructions on where and when to meet your guide, are available at all San Francisco branch libraries and at the S.F. Convention & Visitors Bureau Information Center in Hallidie Plaza.

The Flower Power Haight Ashbury Tour   Walking Tours
520 Shrader #1, San Francisco, CA 94117. 415-221-8442. FREQUENCY & PRICES: Tues & Sat, starting at 9:30a.m. (roughly lasting 2 hours) $15.00 per person

Rachel Heller passionately narrates a walking tour of where the hippie movement of the sixties was centered. She will show you where it all happened: The Summer of Love, the Human Be-in, the Digger feeds, the free Grateful Dead concerts, etc... The tour also points out the forgotten history of the neighborhood and the overlooked Victorian architecture.

Group tours at other times can be arranged by appointment.

Tom's Scenic Trailwalks   Walking Tours

1-800-WOW-WALK (1-800-909-9255) or 510-845-0856. FREQUENCY & PRICES: Daily, mid-morning to mid-afternoon. $49.95 per person

Enjoy a healthful stroll through moss shrouded redwood forests and wildflower meadow. See spectacular vistas of the Pacific Ocean and San Francisco.

Tom's Trailwalk package includes: 3 to 4 miles guided tour at a pace that's comforatable to you. A picnic lunch, fruit juices and drinking water. Door-to-door transportation service.

Victorian Home Walk   Walking Tours

415-252-9485. FREQUENCY & PRICES: Daily, departing at 11a.m. (lasts approx. 2-1/2 hours) $20.00 per person.

Take a trolly bus ride to the best Victorian neighborhoods where tour buses are prohibited. Learn to appreciate the difference between Queen Annes, Edwardians, Italianates and other Victorian homes and mansions.

Wok Wiz   Walking Tours

750 Kearny Street, Suite 800, San Francisco, CA 94108. 415-355-9657, FAX-355-5928. FREQUENCY & PRICES: Daily, 10a.m.-1:30p.m. $25.00 per person w/out lunch. $35.00 per person with lunch.

Experience the flavors of the historical Chinese community. The tours are personalized and are usually kept at a 12 person maximum. Lunch is included at the end of the tour.

Late Night Food

• Castro

Hot 'n Hunky   Hamburgers

4039 18th St. (at Noe). 415-621-6365. Hours: Sun-Thur, 11 a.m.-Midnight; Fri-Sat, 11a.m.-1a.m. 415-621-6365.

Marcello's Pizza   Pizza

420 Castro St. (between Market & 18th). 415-863-3900. Hours: Sun-Thur, 11a.m.-1a.m.; Fri-Sat, 11a.m.- 2a.m.

Orphan Andy's (see Map: Castro – C)   Diner

3991 Market St. (between 17th & Castro). 415-864-9795. Hours: Daily, 24 hours.

Sparkey's (see Map: Castro – D)   Diner

242 Church St. (between Market & 15th). 415-621-6001.Hours: Daily, 24 hours.

The Sausage Factory   Italian

517 Castro St. (at 18th St.). 415-626-1250. Hours: Daily, 11:30a.m.-1a.m.

Late Night Food

• Chinatown

Yuet Lee   **Chinese**
1300 Stockton St. (at Broadway). 415-982-6020. Hours: Daily, 11a.m.-3a.m.

• Delivery

Mr. Pizza Man   **Pizza**
415-285-3337. Daily, 24 hour delivery from several locations.

• Financial

Silver Restaurant   **Chinese**
737 Washington St. (between Grant & Kearny). 415-433-8888. Hours: Daily, 24 hours.

• Haight

John Henry Pizzeria   **Pizza**
551 Haight St. (between Fillmore & Steiner). 415-626-8344. Hours: Sun-Thur, Noon-Midnight; Fri-Sat, Noon-2a.m.

Love 'n Haight   **American and Greek**
553 Haight St. (between Steiner & Fillmore). 415-252-8190. Hours: Sun-Thur, 11a.m.-1a.m.; Fri-Sat, 11a.m.-2a.m.

Papa Doro Pizza Restaurant   **Pizza**
1649 Haight St. (between Belvedere & Clayton). 415-621-7272. Hours: Daily, 11a.m.-1a.m.; delivery 11a.m.-2a.m.

North Beach Pizza (Delivery only)   **Pizza**
800 Stanyon St. 415-751-2300. Hours: 24 hour delivery only.

• Japantown

Denny's   **Diner**
1700 Post St. (between Webster & Laguna). 415-563-1400. **Hours:** Daily, 24 hours.

• Marina

Bepple's Pies   **Diner**
2142 Chestnut St. (between Steiner & Pierce). 415-931-6226. Hours: Sun-Thur, 9a.m.-Midnight; Fri-Sat, 9a.m.-2a.m.

International House of Pancakes   **Diner**
2299 Lombard St. (at Pierce). 415-921-4004. **Hours:** Daily, 24 hours

• Mission

El Zocalo   **Mexican and Salvadoran**
3230 Mission St. (at Valencia). 415-282-2572. Hours: Mon-Fri, 11a.m.-3a.m.; Sat-Sun, 11a.m.-4a.m.

La Rondalla   **Mexican**
901 Valencia St. (at 20th St). 415-647-7474. Hours: Tues-Sun, 11:30a.m.-3a.m. Closed Mondays

Pancho Villa   **Mexican**
3071 16th St. (between Valencia & Mission). 415-864-8840. Hours: Daily, 10a.m.-Midnight

Taquería Can-cun   **Mexican**
2288 Mission St. (at 19th St). 415-252-9560. Hours: Daily, 9a.m.-1a.m.

Taquería San Jose   **Mexican**
2830 Mission St. or 2839 Mission St. (at 24th St). 415-282-0203 or 415-282-0283. Hours: Daily, 8a.m.-2a.m.

• NoMa

Hollywood Billiards (Tenderloin) American
61 Golden Gate (between Taylor & Jones). 415-252-9643. Hours: Daily, 6p.m.-2a.m.

Lori's Diner (see Map: NoMa – A) Diner
336 Mason St. (between Geary & O'Farrel). 415-392-8646. Hours: Daily, 24 hours

Pinecrest Restaurant (Union Square) Diner
401 Geary St. (at Mason). 415-885-6407. Hours: Daily, 24 hours.

North Beach

Basta Pasta Italian
1268 Grant Ave. (at Vallejo). 415-434-2248. Hours: Daily, 11:30a.m.-1:45a.m.

North Beach Pizza Pizza / Italian
1499 Grant St. (at Union). 415-433-2444. Hours: Mon-Thur, noon-1a.m., Fri, noon-3a.m.; Sat, 10:30a.m.-3a.m.; Sun, 10:30a.m.-1a.m. Also 24 hour delivery

North Beach Pizza Pizza / Italian
1310 Grant St. (at Vallejo). 415-433-2444. Hours: Mon-Fri, noon-10p.m. Also 24 hour delivery

Steps of Rome Italian
348 Columbus Ave. (at Grant). Hours: Sun-Thur, 8:30a.m.-1a.m.; Fri-Sat, 8:30a.m.-3a.m.

• Marina $-Green-$

Amici's East Coast Pizzeria Pizza
2033 Union St. (between Webster & Buchanan). 415-885-4500. Hours: Sun-Thur, 11a.m.-Midnight; Fri-Sat, 11a.m.-1a.m.

Bepple's Pies Diner
1934 Union St. (at Laguna). 415-931-6225. Hours: Sun-Thur, 9a.m.-Midnight; Fri-Sat, 9a.m.-2a.m.

Brazen Head Continental
3166 Buchanan St. (at Greenwich). 415-921-7600. Hours: Daily, 5p.m.-1a.m.

Mel's Drive-In (see Map: Marina – B) Diner
2165 Lombard St. (at Steiner). 415-921-3039. Hours: Mon-Thur, 6a.m.-2a.m.; Fri-Sat, 24 hours

• Richmond

Hanil Kwan Korean
1802 Balboa (at 19th Ave). 415-752-4447. Hours: Daily, 10a.m.-2a.m.

Video Cafe Diner
5700 Geary St. (at 21st. Ave). 415-387-3999. Hours: Daily, 24 hours

Lucky Penny Diner
2670 Geary St. (at Masonic). 415-921-0836. Hours: Daily, 24 hours

Mel's Drive-In Diner
3355 Geary St. (between Parker & Stanyan). 415-387-2244. Hours: Mon-Thur, 6a.m.-1a.m.; Fri-Sat, 6a.m.-3a.m.

• Russian Gulch

Coconut Grove Supper Club
1415 Van Ness Ave. (between Bush & Pine). 415-776-1616. Hours: Daily, 5:30p.m.-1:30a.m.

Steve the Greek Greek
1431 Polk St. (between Pine & California). Hours: Mon-Thur, 11a.m.-4a.m.; Fri-Sat, 11a.m.-5a.m.

• SoMa

Hamburger Mary's American
1582 Folsom St. (at12th St). 415-626-5767. Hours: Mon-Thur, 11:30a.m.-12:15a.m.; Fri, 11:30a.m.-1:15a.m.; Sat, 10a.m.-1:15a.m.; Sun, 10a.m.-12:15a.m.

Twenty Tank American
316 11th St. (between Harrison & Folsom). 415-255-9455. Hours: Daily, 11a.m.-1a.m.

Mile High Airline   *415-713-2359*

Being a flight attendant I just had to mention this quirky airline based in San Francisco and mentioned in Skyy Magazine a few months ago. This airline plays on everyone's urge to join the mile high club (although *we* think it's cheating!).

Welcome to flight 69! The pilot greets you with bottle of champagne, flowers, and directions to the bed. "I'll leave you two alone now," he smirks. It's really ... ah ... really ... ah ... it's a fantasy come true.

There's something to be said for *making-it* in the air (without the need to cram the two of you in the lavatory in back). This flight is a private flight for two and, if you're lucky, you'll run into some *tricky* turbulence. Some people get off on it – *really!*

The plane circles the city, providing breathtaking views of the city, its bridges, Alcatraz ... wait, why are we wasting our time – you won't even be paying attention! It lands an hour and a half later, and if that wasn't enough time, you can always practice hangar-landings back home. The cost is around $200, but worth it for the ... *high.*

Now you're ready for a *real* adventure ....

(Editors note: Hey, Jess. Are you a member of the mile-high club? No ... really?!?)

Be-At-Line ...   *415-626-4087*

Where's it happenin' tonight? Call the *Be-At-Line.*

In San Francisco, even the mayor's *son* knows where to party! Michael Brown, son of Mayor Willie Brown, offers a low-down phone guide to San Francisco's nightclub and party scene. He makes this service part of a regular routine, updating it with new tidbits every day. Michael has been part of the city's underground Hip-Hop scene for years. He was there when House came on the make, and he was behind the 80s explosion of "Don't sit on the furniture" house parties. "Wherever I go, clubs or stores, I pick up flyers. Plus, people call me about parties," he was quoted as saying in the entertainment section of the San Francisco Chronicle.

That's exactly what we do here at *Let's Party!* headquarters. Go Michael!

-end-

This is your Passport to Party San Francisco, **Let's Party!** Style. Please present your coupons at the time of ordering, and tip according to the entire bill. That way, you will keep good karma. Enjoy!

111 Minna Street Gallery   SoMa
Club. It's also a gallery.
111 Minna Street
Two for one entry, any day.
Limit two persons.

330 Ritch Street   SoMa
JazzSupper Club
330 Ritch Street
Two for one entry (not valid during special events - call to verify). Limit two persons.

Bahia Cabana   NoMa
Dance Club/Restaurant
1600 Market Street
30% off the cover charge.
Limited to your party.

Big Heart City   SoMa
Dance Club
836 Mission Street
Two for one cocktail.
Limit one offer.

Biscuits & Blues   NoMa
Live Blues Bar/Restaurant
401 Mason Street
50% off entrance charge.
Limit one person.

Blues   Cow Hollow
Live Music Bar
2125 Lombard Street
Two for one entry.
Limit two persons.

Brain Wash   SoMa
Cafe/Laundromat/Live Music
1122 Folsom Street
A cup of coffee with breakfast entree. Mon - Fri only. Limit one person.

Let's Party! **San Francisco**
O F F I C I A L
Party Passport
C O U P O N

Let's Party! **San Francisco**
O F F I C I A L
Party Passport
C O U P O N

Let's Party! **San Francisco**
O F F I C I A L
Party Passport
C O U P O N

Let's Party! **San Francisco**
O F F I C I A L
Party Passport
C O U P O N

Let's Party! **San Francisco**
O F F I C I A L
Party Passport
C O U P O N

Let's Party! **San Francisco**
O F F I C I A L
Party Passport
C O U P O N

Let's Party! **San Francisco**
O F F I C I A L
Party Passport
C O U P O N

Let's Party! **San Francisco**
O F F I C I A L
Party Passport
C O U P O N

Let's Party!

The *Let's Party!* PartyLine: 415-979-4FUN

San Francisco

Café Bastille — NoMa
French Bistro/Bar
22 Belden Place
Free coffee drink with purchase of an entree.
Limit one person.

Cafe Du Nord — Upper Market
Dance Club/Restaurant/Bar
2170 Market Street
One free entrance.
Limit one person.

Cafe Istanbul — Noe Valley
Middle Eastern Cafe/Restaurant
525 Valencia Street
A Chai tea with the purchase of a Mid-Eastern plate. *Limit one person.*

Cafe Mars — SoMa
Bar/Restauant
798 Brannan Street
Free entry.
Limit one person.

Club 181 — NoMa
Dance Club/Restaurant
181 Eddy Street
Two for one entry (not valid for special events). *Limit two persons.*

Coconut Grove — Polk Gulch
Supper Club/Swing & Jass Bar
1415 Van Ness Avenue
A complimentary show for two. Sun-Thur (National Headliner excl.). Reservations req.

Compas Rose — Noma
Piano Bar & Lounge
The Westin St. Francis Hotel (Union Square)
Buy one, get one free, off evening 'tasting menu.' *Limit one offer.*

Desert Moon — Cow Hollow
Bar
3111 Fillmore Street
Two for one any beer.
Limit one offer.

Let's Party! **San Francisco**
O F F I C I A L
Party Passport
C O U P O N

Let's Party! **San Francisco**
O F F I C I A L
Party Passport
C O U P O N

Let's Party! **San Francisco**
O F F I C I A L
Party Passport
C O U P O N

Let's Party! **San Francisco**
O F F I C I A L
Party Passport
C O U P O N

Let's Party! **San Francisco**
O F F I C I A L
Party Passport
C O U P O N

Let's Party! **San Francisco**
O F F I C I A L
Party Passport
C O U P O N

Let's Party! **San Francisco**
O F F I C I A L
Party Passport
C O U P O N

Let's Party! **San Francisco**
O F F I C I A L
Party Passport
C O U P O N

Let's Party!

San Francisco

Fiddler's Green — Wharf
Live Music Bar/Restaurant
1333 Columbus Avenue
20% off the Lunch or Dinner menu per table.
Limited to your table.

Grant & Green — North Beach
Live Music Bar
1371 Grant Avenue
Two for one draft beer of choice.
Limit one offer.

Hamburger Marys — SoMa
Restaurant
1582 Folsom Street
10% off food only.
Limited to your table.

Harry Denton's — SoMa
Brasserie-style Restaurant/Nightclub
161 Steuart Street
Free entry.
Limit two persons.

Hollywood Billiards — NoMa
Pool Hall
61 Golden Gate Avenue
Pay for one hour and get one hour free.
Limit one offer.

Holy Cow — SoMa
Dance Bar
1531 Folsom Street
Two for one draft beer or well drink cocktail.
Limit one offer.

Hotel Utah Saloon — SoMa
Bar/Restaurant
500 4th Street
Two for one draft beer.
Limit to your party.

Infusion — SoMa
Bar/Restaurant/Live Music
555 Second Street
Two Infusions for one.
Limit one offer.

Visit our site – http://EntertainNET.com

Let's Party! **San Francisco**
O F F I C I A L
Party Passport
C O U P O N

Let's Party! **San Francisco**
O F F I C I A L
Party Passport
C O U P O N

Let's Party! **San Francisco**
O F F I C I A L
Party Passport
C O U P O N

Let's Party! **San Francisco**
O F F I C I A L
Party Passport
C O U P O N

Let's Party! **San Francisco**
O F F I C I A L
Party Passport
C O U P O N

Let's Party! **San Francisco**
O F F I C I A L
Party Passport
C O U P O N

Let's Party! **San Francisco**
O F F I C I A L
Party Passport
C O U P O N

Let's Party! **San Francisco**
O F F I C I A L
Party Passport
C O U P O N

The *Let's Party!* PartyLine: 415-979-4FUN

Ireland's 32   **Richmond**
Live Music Irish Bar
3920 Geary Boulevard
Two for one beer.
Limit one offer.

Julie Ring's Heart & Soul   **Russian Hill**
Supper Club
1695 Polk Street
Two for one entry (not valid during special events - call to verify). *Limit two persons.*

Kan Zaman   **Haight**
Middle Eastern Cafe/Restaurant/Bar
1793 Haight Street
Free Hooka with the purchase of one entree.
Limited to your table.

Lovejoy's   **Noe Valley**
Tea Room
1195 Church Street
A free pot of tea with meal.
Limited to your table.

Mad Magda's   **Hayes Valley**
Cafe/Restaurant
579 Hayes Street
Two for one lunch or dinner entrees. Mon - Fri only. *Limit two persons.*

Nickie's BBQ   **Haight**
Dance Bar
460 Haight Street
Two for one entry or admit one free.
Limit two persons.

Noc Noc   **Haight**
Bar
557 Haight Street
Happy hour prices extended to 2 a.m.
Limit one person (stay late!).

Orocco   **Richmond**
Supper Club
3565 Geary Boulevard
20% off dinner (food portion only) Sun-Thur.
Limit to your table.

Let's Party! **San Francisco**
O F F I C I A L
Party Passport
C O U P O N

Let's Party! **San Francisco**
O F F I C I A L
Party Passport
C O U P O N

Let's Party! **San Francisco**
O F F I C I A L
Party Passport
C O U P O N

Let's Party! **San Francisco**
O F F I C I A L
Party Passport
C O U P O N

Let's Party! **San Francisco**
O F F I C I A L
Party Passport
C O U P O N

Let's Party! **San Francisco**
O F F I C I A L
Party Passport
C O U P O N

Let's Party! **San Francisco**
O F F I C I A L
Party Passport
C O U P O N

Let's Party! **San Francisco**
O F F I C I A L
Party Passport
C O U P O N

The *Let's Party!* PartyLine: 415-979-4FUN

Pat O'Shea's   Richmond
Pub/Sports Bar
3848 Geary Boulevard
Two for one on domestic beer, microbrew or well drink cocktails. *Limit one offer.*

Place Pigalle   Hayes Valley
Live Music/Arts & Events Bar
520 Hayes Street
Two for one entry.
Limit two persons.

Sol Y Luna   NoMa
Spanish Supper Club
475 Sacramento Street
Two for one dance cover. After 10p.m. only.
Limit two persons.

South Beach Billiards   SoMa
Pool Hall
270 Brannan Street
Half off regular priced pool, any day, plus $2.00 off T-shirt. *Limit one offer.*

Tarr & Feathers   Cow Hollow
Live Music/Sports Bar
2140 Union Street
Shot of Jägermeister for $2.00 per person.
Limited to your table.

The Mexican Bus   SoMa
Dance Club Tours
119 Bartlett Street
$5.00 off a ticket.
Limit one person.

The Punch Line   NoMa
Comedy Club
444 Battery Street
Two for one entry valid Sun-Thur (except special events -call to verify). *Limit two persons.*

The Top   Haight
Dance Bar
424 Haight Street
Buy one beer and get one free.
Limit one offer.

San Francisco

Let's Party! **San Francisco**
O F F I C I A L
Party Passport
C O U P O N

Let's Party! **San Francisco**
O F F I C I A L
Party Passport
C O U P O N

Let's Party! **San Francisco**
O F F I C I A L
Party Passport
C O U P O N

Let's Party! **San Francisco**
O F F I C I A L
Party Passport
C O U P O N

Let's Party! **San Francisco**
O F F I C I A L
Party Passport
C O U P O N

Let's Party! **San Francisco**
O F F I C I A L
Party Passport
C O U P O N

Let's Party! **San Francisco**
O F F I C I A L
Party Passport
C O U P O N

Let's Party! **San Francisco**
O F F I C I A L
Party Passport
C O U P O N